TWO BICYCLES

Film and Media Studies Series

Film studies is the critical exploration of cinematic texts as art and entertainment, as well as the industries that produce them and the audiences that consume them. Although a medium barely one hundred years old, film is already transformed through the emergence of new media forms. Media studies is an interdisciplinary field that considers the nature and effects of mass media upon individuals and society and analyzes media content and representations. Despite changing modes of consumption—especially the proliferation of individuated viewing technologies—film has retained its cultural dominance into the 21st century, and it is this transformative moment that the WLU Press Film and Media Studies series addresses.

Our Film and Media Studies series includes topics such as identity, gender, sexuality, class, race, visuality, space, music, new media, aesthetics, genre, youth culture, popular culture, consumer culture, regional/national cinemas, film policy, film theory, and film history.

Wilfrid Laurier University Press invites submissions. For further information, please contact the Series editors, all of whom are in the Department of English and Film Studies at Wilfrid Laurier University:

>Dr. Philippa Gates, email: pgates@wlu.ca
>Dr. Russell Kilbourn, email: rkilbourn@wlu.ca
>Dr. Ute Lischke, email: ulischke@wlu.ca
>Department of English and Film Studies
>Wilfrid Laurier University
>75 University Avenue West
>Waterloo, ON N2L 3C5
>Canada
>Phone: 519-884-0710
>Fax: 519-884-8307

TWO BICYCLES

The Work of Jean-Luc Godard
and Anne-Marie Miéville

JERRY WHITE

WILFRID LAURIER
UNIVERSITY PRESS

Wilfrid Laurier University Press acknowledges the support of the Canada Council for the Arts for our publishing program We acknolwedge the financial support of the Government of Canada through the Canada Book Fund for our publishing activities.

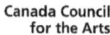 

Library and Archives Canada Cataloguing in Publication

White, Jerry, 1971–, author
   Two bicycles : the work of Jean-Luc Godard and Anne-Marie Miéville / Jerry White.

(Film and media studies series)
Includes bibliographical references and index.
Issued in print and electronic formats.
ISBN 978-1-55458-935-7 (pbk.).—ISBN 978-1-55458-936-4 (pdf).—ISBN 978-1-55458-937-1 (epub)

   1. Godard, Jean Luc, 1930– —Criticism and interpretation. 2. Miéville, Anne-Marie—Criticism and interpretation. I. Title. II. Series: Film and media studies series

PN1998.3.G63W45 2013   791.4302'330922   C2013-903427-7   C2013-903428-5

Cover design by Heng Wee Tan. Front-cover image from New Yorker Films/Photofest, © New Yorker Films. Image from Jean-Luc Godard's *Sauve qui peut (la vie)* (1980). Text design by Janette Thompson.

© 2013 Wilfrid Laurier University Press
Waterloo, Ontario, Canada
www.wlupress.wlu.ca

Every reasonable effort has been made to acquire permission for copyright material used in this text, and to acknowledge all such indebtedness accurately. Any errors and omissions called to the publisher's attention will be corrected in future printings.

No part of this publication may be reproduced, stored in a retrieval system, or transmitted, in any form or by any means, without the prior written consent of the publisher or a licence from the Canadian Copyright Licensing Agency (Access Copyright). For an Access Copyright licence, visit http://www.accesscopyright.ca or call toll free to 1-800-893-5777.

For Jim Bedford and Kate Sibley:
Toujours mon chef, toujours ma doyenne

CONTENTS

Acknowledgements ix

Chapter 1 Introduction 1
Chapter 2 Abandonments 37
Chapter 3 Communication 59
Chapter 4 Realization 95
Chapter 5 Reconsideration 137
Chapter 6 Conclusion 159

Appendix 1 *Cinéma Pratique's* Interview with Jean-Luc Godard 165
Appendix 2 Interviews with Anne-Marie Miéville 173

Notes 183
Bibliography 189
Index 197

ACKNOWLEDGEMENTS

Writing this book has been a very long road. I began it as a childless Albertan; I finish it as a Nova Scotian father of two school-age boys. It began with the support of James Naremore and Joan Catapano, and I have remained grateful for that throughout this process. It was brought to fruition by Lisa Quinn, WLU's indomitable editor, and I am also grateful for the faith and confidence she has always shown.

That process unfolded in the context of very supportive colleagues at several institutions. At the University of Alberta, I am especially grateful to my compadres in Film Studies: Bill Beard, Liz Czach, and Elena del Río. In Halifax, I am in the perpetual debt of Sol Nagler and Darrell Varga (both of NSCAD University) and Jen VanderBurgh (Saint Mary's University), and I am proud of the little cine-critical fleet that we are assembling together. At Dalhousie, I have been supported by the Canada Research Chairs program, and I am very happy to acknowledge their role in this.

A number of undergraduates have helped here, and I thank them. When I was at the University of Alberta, I drew on the support of David Burke, Olivier Creurer, Conor Morris, Celia Nicholls (now studying at the University of Warwick), and Kate Rennebohm (now studying at Harvard University). At Dalhousie University, I am grateful to Emily Macrae (a student at the University of King's College). All of them, it is worth noting, are also alumni of the Telluride Film Festival's Student Symposium.

Marcy Goldberg (Universität Zürich) was very supportive of this project early on, and I always think of her as my most trusted "Swiss connection." I am certainly grateful to her for giving me permission to reprint her translation of an interview with Anne-Marie Miéville. On that front, thanks also to Danièle Hibon (Galerie nationale du Jeu de Paume) and Janine Euvrard (*24 Images*'s Paris correspondent) for permissions to reprint.

D. B. Jones (Drexel University) and Marsh Murphy (Metro Cinema Society) were the first colleagues to read bits of this, and they gave me good support and, just as important, skeptical criticism. I am also grateful for feedback and advice from Jonathan Rosenbaum.

On the matter of seeing material, not always an easy task with these two, I have numerous debts. Denis Lacroix (University of Alberta) was a great help in acquiring copies of the television material; he is a real librarian's librarian and a very good teacher, and I miss his wise counsel a lot. That is also true of Pierre Véronneau (Cinémathèque Québécoise), who helped out with some of the darker corners of the 1980s. Oksana Dykyj (Concordia University) is the keeper of the records of Godard's time in Montreal, and I thank her for her help. Douglas Morrey (University of Warwick) provided an indispensible and totally fascinating DVD for me at a crucial juncture, and I am very grateful indeed.

I owe a great deal to Tom Luddy. For my purposes here, I will just thank him for talking to me about his time working with Godard and for clarifying some of my thoughts about Godard's use of video. And I will also say that over the past few years I have developed a new test for starting a research project, which I hereby dub "the Luddy Litmus": if it turns out that Tom has played some key role in making this part of world cinema more widely known and understood, then I know that it constitutes a project worth pursuing.

Sasha and Bubba have improved my French a lot; they have also improved my life immeasurably in every imaginable way. And Sara Daniels, as always, deserves the biggest thanks of all.

Chapter 1
INTRODUCTION

The work of Jean-Luc Godard is both voluminous and widely celebrated. This is as it should be; he is a great filmmaker, someone who has spent a career rigorously rethinking the fundamentals of his medium (film) and its neighbouring media (television and video). Anne-Marie Miéville's work as a filmmaker seems, at first glance, to pale in comparison. She has directed several noteworthy works, and to judge from them, it might seem that she could be filed under the category "interesting Swiss filmmaker," hardly a classification that would offer a central place in the history of postwar cinema. That would be a mistake. The greater mistake, though, and the more common one, is to conflate "the films of Godard and Miéville" with "the films of Jean-Luc Godard." The frequency with which that mistake is made is no doubt a result of the considerable international fame that Godard accrued during the 1960s as part of the French *nouvelle vague* (hereafter, the New Wave). When such fame is attached to a single name, it can become hard to see beyond that name. This sort of myopia is explicit in Andrew Sarris's 1970 interview with Godard and Jean-Pierre Gorin, who were at that time making films together and signing them as "Groupe Dziga Vertov"; Sarris writes there how Godard "walked in with his assistant Jean-Pierre something or other" (51). Critics often seem to consider some of Godard's very best work to be made by him and his girlfriend, Anne-Marie something or other.

Of course, this is not the case at all, as it was not the case with Gorin; one of my first tasks in this book is to lay out some of the problems that the films of "Godard and Miéville" pose for understandings of authorship in cinema. I do that, in small part, by following scholars such as Michael Witt and Catherine Grant and proposing that the clearest, most illustrative comparison point for Godard and Miéville is the work of Jean-Marie Straub and Danièle Huillet. Godard and Miéville pose similar problems in terms of their status as avant-garde artists; thus, I also lay out some of the ways in which their work is both more and less radical than it may at first appear. It is the French critic

Serge Daney who lays out this "Godard paradox" more elegantly than any critic I know of, and his notion of the Godard paradox serves as a segue into a brief discussion of Daney's work and its usefulness as a "way in" to Godard and Miéville's films, videos, and television programs.

Once through the preliminaries (Chapter 1, "Introduction"), I divide this book into four parts that more or less move forward chronologically, and that seek to integrate some of the work that Godard and Miéville have done individually with the work they have done together. In Chapter 2, "Abandonments," I give some basic discussion of projects that Godard, or Godard and Miéville, began but abandoned. There are quite a few such projects, and I believe that seven of them are important for understanding the kind of work that Godard and Miéville have done together: the film *One P.M.* (which Godard began with D. A. Pennebaker in 1968 as *One A.M.* and Pennebaker finished in 1971), the video project *Moi Je* (which Godard began work on just before leaving Paris for Grenoble, where he set up shop with Miéville in 1973), aborted projects in Quebec and Mozambique, an abandoned feature film for Francis Ford Coppola's Zoetrope Studios (which was to have been called *The Story*), a basically unsuccessful attempt to work with Jean-Pierre Beauviala to create a new 35 mm camera, and an abandoned project to commemorate the seven hundredth anniversary of the Swiss confederation.

In Chapter 3, I move on to a discussion of the three films and two television series that Godard and Miéville first made together in the 1970s, work that exists in a curious state, between film and video; I call this chapter "Communication," which is a persistent concern for them during this period. "Communication" begins with three feature films that use video imagery—*Ici et ailleurs* (1974), *Numéro deux* (1975), and *Comment ça va?* (1976)—and concludes with two television series—*Six fois deux: Sur et sous la communication* (1976) and *France/tour/détour/deux/enfants* (1979). Following that, in Chapter 4, I discuss the feature-length work that Godard and Miéville made together during the 1980s, work that is clearly influenced by the tele-video experiments of the 1970s, but which also represents a conversation with both the aesthetic that Godard forged during the New Wave and which Miéville was then developing on her own. I call this chapter "Realization" because, in many ways, it is where their collective practice is at its peak; they were moving very easily between narrative and poetic works, between film and video, between short- and feature-length works, as though the differences between them meant nothing. That chapter begins with *Sauve qui peut (la vie)* (1980) and ends with *Soft and Hard* (1985) and includes discussion of roughly contemporary films such as Godard's *Lettre à Freddy Buache* (1981) and Miéville's *How Can I Love* (1983) and *Faire la fête* (1986). In Chapter 5, I discuss the short film and videos that have defined their work since the late 1980s, and try to show the degree to which it carries forward the ideas of the work that had come before it but nevertheless marks a turning inward that is different in degree to their earlier films, videos, and television programs. I call this chapter "Reconsideration," which begins with *Le Rapport Darty* (1989) and ends with the film they made for the Expo nationale suisse, *Liberté et patrie* (2002).

To a great extent, this book is devoted to what has become informally known, at least in English-language criticism, as "Late Godard." This term is usually used pejoratively, and Gerald Peary's report for the *Boston Phoenix* from the 2002 Cannes premiere of Godard's *Éloge de l'amour* (2001) is typical: "We were prisoners to the usual 'late Godard,' 'extreme Godard,' the gnomic mishmash which the once-essential filmmaker has been giving us for more than two post-Vietnam, post-68, death-of-cinema, living-in-Swiss-exile decades." When Godard was, in 2011, awarded an honorary Oscar for lifetime achievement (known as a Governor's Award), Terrence Rafferty's tribute in the *New York Times* managed to present his entire career without naming a single film after *Weekend* (1967). Bad enough that the term "Late Godard" leaves out Miéville (whom, needless to say, Rafferty's *New York Times* piece never even mentions); in English-language discussion of his work, it has become a kind of a cue for the dismissal of difficult work and a simultaneous nostalgia for some sort of lost innocence of franco/cinephilic youth.

I am more sympathetic to French-language summaries like René Prédal's sense of "les trios âges de Godard," although finally I think this, like similar discussions in English, is inadequate for my task here as well. In a 1989 article of that title, Prédal laid out what he saw as the main periods of his work:

> From 1959 to 1968, Godard, in his 30s, is paradoxically defined by both a triumphant cinephilia and a reinvention of the seventh art. It's then that he embodies auteur cinema with films like *À bout de souffle* or *Le Mépris*. The 70s, the period of his 40s, provoked a typical mid-life crisis. The questioning of fundamentals leads first to an experience with militant cinema, filmmaking collectives, and then regionalisation; he set up shop in Grenoble and discovered video, which led to two TV series. With *Sauve qui peut (la vie)*, Godard begins the period of the 1980s and his 50s. He returns to his roots in the Swiss canton of Vaud by setting up near Nyons, just as his creative explosion gives him a multimedia dimension that—having first been about expression when he set up the base for an auteur cinema in France, then about information or more precisely a counter-information opposed to national TV networks and big distribution outfits—now has as its priority questions of communication. ("Les trois âges de Godard," 13; my translation [hereafter "m.t."])

Prédal is touching on many of the issues at the heart of my discussion here, and the second two of these "three ages" correspond roughly to Chapters 2 and 3 of this book. More importantly, I am in full agreement that the story of Godard's post-1960s work is the story of his and Miéville's turn toward "communication" as a central interest. But I do not accept at all the contention that the 1970s represents some sort of mid-life crisis, "*le syndrome typique de la mi-vie*," as Prédal puts it. This is a fairly common way of describing Godard in the 1970s. The chapter in Antoine de Baecque's biography of Godard that is devoted to 1973–79, for instance, is called "L'Exil." Richard Brody's biography was spun off from a 2000 *New Yorker* profile of Godard, called "Exile in Paradise," which is based in part on an interview with Godard he conducted in June 2000; his 2008 *New Yorker* article, called "Auteur Wars," ends with Brody citing a 2007 interview Godard gave to *Die Zeit*: "Today I feel rather like an exile in my own land. In the land of cinema" (65). Writing in 1980, Colin MacCabe states that "[i]f there is a time when Godard can be considered to have abandoned filmmaking, it is not in the aftermath of 1968 but in the period when he left Paris and with Anne-Marie Miéville set up a company called Sonimage at Grenoble in the French Alps" (*Images, Sounds, Politics*, 23).

Even Godard himself has dismissed a lot of the work that he and Miéville did during this period of living in Grenoble and working with video. But I agree with Brody's assessment that "his activities there were of far greater importance than he allowed" (374). The 1970s is the period when Godard leaves the metropolis for good, starts working with Miéville, branches out into video and television in a serious way, and really becomes, with Miéville, an artist who is working with multiple media and with multiple formal and structural approaches. It is the period of films that mix in video images, complex montages that exist alongside extremely long takes, and a graceful interweaving of narrative and elliptical approaches. This is as true of films like *Numéro deux* (1975) and television work such as *Six fois deux: Sur et sous la communication* (1976) as it is of films like *Sauve qui peut (la vie)* (1979) and television work such as *Soft and Hard* (1985). This is a period not of exile, nor of mid-life crisis, nor of abandonment; it is a period of experimentation and genuine independence.

In keeping with this general sense, my overall task in this book is to reframe Godard and Miéville as artists whose collaboration has been shaped by a flexible, innovative approach to cinema and ideology alike, and thus to show that the Grenoble work is not some sort of lacuna but instead a key part of a very rich cinematic oeuvre. I am in broad agreement with Michael Witt's assessment of Godard that "he is as much a multimedia poet in the manner of Jean Cocteau as a feature-film director in the lineage of Hitchcock or Hawks" ("Shapeshifter," 75), and much the same could be said of Miéville. As this talk of exile and mid-life crises suggests, this is a very different kind of critical narrative than the one that has dominated discussion of Godard, in both French and English. As I mentioned above, a lot of that discourse seems to go something like this: "He was once this fabulous New Wave director; then he went all political and wonky, had this weird video phase, and now makes movies that are insufferably difficult and cranky." The analysis I want to offer is also different from the discourse around Miéville, which, especially in English but in French as well, is so minimal as to be difficult to satirize in a comparable manner. By way of trying to make up for this absence, I open each of the chapters of this book with a discussion of some part of a film that Miéville made on her own; this doesn't quite equal the degree to which my discussion sometimes wanders into work that Godard did on his own, but I hope it comes close. Between these discussions and the Miéville interviews in this book's appendix, the only films that she made on her own that do not receive some discussion are 1989's *Mon cher sujet* (a quiet, gentle film about intergenerational misunderstandings between women) and 1997's *Nous sommes tous encore ici* (which features a self-deprecating performance by Godard as a shambling pain in the butt who always wears a silly-looking toque and annoys his long-suffering partner by putting water into glasses of very nice wine). My regrettably brief discussions of Miéville's solo films are my effort to offer some modest check against what Kathleen K. Rowe (in an article I discuss later) calls "our critical ignorance" of Miéville's work as a filmmaker (50). This ignorance has been ameliorated slightly by events such as the Miéville retrospective that Paris's Jeu de Paume staged in 1998, or the group of English-subtitled prints of Miéville's films that the Swiss cultural agency Pro Helvetia circulated in 2002. Still, though, Miéville tends to be eclipsed by her more famous partner, and this is, I believe, a problem. For while they both did their best work together, they are each major filmmakers, and they deserve equal consideration. Catherine Grant is quite right to say that "film artists are not properly individual creators but, rather, embodied sites where words and audio-visual forms inscribe or install themselves. For Godard and Miéville, this plural site starts with Sonimage, the beginning of the collective creative ferment that frames all their later work, together and apart, and (re)creates them as 'different' filmmakers and dual authors" (117).

CORPUS

Just to make matters explicit, I conceive of the work of "Godard and Miéville" to be made up of films, videos, or television programs that were either directed by both, written by both, or written by one and directed by the other. The following is a list of such works (whose dates I take from the filmography contained in Nicole Brenez et al.'s *Jean-Luc Godard: Documents*):

> *Ici et ailleurs* (1974)[1]
> *Numéro deux* (1975)
> *Comment ça va?* (1976)
> *Six fois deux: Sur et sous la communication* (1976)
> *France/tour/détour/deux/enfants* (1979)
> *Sauve qui peut (la vie)* (1980)
> *Prénom Carmen* (1983)
> *Je vous salue, Marie* (1985) and *Le livre de Marie* (1985)[2]
> *Détective* (1985)
> *Soft and Hard* (1985)
> *Le Rapport Darty* (1989)
> *L'Enfance de l'art* (episode of the anthology film *Comment vont les enfants?*, 1990)
> *Pour Thomas Wainggai, Indonésie* (episode of the anthology film *Contre l'oubli*, 1991)
> Commercial for the Swiss cigarette company Parisienne People (1992)
> *Deux fois cinquante ans de cinéma français* (1995)
> *The Old Place* (1998)
> *Dans le noir du temps* (episode of the anthology film *10 Minutes Older: The Cello*, 2002)
> *Liberté et patrie* (2002)

With a few exceptions, most of Godard and Miéville's work together is available on video (although not all of it in Region 1/NTSC). *Le Rapport Darty* is nearly impossible to see; Nicole Brenez writes that "the film has currently been banned by Darty, who refuses to allow it to be distributed or shown" ("The Forms of the Question," 177), and I deal with that fact when I discuss it in Chapter 4. The television series *Six fois deux: Sur et sous la communication* and *France/tour/détour/deux/Enfants*, as well as the "television film" *Soft and Hard*, are available in North America only at extremely high institutional prices,[3] although *Soft and Hard* is available as part of a reasonably priced box set, with Spanish subtitles only, from the invaluable Barcelona distributor Intermedio. The anthology films *Comment vont les enfants?* (1990) and and *Contre l'oubli* (1991) were both released on VHS in France, although both are now out of print and very hard to come by. The commercial that Godard and Miéville directed for the cigarette Parisienne People was available, at the time of this writing, on YouTube; I have not been able to find it anywhere else. Despite relatively minor difficulties like these, I mean for this book to be a companion for someone who wants to work his or her way through more or less the entire body of work of Godard and Miéville.

My conception of this corpus leaves out a few important Godard films where Miéville seems to have had some role. I have thought the most about whether to include *Passion* (1982) as part of the Godard–Miéville corpus. The filmography of Antoine de Baecque's 2010 *Godard: biographie* states that the screenplay ("*scénario*") for *Passion* was written by Godard, Miéville, Romain Goupil, and Jean-Claude Carrière; the filmography of Alain Bergala's *Jean-Luc Godard par Jean-Luc Godard*, t.2, has the credit "*Scénario et dialogues: Jean-Luc Godard et Anne-Marie Miéville*" (480). This is not supported by the onscreen credits of the film (which credit Miéville only with "*Photos et conseils*"), nor by the filmographies of Brenez et al.'s *Jean-Luc Godard: Documents* (432), Michael Temple et al.'s *For Ever Godard* (44), or Shafto's filmography for Colin MacCabe's *Godard: Portrait of the Artist at Seventy* (361), none of which mention Miéville as a collaborator. Miéville has similar credits in other parts of Godard's work; she is credited as a still photographer on *Tout va bien* (1972), as art director on *Nouvelle Vague* (1990) and *Notre musique* (2004), and under "Logos" (along with nine other names) on *Film socialisme* (2010). She provided narration for Godard's contribution to the TV film *Le changement à plus d'un titre* (1982) and was producer on the TV work *Le dernier mot* (1988), part of the television anthology *Les Français vu par....* I am reluctant to include these as central because even though most of Godard's films are famously minimalist when it comes to screen credits, it does seem that if he had wanted to signal that these were genuinely collaborative works, then some indicative credit would be given to Miéville. I also leave out of the central corpus the Miéville films in which Godard stars: *Nous sommes tous encore ici* (1997) and *Après la réconciliation* (2000), although I discuss the latter by way of introducing Chapter 5. Indeed, much of this work that I mention as exclusions will come up at some point in the discussions that follow.

BIOGRAPHICAL

I do not want to dwell too much on biographical details, although it is helpful to know some basics of both Godard's and Miéville's career before they began working together. One reason for this is that the imbalance between what is available about the two is considerable. Over the course of several decades now, Godard has been the subject of truly enormous amounts of critical and scholarly attention. This includes Colin MacCabe's 2003 biography *Godard: A Portrait of the Artist at Seventy*, Richard Brody's 2008 biography *Everything Is Cinema: The Working Life of Jean-Luc Godard* (and unless otherwise noted, when I cite Brody this is the work I am referring to), and Antoine de Baecque's aforementioned 2010 *Godard: biographie*. Readers interested in the details of Godard's life thus have good places to go in both French and English (and I frequently refer to all three books throughout this discussion). Readers interested in the details of Anne-Marie Miéville's life are less fortunate, although not as forlorn as they once were. Richard Brody's book, for instance, recovers a bit about Miéville. He writes that she was "born in 1945, [and] was active with the local Swiss group Rupture pour le communisme.... Her family, like Godard's, was from the canton of Vaud in Switzerland, and, also like him, she had moved to Paris. There she briefly sang pop music, and then took up photography. She worked at a pro-Palestinian bookstore in Paris and helped Godard make contact with Palestinians and sympathizers there while he worked on *Until Victory*" (359). *Everything Is Cinema* also offers some detail about her family life, her alienation from her children, and so on (612–13).

One basic in any biographical sketch of Godard is that, like most of the filmmakers of the New Wave, he began as a film critic for the legendary French film magazine *Cahiers du cinéma* and moved from there into making films. In this book, I do not deal much with Godard's earliest films, which is to say his New Wave films—famous works such as *À bout de souffle* (1960), *Le Mépris* (1963), *Pierrot le fou* (1965), *Masculin féminin* (1966), and so on—not only because almost every book-length study of Godard deals with them in great detail, but also because I believe they are very different from the work that he made with Miéville. The degree to which Godard's early biography echoes the common trajectory of the French New Wave actually is deceptive. His early political sympathies are hard to suss out; both Brody and de Baecque make some hay of what seems to be his youthful right-wing sensibilities. De Baecque is more explicit on the subject than Brody, despite Brody's overall argument about Godard that he is something of a soft anti-Semite. Early in his book, de Baecque quotes a 1998 interview Godard gave to *Les Inrockuptibles* in which he said of his youth that "I thus had a right-wing formation, even without knowing it or really being aware of it, since I was so young" (10; m.t.). And while Brody mentions the references to Jean Parvulesco in *À bout de souffle* (the famous writer whom Jean Seberg interviews is named Parvulseco) by identifying him as an "extreme rightist philosopher" (6) and calling him Godard's "Geneva friend" (62), Hélène Liogier has written on Jean Parvulesco's admiration for the New Wave in great detail, and de Baecque quotes her scholarship on the question. Liogier recounts that the essays on the New Wave that Parvulseco wrote for the Falangist film magazine *Primer Plano* during the Franco era argued that the New Wave's films were "totally impregnated with the ideals of the extreme right" (130, m.t.). She writes that in one essay Parvulseco published in 1960, "According to him, the members of the New Wave were impregnated by an 'intellectual fascism.' Their philosophy was nihilism. They put the mentality of youth up on the screen, having a great love of freedom and fascinated by death, violence, and crazy love.... He felt that the films of the New Wave were anti-conformist, anticommunist, antidemocratic and anti-socialist" (134, m.t.). But the late 1960s saw Godard turn sharply leftward, in a way that is quite distinct from many of his New Wave contemporaries. One important part of this transition is the 1967 omnibus film *Loin du Vietnam* (1967), an anti–Vietnam War film produced by Chris Marker's production group SLON (Société pour le lancement des œuvres nouvelles) that included contributions from Godard, Alain Resnais, William Klein, Joris Ivens, Claude Lelouch, and from Marker himself (Agnès Varda participated in the post-production, but the sequence she shot was not included in the final film).

The crucial turning point is clearly May 1968, with its now-legendary strikes, demonstrations, and talk of revolution. De Baecque wrote: "The year 1968 represents a key moment in the life of Jean-Luc Godard. At the age of 38, it was a rupture along whose lines he reconstructed his existence" (391; m.t.). Reviewing de Baecque's biography for *New Left Review*, Emilie Bickerton has written about the importance of *Masculin féminin*, *Weekend*, and *La Chinoise*, arguing that "[i]t is also worth recording that 1968 did not push Godard, he was already walking away—all these films were made before the Langlois affair and the May upheavals" (154). But there is a significant difference between works such as *Masculin féminin* and *Weekend* and the work that he made with Miéville, and it is the material he made around 1968 that forecasts this shift. His series of *Cinétracts* (1968), collections of shorts that were both about and shown during some of the demonstrations and strikes, is an example of this shift away from conventional narrative (be it a push or a walk). Godard followed this up with a few comparably ambitious if often troubled or uncompleted films, such as his collaboration with American documentarian D. A. Pennebaker *One A.M.* (1968) / *One P.M.* (1971), *One Plus One* (1968, released in a slightly different version as *Sympathy for the Devil*)⁴ and *Le gai savoir* (1968), which in the next chapter I argue is an important "transitional film"). He followed these films with the work of his Groupe Dziga Vertov, or Dziga Vertov group, all of which were explicitly committed to leftist politics and social transformation, as well as being made completely outside of the formal or mode-of-production norms of narrative cinema. These films, when they had credits at all, were signed not by Godard but by the "Groupe Dziga Vertov."⁵ Many although not all of these were directed by Godard and Jean-Pierre Gorin; the films made under the Dziga Vertov name are *British Sounds* (1968), *Pravda* (1969), *Vent d'est* (1969), *Lotte in Italia* (1970), and *Vladmir et Rosa* (1970). Godard and Gorin also co-directed the feature film *Tout va bien* (1972) and the essay film *Letter to Jane: An Investigation about a Still* (1972); the former stars Jane Fonda as a television journalist, and the latter is a deconstruction of a photograph of Fonda in North Vietnam. Although the films vary in style, they all strongly bear the mark of post-1968 French leftism, centring on issues such as student uprisings, Hollywood imperialism, internationalism, and Maoist-flavoured variants of socialism. None of these films (except for *Tout va bien*) are narrative in any way; they integrate interviews, direct address to the camera, extremely artificial *tableux-vivants*, and so on. They represent the part of Godard's work where he stands the furthest from conventional cinema.

The other crucial difference between Godard and his contemporaries in the New Wave is his complex sense of nationality. "It would be hard to overemphasise the degree to which Godard is both French and Swiss," Colin MacCabe writes, "both a cultured and cosmopolitan member of elite Parisian society and a solid Swiss burgher, in many ways a typical representative of the canton of Vaud" (*Portrait of the Artist*, 4). This biographical nugget really does provide an important route into Godard's films, one that helps make the connection with Miéville (who also holds both French and Swiss nationality) more central than it has tended to be in discussions of his films (in both French and English). Godard is certainly on the cutting edge of cinema, but many of his films, and especially the ones he made with Miéville after the end of his Dziga Vertov period, have a distinctly self-contained and domestic quality to them. They are, at least in terms of their narrative, very clearly the products of two solid Swiss burghers. This sensibility is not simply biographical speculation; it is borne out by the films themselves, as I try to show throughout this book.

AUTHORSHIP

Godard has long been implicated with arguments around cinematic authorship. A lot of this is because of what he wrote for the *Cahiers du cinéma* during the 1950s, which was a sort of "golden age" for auteurism, for a director-centred approach to film criticism. But the auteurism of the *Cahiers du cinéma* is a lot more complicated than it may at first seem, and actually provides a good way into the work of Godard and Miéville.

Godard's aggressive challenge to authorship begins with the Dziga Vertov period of the late 1960s and early 1970s that I have just mentioned. Michael Witt writes that "May 68 functioned for Godard as a watershed in terms of rethinking his relation to his star status and the type of cinema within which such a status constructed him.... Godard's translation from auteur to quasi-anonymous group participant constitutes a remarkable concrete demonstration of the Structuralist challenge to authorship on a then massively *fêted* living artist" (*On Communcation*, 7). The touchstone essay during this period is certainly Roland Barthes's 1968 "La mort de l'auteur" (which strongly influenced Michel Foucault's 1969 essay "Qu'est-ce qu'un auteur?") This Barthes essay is not that clear an example of structuralism, but it offered ways for people who, in the wake of the furors of May 1968, sought to radically rethink the ways that expression, subjectivity, and socio-cultural formations interacted with one another.

It is worth pointing out, though, that André Bazin had criticized auteurism in the pages of the *Cahiers du cinéma* in a way that strongly anticipates this sort of work. Bazin was a founding editor of the *Cahiers du cinéma* and served as editor until his death in 1958; he also served as a kind of father figure to many of the young critics working there, some of whom, such as Godard, went on to become the filmmakers of the New Wave. Writing in 1957, Bazin emphasized the need to look at a film as an autonomous aesthetic object. He did this in a way that was very close to the structuralist emphasis on the mechanics of communication. He also rejected fuzzy-headed ideas about greatness or personal genius. "I feel that this useful and fruitful approach, quite apart from its polemical value, should be complemented by other approaches to the cinematic phenomenon which will restore to a film its quality as a work of art" ("De la politique des auteurs," 116/"On the *politique des auteurs*," 258). He even previewed structuralism's obsession with systems by asking rhetorically of Classical Hollywood "why not then admire in it what is most admirable, i.e., not only the talent of this or that filmmaker, but the genius of the system" (ibid.,116 / 258). Roland Barthes's sense of the real means of interpretation can be seen chez Bazin, a full eleven years before Barthes laid it out in his celebrated essay "La mort de l'auteur." There Barthes wrote of "the necessity to substitute *language itself* for the person who until then had been supposed to be its owner" ("La mort de l'auteur" 41 / "Death of the Author" 168; emphasis mine). Bazin's emphasis on a film's "*valeur d'œuvre*" is very close to Barthes's desire to reclaim *the language itself* from the author. "'*Auteur,' sans doute*," Bazin wrote, "*mais de quoi?*" ("De la politique des auteurs," 117). This is the question Barthes was asking too, by way of asking people to return to *language itself.* Language itself, communication itself: that is what is really at issue for both Barthes and Bazin, and that question of communication was a key obsession for Godard and Miéville in their 1970s work.

Perhaps it is this general reticence around authorship that helps to explain the difficulty of puzzling out the exact nature of Godard and Miéville's collaboration. In English-language scholarship dealing with their work together, it is something of a ritual to mention how Miéville does not give interviews about the work she has done with Godard. "We tried to communicate with her directly, by sending her questions about her views on these projects, her working methods, and her film, photographic or written work apart from Godard," the editors of the feminist film journal *Camera Obscura* wrote in 1982. "Unfortunately, there was no response" (5). Kathleen K. Rowe wrote in 1990 of how "little is known about Anne Marie Miéville's role in the Sonimage collaboration. Our critical ignorance complicates how we evaluate the issues of sexual representation and institutional power surrounding Godard and Miéville's work" (50); she then recounts *Camera Obscura*'s difficulties in contacting her.

John Gianvito wrote in 1993 that Miéville "has revealed few details about her life and given few interviews" ("Anne-Marie Miéville," 125). After saying that "the near-total absence of interviews with Miéville in which she talks of her collaborative work with Godard poses a problem for the researcher," Michael Witt notes in his 1998 dissertation on Godard and Miéville's production company Sonimage that "[s]he has also not responded to my attempts to contact her in the course of research for this thesis" (11). Catherine Grant, in a 2004 essay, also recounts the *Camera Obscura* difficulties and notes that "they don't say that they have attempted to contact Godard, or that they would be interested in so doing. Only Miéville, it seems, can clear these matters up, and she is silent" (107). This book is no exception to the trend. I sent four faxes to Miéville (in French, to Rolle, where both Godard and Miéville have lived since the late 1970s) and spoke with her on the phone twice; I never got anything beyond a broken promise to get back to me with an answer as to whether she and Godard would consent to an interview. I also sent four faxes to Godard (two to Rolle, and two to different numbers in Paris; three times in French and once in English), asking to interview him and Miéville together, and never received any response. I also sent a fax to Ruth Walderburger, the producer of Godard films such *Notre musique*, *Éloge de l'amour*, and *Film socialisme* (to her office in Zurich and in English); I received no response from her.

The situation is somewhat different in French. Miéville has given interviews, sometimes with Godard, but as far as I can establish, they were mostly about the films she has made as a director. Godard and Miéville did a question-and-answer session with high-school students at the 2001 Sarlat film festival, but they were basically talking about Miéville's film *Après la réconciliation*, which had been screened at the festival; a transcript was published in *Cahiers du cinéma* 552 (December 2000). Miéville was interviewed by Janine Euvrard on her own in 1994 for the Montreal film magazine *24 Images*, on the occasion of her film *Lou n'a pas dit non* (1994) (I reproduce that in full in Appendix 2). Miéville was also interviewed on her own in 1998 by Danièle Hibon for a booklet published to accompany a retrospective of her films at Paris's Jeu de Paume gallery (the full text of that is also reproduced in Appendix 2). None of these dialogues shed any light whatsoever on the details of her collaboration with Godard. The lone exception that I know of is an interview that the couple gave to Phillipe Azoury and Olivier Seguret of the French daily *Libération* on December 27, 2000, also ostensibly about Miéville's film *Après la réconciliation* (it is printed on the page facing Seguret's review of that film). The interview came to my attention because the last line of the bit I quote here opens Catherine Grant's article on Godard and Miéville. Godard summarized the issue of their collaboration in this way:

> To come back to your first question [about the chemistry between them while filming], I'd like to speak about something that's always been unfair for Anne-Marie. When someone asks us "How do you work together?" we should reply: "Like two filmmakers who get along well, who do things separately or together ..." The Straubs work in tandem, on the same bike, one in front of the other. We have two bikes. (23; m.t.)

It is telling that the only substantive discussion of their collaboration comes in an evocation of the films of Jean-Marie Straub and Danièle Huillet (a comparison that Grant's article unfolds a bit). They are another cinematic couple whose collaboration has always been something of a mystery, and whose work is too often conflated with that of the male member of the duo. Michael Witt has written about this comparison in similarly authorship-related terms; in his

1998 dissertation, he suggests that "Miéville and Godard are equally implicated at every stage of the Sonimage project, producing a unique and *genuinely* collaborative body of work (the work of Jean-Marie Straub and Danièle Huillet perhaps provides a close model)" (10). These similarities with Straub–Huillet are about more than just authorship and collaboration, and I deal with their intellectual intersections shortly.

Miéville thus remains a slightly mysterious figure, something that is not true of Godard in the same way. He has, over the course of his fifty-plus years in cinema, given countless interviews on his own. David Sterritt's 1998 anthology *Jean-Luc Godard: Interviews* is a fine survey of that terrain, but Miéville is almost never mentioned (she comes up very briefly in a 1981 interview Godard did with Pauline Kael [123] and more briefly still in the introduction to Katherine Dieckmann's 1985 interview about *Je vous salue, Marie*). Brody seems to have spoken with her as part of his work for *Everything Is Cinema*, and as I said earlier, he is able to share some biographical material but offers basically nothing as to the details of their working relationship. Much the same is true of Colin MacCabe's biography *Godard: A Portrait of the Artist at Seventy*. Whether this is because Godard and Miéville themselves never told the two about the details of their collaborations or because they were never asked is not clear in either case.

This is all to say that a book examining "Godard and Miéville" is a fraught affair. Trying to suss out who did what on which films, which is never a particularly good idea, is an especially futile effort in this case. Interviews with filmmakers can point in interesting directions, but they are far from being indispensable for a critical treatment of their films, and an interview seems especially questionable given Godard's famous unreliability as a self-chronicler. I do have cause to quote some Godard interviews as we move forward here, but I always try to square what he says with direct examples from the films themselves. Antoine de Baecque's frank dismissal of the usefulness of interviewing Godard, has been, for me, instructive. He writes in the first pages of his biography: "So, a Godard biography. But how to proceed? First off, without Godard; as a first condition he was warned but not consulted during this book's conception, on the assumption that he is definitely the worst placed person to talk about his work. He's a brilliant and stimulating filmmaker, but as an autobiographer is disconcerting, dithering and secretive, and the archives that he has preserved are partial and unavailable" (11; m.t.). But it does not follow from this that critics should abandon an interest in the work that Godard and Miéville have done together and simply treat Godard as an abstracted author, along the lines of what Peter Wollen famously did when he insisted that "Fuller or Hawks or Hitchcock, the directors, are quite separate from 'Fuller' or 'Hawks' or 'Hitchcock' the structures named after them, and should not be methodologically confused" (*Signs and Meaning*, 168). Most studies of Godard seem to do this unconsciously, grouping together every film with the name "Jean-Luc Godard" in the credits as though there was no distinction to be made between Godard and Miéville, two filmmakers who work together, and "Godard," a structure named after one of them. I believe that Colin MacCabe is quite right to say, of the work of the 1980s and 1990s, that "this period, which is impossible to understand outside of his enduring partnership with Anne-Marie Miéville ... while less well known than the films of the sixties, [marks] an aesthetic and intellectual achievement to rival the early decade" (xiii). To my mind, "Godard and Miéville" represents the best work in the oeuvres of both "Godard" and "Miéville," and it is only right that both partners be acknowledged equally. But beyond that I think a critic should tread carefully, worrying less about what filmmakers say about the details of their shared production methods than the films that emerge from those collaborations. I therefore strive to follow to a Bazinian "middle line" on the question of Godard and Miéville's authorship. Without a doubt, they are *both* auteurs. But of what?

Indeed, I heartily concur with MacCabe's statement that Godard is "unthinkable without the philosophical and critical thinking of André Bazin" (*Portrait of the Artist*, 58). That is true of Miéville as well, partly because of Bazin's status as a supportive skeptic of the *politique des auteurs*, but equally importantly because of Godard and Miéville's ongoing investment in a realist aesthetic, an aesthetic whose ethical framework was central to Bazin's thinking about cinema and its photographic essence. MacCabe traces this to Bazin's 1945 essay "L'ontologie de l'image photographique," which he sees as seminal for the filmmakers of the New Wave clustered at the 1950s *Cahiers du cinéma* (*Portrait of the Artist*, 62). It is in this essay that Bazin calls attention to the role of the world outside the mind of the artist in creating a photographic image in a way that is quite consistent with his desire in the "politique des auteurs" essay to move beyond plumbing the depths of a lone artistic genius. He writes that photography "has an effect upon us of a natural phenomenon, like a flower or snowflake whose beauty is inseparable from its earthy origin" (*Qu'est-ce que le cinéma?*, 13 / *What Is Cinema?*, 7). This awareness runs throughout Godard and Miéville's work, which is marked by a tension between earthly origins and highly composed beauty. The hypnotic long takes that so define the television series *Six fois deux: Sur et sous la communication* (1976), like the images of rolling green fields of *Sauve qui peut (la vie)* (1979), the softly dark interiors of the *Arte* office in their contribution to the omnibus film *Contre l'oubli* (1991), and the images of French trains rolling though a verdant vaudois landscape in *Liberté et patrie* (2002), derive their beauty from their rootedness in physical reality, although that is where their beauty *begins*. It is easy to caricature Bazin as someone who placed a naive faith in the degree to which cinema offers unmediated access to a piece of reality. He, like his students Godard and Miéville, understood very well that earthly origins are an inseparable *part* of the beauty of cinema, not the whole story.

GENDER

Godard has had a very complicated relationship with gender, specifically with representations of women. A critic looking at Miéville's corpus separately from Godard, though, could easily come to the conclusion that her films would be very interesting for feminist film critics. They are perhaps not as inarguably key as those of Chantal Akerman, but Miéville's work on her own is certainly as suggestive and complex as, say, the work of Ulrike Ottinger. And so there is little question that part of the story of Godard's collaboration with Miéville is the story of him becoming more interesting when it comes to representations of gender. Akerman, Ottinger, or Godard and Miéville all make films that are defined by very complex representational strategies of all sorts, and their films (more so than the films of Straub–Huillet, for example) engage with and radically revise cinematic representation *via* gender.

In English-language film criticism and theory, Godard and Miéville's work has attracted much sympathetic attention from feminist critics, and the most celebrated of them all, Laura Mulvey, has written quite a bit about Godard's evolution on matters of gender and that evolution's connection to Miéville. In a 1985 essay she co-wrote with Colin MacCabe (and later published in her book *Visual and Other Pleasures*), Mulvey writes that "Godard slides continually between an investigation of the images of women and an investigation which uses those images. It could be argued that since his collaboration with Anne-Marie Miéville this sliding has to a certain extent diminished as the problems of male sexuality have been introduced directly into the content of the films" (52–53). In an essay originally written for the catalogue to MoMA's 1992 Godard retrospective and subsequently revised for her 1996 book *Fetishism and Curiosity* (the version I am citing here), she traces the evolution of his political "triads." In the 1960s, the triad was "cinema, the woman's body, consumer society"; in the 1970s, it was "[t]he cinema, the body, the factory"; in the 1980s, it becomes "cinema, the woman's body, 'nature'" (78). Clearly a key factor here is the emergence and then deepening of the connection to Miéville, although Mulvey goes on to point to the importance of a film that Miéville appears to have been only tangentially connected to: "*Passion* is a watershed film, a point at which Godard's changing aesthetic and political priorities take shape. *Carmen* is a transitional film, a film of crisis marking the distance that lies between *Passion* and *Je vous salue, Marie*" (78). For other English-language feminists (and for me, as well), the key film is the one they finished just before *Passion*, 1979's *Sauve qui peut (la vie)*. The special issue of *Camera Obscura: A Journal of Feminism and Film Theory* devoted to Godard and Miéville has an image from *Passion* on the cover but spends a lot more time talking about *Sauve qui peut*. For Elisabeth Lyon, a sequence where Marguerite Duras is heard offscreen, partially via a radio interview that is playing in the lead character's car (he is called Paul Godard, and his estranged partner is called Denise), and yet is never actually seen on screen, is key:

> It is around these issues of the representation of women's desire at stake in the Duras episode that language later becomes a vehicle (quite literally) for aggression.... Denise accuses Paul of always wanting to think for her, an accusation which turns Godard/*Godard*'s idealized appropriation of women's desire (Duras and the idea of *parole de femme*) into subsequent aggression against the actual possibility of difference in the fiction; here in the form of Denise and her work. (9)

This "Duras episode" is one of the more self-aware and more gently absurd sequences in the film; it is important in no small part because it so clearly tries to stake out a political position on gender and representation. I am much more sympathetic to this "*Camera Obscura*" position of centralizing *Sauve qui peut*, a film that is, I go on to argue, a watershed in their work together for many reasons, one of which without question is its highly nuanced arguments about gender representation.

Indeed, one way of thinking of the difference between "Godard and gender" and "Godard–Miéville and gender" is to think of the difference between being aligned with the cinephile branch of the French New Wave and being aligned with the politicalized, cinema-friendly wing of the *nouveau roman*, the group of which Duras was the leading light. The key document here is clearly the special double issue of the *Cahiers du cinéma* devoted to Duras. It was number 312–13, published in June 1980, and titled *Marguerite Duras: Les yeux verts*; it was coordinated by Serge Daney, Pascal Bonitzer, François Regnault, and Charles Tesson. It is a collection of articles about, interviews with, and texts written by Duras, all of which have something to do with the cinema. In one interview where she is being asked about her favourite filmmakers, the questioner simply asks

"Godard?" and she replies: "He is one of the greatest. The greatest catalyst of world cinema" (37; m.t.). Elsewhere, she talks about the experience of *Sauve qui peut (la vie)*, with imagery that is appropriately chaotic and occasionally absurd:

> Last year Godard asked me to shoot a short sequence in his film, which at the time was called *Sauve qui peut (la vie)*. I didn't want to shoot, I only wanted to do an interview with him. So he asked me to come, in October of 79, and I went, it was to be at Lausanne, he told me that it would all be set up, the time and place for the interview. So he took me into a school—it was recess time, or dismissal time, I don't remember anymore—and it was under a wooden staircase that the students used. So we did the interview. I didn't understand anything he said to me. He didn't understand anything I said to him, and not only because of the infernal noise in the school, but no matter, that was the interview. At the end he said, "To think that I asked to you to come from Paris to talk in this of all places." After I knew him a little better it was OK and I came to really like him. It seemed to me that he and I had experienced inverse problems with the cinema, especially in the sound–image relationship. (25–26; m.t.)

The sorts of sound–image problems that Duras is alluding to are, as Lyon keenly observes, a considerable part of the way in which *Sauve qui peut* uses language and its limitations as a means to evoke the ways that dominant and sexist cinematic representation often amounts to an aggression against difference. Disruption of realist form via unconventional sound–image relationships, as well as unconventional narrative structures, is indeed a key way that Duras's cinema enunciates a commitment to difference, very much including sexual difference. Writing of how Duras's cinema draws attention to that which conventional cinema always renders invisible or naturalized, Roseanna Maule writes in the introduction to her anthology on Duras and cinema that "[t]his book assumes that Duras' dismissal of the structuring mechanisms of film narrative and enunciation represented by the figure of the *grand imagier* is the fundamental characterizing trait of her film-making practice and a central point of reference for discussing her films" (26). What defines the organization of Duras's cinema, for Maule, is "the major presence of female voices, both off-screen and in voice over.... These voices ostensibly substitute for the narrative continuity otherwise missing in Duras's films and place enunciation on the side of feminine identity, traditionally undermined in narrative cinema" (30). Duras's 1975 film *India Song* is a case study there, a film that radically disrupts conventional realist narration and centralizes an explicitly female subjectivity in the process. These kinds of voices that Maule alludes to, voices that substitute for narrative continuity, can also be heard in the Godard and Miéville film of the same year, 1975's *Numéro deux*, a work that eschews a unified narrative voice in favour of a series of voices—onscreen, off-screen, and in voice-over—many of which are women's voices (such as Miéville's).

Duras was highly committed to what she called "*l'autre cinéma*." She describes that by way of a conclusion to *Les yeux verts*: "When I don't manage to resolve my films in terms of cinema's traps, when they remain suspended, as constant questions, when I cannot deliver myself from their thought, I'm making cinema then" (91; m.t.). Making that kind of cinema, a cinema that lives as a constant question and in so doing avoids the traps of conventional representation, is obviously important for any artist trying to rethink such existential basics as gender. That attempt at rethinking is a good way of defining the practice that Godard and Miéville spent their shared career developing.

THE IMPORTANCE OF SERGE DANEY

Jonathan Rosenbaum has written (in an article called "Daney in English: A Letter to *Trafic*") of how he tried to tell the editors of an American university press that "bringing out a collection of Serge's film criticism in English was an urgent matter and a first priority, almost comparable in some ways to what making Bazin available in English had been in the '60s." It is no surprise, then, that Daney's thought on cinema and television is also central for Godard and Miéville. Like Bazin, Serge Daney was a creature of the *Cahiers du cinéma*; he started writing for the magazine in 1964 and was the editor from 1973 to 1981. And like Godard, Daney became impatient with the magazine's auteurist assumptions, and in the late 1960s and early 1970s, he wrote articles and participated in round tables that sought to move cinema toward a conceptual framework that was more explicitly political and more scientific. And like Godard again, Daney spent the late 1970s and 1980s trying to get "back to cinema," moving between film, television, and video in a search for new ways of understanding the relationship between images, the societies in which they existed, and the people who produced and consumed them. Godard and Miéville have made no secret of their admiration for Daney's work. Their film *Deux fois cinquante ans de cinéma français* (1995) contains a montage of their pantheon of criticism (images of their faces with their names superimposed over them and excerpts from their writing read by Godard or Miéville on the soundtrack); the names are Denis Diderot, Eugène Fromentin, Elie Faure, Georges Sadoul, Jean Epstein, Jean-Georges Auriol, André Malraux, Jean Cocteau, Robert Bresson, André Bazin, Maurice Schérer (Éric Rohmer), François Truffaut, Jacques Rivette, Marguerite Duras, and Serge Daney. Part of Godard and Miéville's attraction to Daney's writing is no doubt due to his intersections with their own interests (such as the play between film and television, which I discuss shortly). But part of this attraction is no doubt also due to the fact that Daney wrote eloquently about the films and television programs that they made.

Although Godard comes up throughout Daney's writing, his earliest attempt to tackle it directly was the 1976 essay "Le thérrorisé: pédagogie godardienne," published in *Cahiers du cinéma* 262–63. The topic here was basically the films that Godard had made with Gorin, and he treats *Tout va bien* (1972) in some detail. But equally central to the analysis is *Ici et allieurs* (1974), initiated by Godard and Gorin and finished by Godard and Miéville. As I argue shortly, this is another important "transitional film," a work that ends one collaboration and begins another. To a great extent, the difference between these phases is the difference between urgency and meditation; the difference between Paris and Rolle (the small village in the Swiss canton of Vaud, where, as I discuss in Chapter 3, the two moved in the late 1970s); or the difference between a pared-down, interview-heavy work like *British Sounds* (1969) and a brooding, lyrical work like *Soft and Hard* (1985). Daney writes in "Le thérrorisé" that "Godard's pedagogy consists in forever coming back to images and sounds, pointing to them, matching them, commenting on them, putting images within images and sounds within sounds, criticizing them, like so many insoluble enigmas: not losing them, keeping them in sight, *keeping them*" (*La rampe*, 92 / "Theorize / Terrorize," 120; italics his). In *Ici et allieurs*, we can see Godard, as he will go on to do with Miéville, trying to *keep* these images, rather than to throw them right back into some sort of ongoing struggle. The struggle of the Fatah fighters of the "*allieurs*" part of *Ici et allieurs* is, after all, finished, as Daney knows very well: "They—or other fedayeen like them—died in 1970, assassinated by Hussein's troops" (*La rampe*, 94 / "Theorize / Terrorize," 121). The purpose here is not, as it was in Godard's Dziga Vertov days, to use the cinema as a means in an ongoing struggle. The function of films such as *Ici et allieurs*, and the work that followed it, is to use the cinema to comment, layer, and match; the purpose is to keep these images in sight, to prevent their disappearance.

But the most fruitful of Daney's engagements with Godard's work, to my mind, is a short essay he wrote for the *Revue Belge du cinéma* in 1987 called "Le paradoxe de Godard." This is where he sets out a schema for a different sort of avant-garde, one that is oddly respectful of convention. "A love of cinema desires only cinema," Daney wrote there, "whereas passion is excessive; it wants cinema but it also wants cinema to be something else, it even longs for the horizon where cinema risks being absorbed by dint of metamorphosis, it opens up its focus into the unknown" ("Le paradoxe de Godard," 7/"The Godard Paradox," 68). A love of cinema is, of course, at the core of the work of Godard the cinephile, Godard of the metacinematic New Wave; this is most visible in films like À bout de souffle (1960), Bande à part (1964), and Alphaville (1965). And a desire for cinema to be something else is equally central to his post-1968 work, from Cinétracts (1968) forward; these films really do try to make cinema into something new in the way that they utterly reject conventional film language and stand completely outside of the conventional distribution and exhibition networks. This is quite visible in the Dziga Vertov work, but also in films such as One Plus One (1968) and Le gai savoir (1968). But it is in his work with Miéville that he really becomes *both* kinds of filmmakers, someone who wants to love the cinema but who also wants to move it beyond convention, beyond what it has been so far. Only the work of Godard and Miéville embodies this new, paradoxical avant-garde. Daney goes on to write:

> Godard has been so easily described as an "enfant terrible," an "avant-garde filmmaker," an "iconoclast" and a "revolutionary" that we have failed to notice that right from the start, he respected the rules of the game.... In fact, Godard is troubled by the absence of rules. There is nothing revolutionary about Godard, rather, he is more interested in radical reformism, because reformism concerns the present. ("Le paradoxe de Godard," 7/ "The Godard Paradox," 71)

This is a very precise description of Godard and Miéville. The revolutionary aspirations of the Dziga Vertov group have been left behind in favour of a radical reformism that operates both on the level of form (which we can see, for instance, in a film like Détective [1985], which begins with the conventions of a crime film only to utterly flummox them) and on the level of politics (which we can see, for instance, in a film like The Old Place [1998], which, as I discuss below, uses montage to try to lay out the age-old argument that art and commerce have a troubled relationship). This "present-ism" that Daney evokes is everywhere in Godard and Miéville; their work engages—equally vigorously as it does with problems of politics and of form—with the look and feel of everyday life. Like good Bazinians, Godard and Miéville are making films about their world as they find it.

A more melancholy connection between Godard and Daney is to be found in the interview that they did in 1989. This was from the beginning intended to be part of Godard's massive video series Histoire(s) du cinéma (1988–2004), and was eventually integrated into episode 2A, Histoire(s) du cinéma: Seul le cinéma (1997). Video footage of Daney sitting at a table talking (he is awkwardly framed in the background; Godard is in the foreground) accounts for about two-thirds of that episode. It was originally published in *Libération* on December 26, 1988 and was republished in *Cahiers du cinéma* 513 (1997) upon the completion of *Seul le cinéma* (part of this was also published in an English translation in Raymond Bellour's anthology *Son + Image*, although not the passage I reproduce below). Godard and Daney's discussion is wide ranging and in some places melancholy; like Godard's *Histoire(s) du cinéma* overall, there is in the interview a fair bit of melancholy about the failure of film to transform the world. But there are also instances of Daney and Godard making common intellectual commitments explicit; one example of this is when they talk about television:

> S. DANEY: This dual heritage of television is very interesting. French television is mostly built as a continuation of the French tradition of Quality Cinema, of drama. At the same time, in the 1950s, a few great filmmakers like Rossellini, or even like Bresson or Tati, who didn't necessarily work for television, anticipated this apparatus of television, seeing that they could obtain other very powerful effects with the memory of cinema, that is to say film. You all were critics, then filmmakers at this moment, and you alternated between the two. There was never an anti-television discourse on the part of filmmakers like Welles, Hitchcock or Tati. There was thus a sort of happy incest at the beginning, which has since become unhappy.
>
> J-L. GODARD: ... You mustn't conflate the terrain and the tool: television isn't a terrain, it's a tool.... Television is something staggering because of its popularity. Cinema, the novel, European-inspired painting have each done some part of the things they can do: the child has grown up. But in a way television hasn't done this: and in light of its universalism and its popularity, this is a global catastrophe. ("Dialogue entre Jean-Luc Godard et Serge Daney," 50; m.t.)

This sense of the possibility of television, and the delicate tension between its status as a distinctive medium with its own prosperities and its status as a place for serious filmmakers, is quite consistent with what Daney had written about television elsewhere. Daney left the *Cahiers du cinéma* in 1981 and became a film critic for the leftist daily *Libération*. In 1987, he spent 100 days watching six television channels and writing a column called "Le Salaire du zappeur" (a pun on the French title of the 1953 film *Wages of Fear: Le Salaire de la peur*); these columns were collected in a 1993 edition of the same title. In the essay that concludes that collection, titled "Back to the Future," he writes of his "*théorie de l'inceste ciné-télé*" (186). He goes on to say that "the real impact of filmmakers like Vertov, Rossellini, Bresson, Tati, Welles, Godard, or Straub (among others) lies in their unstable positioning between the poetic requirements of cinema and the progress of the mass-mediation (mass-mediatisation) of the world" (186–87; m.t.). This is a defining characteristic of Godard and Miéville's work: the tension between poetics and progress, between cinema and "mass-mediation." Daney's work, especially the part that dealt directly with television, was always about discovering the new life created by such tensions (or such conflicts and contradictions, as he might have said in his more Marxist, *Cahiers du cinéma* days).

COMPARISONS

A few comparative notes can give a good sense of the ways in which Godard and Miéville are, following Daney, different kinds of avant-garde artists, rather than simply an extension of the New Wave. The work of three filmmakers can help steer us toward a clearer understanding of that Daney-esque sense of the avant-garde: Jean Rouch, and the husband-wife team of Jean-Marie Straub and Danièle Huillet.

Jean Rouch was a French ethnographic filmmaker who built his reputation on the critical, playful quality of his documentaries.[6] Most of these were filmed in west Africa in which Rouch had an abiding interest (he was born in Niger). His most famous film is probably *Chronique d'un été* (1960), where he and co-director Edgar Morin turned their cameras on what Morin called Rouch's "own tribe": Parisians. MacCabe has argued for the Godard–Rouch connection, seeing it as further evidence of Godard's Bazinian sensibilities; MacCabe was himself following Luc Moullet's 1962 essay on Godard. Alluding to Rouch's celebrated films *Moi, un noir* (1958) and *Les maîtres fous* (1955), Moullet wrote of Godard's first feature film that "*Breathless* is kind of 'I, a white guy,' or the story of two crazy masters" (26; m.t.). Godard himself had written rapturously about both of Rouch's films. He wrote in the March 11, 1959, issue of the magazine *Arts* that "*Moi, un noir* is, effectively, both the most audacious and the most humble of films" (*Jean-Luc Godard par Jean-Luc Godard* t.1, 177; m.t.). Writing in *Cahiers du cinéma* 94 (April 1959), he said that "there is no film more moral than *Birth of a Nation* and no film more spectacular than *Moi, un noir*" (*Jean-Luc Godard par Jean-Luc Godard* t.1, 182; m.t.). Leaving aside the matter of the morality of *Birth of a Nation* (1915) (a film beloved by many French cinephiles despite the heroic status it accords to the Ku Klux Klan), this does make clear the high esteem in which the early Godard held Rouch. It is not hard to see why this is the case. Early New Wave films made prodigious use of on-location shooting with lightweight cameras and sound gear, and generally worked very hard to cultivate the creative tension—or the dialectic, as some of them might later say—between spontaneity and fiction. Rouch's films were built on just this tension, frequently featuring people who would "play" themselves, "perform" their everyday lives, and as his career moved forward, he did so using cutting-edge technological developments in portable cameras and sound. He is, aesthetically and thematically, the grandfather of the New Wave. His connection to early Godard is obviously important, but his importance to Godard and Miéville is less clear. As I have said above, the films that Godard has made with Miéville are substantively different from the work he did as part of the New Wave; in many ways this is a matter of a heightened reliance on montage and, in turn, a decreased interest in the energetic newness of location shooting.

One way of explaining the shift from "Godard" to "Godard and Miéville" is to suggest that it is about the movement from films that suggest a comparison with those of Jean Rouch to films that suggest a comparison with those of Jean-Marie Straub and Danièle Huillet. Although Richard Roud's groundbreaking 1971 book on their films is called just *Straub*, it was more typical to refer to the films they made together as being "Straub–Huillet" films (or, sometimes, as films made by "the Straubs," as Godard himself did).[7] The fact that "Straub–Huillet" was also the name of their production company made this even more natural. Despite the aforementioned qualification that Godard offered about "the Straubs" working on a tandem bike but he and Miéville having two bikes, I think it is regrettable that the nomenclature "Godard and Miéville" has not become equally second nature.

The similarities here are about more than taxonomy, or bicycles; Straub-Huillet and Godard–Miéville are, in many films, evincing a very similar set of formal and thematic concerns. Cryptically acknowledging their female partners, Pascal Bonitzer argued in a 1976 issue of the *Cahiers du cinéma* that "Straub and Godard (these names, for what they are worth, should at least be doubled, or linked up with another one) are situated at two extremes of cinematic modernity" ("J.-M. S. et J.-L.G.," 5; m.t.). Bonitzer's essay is an attempt to situate Straub–Huillet and Godard–Miéville as the dual flag carriers of radical cinema's highest idealism. Alluding to Straub–Huillet's then-most-recent film *Moses und Aron* (1973), he writes "Moses *and* Aaron: Straub and Godard's operations unspool like one and another, one in another, one wrecked in the wreck of the other" (10; m.t.). Straub–Huillet are best known for *Moses und Aron* as well as films such as *Chronik der Anna Magdalena Bach* (1968), *Klassenverhältnisse* (1984), all of which aspire to a kind of semi-musical transcendence of film language, a transcendence that is sharply tinged with politics. "He may construct his films from the most realistic materials," Roud writes of Straub (meaning to say Straub–Huillet, no doubt), "and yet the result is a musical structure which transcends realism—but without rejecting it" (11). He could just as easily be describing the Bazinian-tinged practice of Godard and Miéville. Now, the gap between Godard and Miéville's work and Straub–Huillet films such as *Anna Magdalena Bach* or *Moses und Aron*, which are literally dealing with music, may at first seem considerable. But the "musical structure which transcends realism—but without rejecting it" is an ethic that also keenly informs Straub–Huillet's representation of landscape, which is a recurring although not very widely discussed concern of theirs. I see Godard and Miéville not necessarily in the flat, still acting and camera style of Straub–Huillet's *Klassenverhältnisse* nor in the studied compositions and steady camera movements of their *Moses und Aron*, but in the lush, patient evocation of the landscape of Metz and its surroundings in their short film *Lothringen!* (1994).[8]

That film (like some key sequences of *Moses und Aron*) features the 180-degree pans and the characters and voice-overs addressing history and geography in flat, self-aware tones that are so familiar from their other films. But there is also a very real pastoral sensibility here, a palatable desire to lyricize the *terroir* of the Lorraine valley (this sensibility is actually quite visible in parts of *Moses und Aron* as well). Here we see them intersecting with important parts of Godard and Miéville works like *Sauve qui peut (la vie)* (1979) or *Soft and Hard* (1985)—which are, as I discuss in due course, important in no small part for their status as meditations on the landscape of the area around Lac Léman (known in English as Lake Geneva)—or their television series *France/tour/détour/deux/enfants* (1979)—which is, as I also discuss, a meditation on suburban / provincial life and its connection to transcendence. Straub–Huillet are too easily dismissed as obscurantist, elitist Marxists, making films that deny their viewers pleasure in the name of some higher political purpose; it would be easy to say something similar about the work of Godard and Miéville. In both cases there is a poetic sensibility at work, one that is often deeply rooted in a specific place: the Lorraine valley, Lac Léman, and so on.

INSTITUTIONS

The importance of a sense of place is also a good way into understanding Godard and Miéville's unusual institutional situation. Like the details of their biographies or their collaborative division of labour, their succession of production companies is something in which it would be very easy to get involved. But just as it was helpful to know a little bit about their lives by way of focusing attention on specific aspects of the films themselves, some discussion of their production arrangements does help bring their concerns into slightly sharper focus.

To a great extent, the history of "Godard and Miéville" is a history of the work they did together after Godard left Paris. MacCabe writes that "on 1 December 1973, Anne-Marie Miéville became the legal representative of a company with the name of Sonimage.... when she assumed control of Sonimage she was living in Paris at 76, boulevard Saint-Michel" (*Portrait of the Artist*, 239). Michael Witt has also recalled the company's Paris lineage, writing that while he was in the United States on a tour to promote *Tout va bien* (which he co-directed with Jean-Pierre Gorin), "Godard purchased some of the video equipment with which to set up the first Sonimage studio in Paris ... in early 1973. The Paris-based Sonimage video *atelier* [workshop] was established by Godard with Anne-Marie Miéville" (*On Communication*, 1). But Witt goes on to say that "[d]ecentralisation is a central defining premise to the Sonimage practice: the relocation of Sonimage to Grenoble constituted first and foremost a move *from* Paris, a desire to resist the political and cultural hegemony of the capital" (*On Communication*, 3). The Sonimage idea, the desire to create a self-contained workshop that relied heavily on emerging video technology, would not really flower until Godard and Miéville left the metropolis. Brody traces this departure to Godard's desire to collaborate with cameraman and cinéma-vérité innovator Jean-Pierre Beauviala. Indeed, Antoine de Baecque writes of the 1970s that "the most essential technological team-up of this period is surely that of Jean-Pierre Beauviala" (523; m.t). In the late 1960s, Beauviala's camera manufacturing company Aaton was based in the French alpine town of Grenoble, where he was working on the technology to shoot in synchronous sound without a cable-connected camera and tape recorder. He was very involved with the *Cahiers du cinéma*, which published a four-part interview with him (in nos. 321–25) and listed him on their masthead as their "*Conseiller scientifique*" though the 1970s. Brody recalls how "[a]fter meeting Beauviala, Godard remained in contact with him, learned of his camera project, and took an interest in it. Godard asked Beauviala to move to Paris, but Beauviala refused. The next logical step was for Godard to follow him to Grenoble" (373). The Grenoble collaboration did not last very long; however, Beauviala was an important figure for Godard and Miéville for some years to come. Brody suggests that "Aaton was to be the model for Godard and Miéville's new company, Sonimage.... Beauviala was in business to make money, but to do so by producing a highly technical product (in Aaton's case, cameras; in Sonimage's, films)" (375). Beauviala remained close to Godard and Miéville professionally for the next decade or so. Starting in the late 1970s, he began design work on a lightweight 35 mm camera, which was intended to be used first on Godard's aborted Francis Ford Coppolla–sponsored film project *The Story*, then on

Sauve qui peut (la vie), although was not actually used until *Prénom Carmen* (1983), and even then not very successfully. I discuss that camera and the problems that surrounded its design in Chapter 3, "Abandonments."

This should all give a sense of the degree to which Godard and Miéville's interest was part of a project of regionalization, which is a particularly important issue in both France and Switzerland, although for very different reasons. As a legacy of the revolution, which unified a diverse set of territories into a republic with a Paris-based government that sought to treat all citizens equally (and was therefore blind to any religious, linguistic, ethnic, or regional identifications), centralization has long been a characterizing aspect of French governance. Many groups have historically chafed against this centralization, generally in the name of linguistic or cultural distinctiveness. The Basques and the Bretons, for example, have both long had separatist movements. During the 1970s and 1980s, there were some concessions by the French state in the form of widespread regionalization programs, many of which had a linguistic and cultural emphasis, which logically included cinema and especially television. Michael Witt's *On Communication* engages with this aspect of Sonimage's work, partially by commenting on the work of René Prédal, who, as Witt points out, connects this regionalization to Godard's post-1968 period in his 1984 history of French cinema. This is the way Prédal describes the move from Paris to Grenoble:

> In leaving the capital, Godard was giving the tedious notion of regionalisation its real sense. The experience of Sonimage was also an example of his desire to set up, in the countryside, a genuinely living culture, almost ten years before the official recognition of this movement, with the creation of eight cinemas, which are in operation today. (*Le cinéma français contemporain*, 238; m.t.)

Part of what is going on in the Sonimage practice, then, is a move to divorce regionalism from the folkloric, to rediscover the political radicalism and freedom from constraint that comes from being autonomous from an all-controlling metropolis. The 1960s and 1970s saw a great deal of this kind of regionalist discourse emerge all over Europe. In Ireland, it was particularly linked to mass media, as the 1970s and 1980s were marked by pirate broadcasts (first radio, then television) in Irish Gaelic, broadcasts inseparably linked to parallel movements for cultural and economic autonomy from Dublin (governance of the Republic of Ireland was, and remains, nearly as centralized as that of France). In Switzerland, the regionalization movement of note was both more militant and more about governance. The 1960s and 1970s saw the transformation of the quest for a new, French-speaking canton of Jura, which was independent of the canton of Berne and a full member of the Swiss confederation. The Jura movement was ultimately successful, and following the success of a Jura-wide referendum in 1974 and a series of "cascading referenda" meant to establish a geographically contiguous entity, the new canton came into being on January 1, 1979. This was one of the real success stories of European regionalism of the post-1968 era. Godard and Miéville, both citizens of the francophone canton of Vaud, could not have been unaware of it (I discuss this in a bit more detail in Chapter 5, when I deal with their 2002 film *Liberté et patrie*).

Indeed, another way of explaining the shift from the "Godard" of the New Wave to "Godard and Miéville" is to suggest that (even though he and Miéville lived and worked in Grenoble for a time) it is about the difference between a French outlook and a Swiss one. In vivid contrast to France, Switzerland has always (except for a brief period under Napoleonic puppet government, which I discuss more in Chapter 5) been characterized as a loose federation of very different cantons, to which nearly all powers (except for defence, foreign, and monetary policy) are devolved. In vivid contrast to France where the capital of Paris casts a huge shadow, the Swiss do not even use the term "capital"; Berne is known in French as "*la ville fédérale*." In his 1992 essay "Eight Obstacles to the Appreciation of Godard in the United States," Jonathan Rosenbaum cites as number 6: "The move from Paris." Comparing Godard with Michael Snow and Chantal Akerman, he writes there that "[t]he same unconscious form of imperialism that has tended to ignore both the Belgian aspects of Akerman's work and the Canadian aspects of Snow's has resisted regarding the bulk of Godard's work since *Every Man for Himself* [*Sauve qui peu (la vie)*] (1979) as Swiss. This has unfortunately obscured the degree to which Godard's Swiss identity might be construed as a significant factor in the meaning of his recent work ..." (201). Rosenbaum is starting with *Sauve qui peut (la vie)* because that was the first film that was made by Sonimage from their Rolle location. But I think that Godard's Swiss identity might be construed as "a significant factor in the meaning of" all of the work that he and Miéville have done together. This kind of regionalism, this push for a more localized, self-sufficient cinematic practice that is at the core of their Sonimage operations, is much closer in spirit to the Swiss idea of federalism than it is to French republicanism.

This "Sonimage practice" is about more than simply forming a production company outside Paris; it is about autonomy. In the 1970s, Godard and Miéville began to acquire video equipment, which was at that time on the technological cutting edge but which also required much less technical expertise to operate (no labs, fewer technicians, and so on). "The growth of video technology seemed to offer the possibility of gaining some autonomy at every level of production," Colin MacCabe writes, "and Sonimage was set up with a considerable stock of video equipment. At the time Godard seems to have considered, at least in interviews, the possibility of alternative distribution ... which would operate as though Sonimage was a handicraft industry with customers ordering video programmes for particular purposes" (*Images Sounds Politics*, 23). Even after the name of Godard and Miéville's production company had to be changed for legal reasons, this "Sonimage practice" has remained. Godard and Miéville's shared atelier has had three names: Sonimage, JLG Films, and, since 1989, Peripheria. This is how Godard explained the shifts, in that same 1998 interview with Alain Bergala:

> At the beginning, it was called Sonimage. Then, because the name was taken, we called it JLG Films. As this new name did wrong by Anne-Marie Miéville, we changed it. Jack Lang, who had to help us get set up at La Fémis,[9] told us that since we were on the periphery, we could only call it Peripheria. That's stuck. (*Jean-Luc Godard par Jean-Luc Godard* t.2, 11; m.t.)

As he was recalling that failed project for the French film school La Fémis, Godard wrote (in an article published in *Le Monde* in 1991 called "Rapport d'inactivité") that "[t]he Peripheria workshop (an editing suite, a library, a production office) seeks to put, under one roof, all the components that the eyes and the hands need to make an entire film, with the exception of lab work—but including optical sound recording, in particular digital coding" (*Jean-Luc Godard par Jean-Luc Godard* t.2, 249; m.t.).

Independence is thus the key element of the "Sonimage practice." That is certainly how de Baecque presents it in his *Godard: biographie*; echoing Daney's "Godard paradox," he writes that "[u]p to the present day, Godard works independently; someone orders a film from him and he makes it like he wants to, with other people's money, within and against the system at the same time" (520; m.t.). In a 1998 interview with Alain Bergala, Godard was explicit about the degree to which he and Miéville were seeking, in essence, to be left alone to work, and talking about Miéville's preference to take care of all business matters relating to film production, Godard said that "[s]he can't make films any other way. This isn't someone who, like this or that filmmaker, has a producer who does everything. We like to do everything" (*Jean-Luc Godard par Jean-Luc Godard* t.2, 11; m.t.).

This was a considerable shift in production mode from the days of the French New Wave, a movement whose films were made in a way that was informal relative to mainstream cinema but which was still basically commercial. And so, at the time, plenty of commentators tried to explain the degree to which Godard was, after joining forces with Miéville in 1972, changing the ground rules. In 1976, *L'Avant-scène cinéma* published a special issue reproducing excerpts from scripts and documents connected to recent Godard films, with a special section called "Les films invisibles," which featured *Le gai savoir* (1968), *Cinétracts* (1968), *Un film comme les autres* (1968), and all of his Groupe Dziga Vertov films. The anonymous introduction to the section tried to make sense of this radical break from the other films it was documenting (1963's *Les Carabiniers* and 1965's *Pierrot le fou*), mostly via a summary of other interviews that Godard had given. The introduction recalls how in 1973, "Jean-Luc Godard separates from Gorin, and takes his name back. In going to Grenoble, he undergoes a technical conversion—from film to video—and a new education in solitude" (52; m.t.). Expanding on this new interest in solitude, the introduction quotes an interview he gave to the now-defunct amateur film magazine *Cinéma Pratique*'s Philippe Durand in 1973, which I reproduce in full in Appendix 1 of this book. I reproduce it in full because it is not a well-known document, but I would argue that it constitutes Godard's first real engagement with what will become the "Sonimage practice," a radically decentred approach to cinema that is made possible by low-end gear such as home movie and video technology. The one part of that interview that is often invoked is when Godard tried to claim a political mandate for home movies, and he said in that interview that:

> As for me, I've become aware, after fifteen years of cinema, that the real "political" film that I'd like to end up with would be a film about me which would show to my wife and my daughter what I am, in other words a home movie—home movies represent the popular base of the cinema.
> (*Cinéma Pratique* 157 / MacCabe, *Images Sounds Politics*, 23)

This invocation of the home movie illustrates the degree to which Godard and Miéville's work is also quite close in spirit, and in mode of production, to another filmmaker whose sense of the avant-garde is quite close to the paradoxical conservatism evoked by Serge Daney in his "Godard Paradox" essay: Stan Brakhage. Brakhage's films (he made nearly 400 in all) reject conventional film language utterly; most of them are silent, almost none of them have narratives, and they run anywhere from less than a minute to over four hours. Criticism and interpretation of Brakhage films is famously challenging, although as someone who has published articles on Brakhage, I reject the myth that it is impossible. A similar myth has grown up around Godard and Miéville's toughest work, one that is echoed in Colin MacCabe's assessment of their massive television series *France/tour/détour/deux/enfants* (1979): "To do justice to the complexity, beauty, and pessimism of these programs is impossible; their enormous originality and control of the video image defy analysis" ("Betaville," 61). Change the word "video" to "film" and you have an assessment of Brakhage that is, like MacCabe on *France/tour/détour/deux/enfants*, both quite right about the command of the medium on display and quite wrong about the impossibility of criticism.

Indeed, although his films look very different from Godard and Miéville works, there are very real elements of intersection between the Swiss couple and Brakhage. There is, for instance, a recurring shot in the first episode of *France/tour/détour/deux/enfants* of a naked, pregnant woman with a circular, iris-image close-up of a baby's face, which startlingly recalls the layered image of a baby's face in Brakhage's *Dog Star Man* (1964). And like Godard speaking in *Cinéma Pratique*, Brakhage embraced the term "amateur filmmaker." Brakhage argued in a 1972 essay called "In Defense of Amateur," in terms that seem just as startlingly familiar to those who have read that *Cinéma Pratique* interview, that "I have worked alone and at home, on films of seemingly *no* commercial value … 'at home' with a medium I love, making films I care for as surely as I have as a father cared for my children. As these home movies have come to be valued, have grown into a public life, I, as a maker of them, have come to be called a 'professional,' an 'artist,' and an 'amateur.' Of those three terms, the last one—amateur—is the one I am most truly honored by" (*Brakhage Scrapbook*, 162). This was because, as he points out, "'Amateur' is a word which, in the Latin, meant 'lover'" (ibid). And just as Daney bristled at the sense of Godard as an avant-gardist, Brakhage repeatedly rejected this label, preferring "independent film," and sharply resenting the appropriation of the term by low-budget conventional-narrative filmmakers. He mostly did this in conversation and informal introductions, although he wrote in a 1979 letter to Bill and Stella Pence that "I have personally given up trying to represent 'The Avant-Garde' (detestable term) and/or whatEVER you want to call it—the independent film."[10] It was independence, the ability to work at home, by oneself and *about* oneself, that Brakhage prized, not some falsely teleological sense of moving a medium forward. "I am guided primarily in all creative dimensions by the spirit of the home in which I am working," he wrote in the "Defense of the Amateur" essay (168).

So it has been for Godard and Miéville, whose work is as keenly inflected by the landscape of region around Lac Léman as Brakhage's was by the Rocky Mountains (he lived for many years in the mountains of Colorado before moving to Boulder in 1988, rather neatly inverting Godard and Miéville's move from Grenoble to Rolle), and is just as formed by their shared domestic obsessions as Brakhage's was defined by the life of his family. This is part of what has led feminist and gay critics to sharply reject Brakhage's vision of film practice, and I believe is partly what led J. Hoberman to write—in a celebratory essay about Andrei Tarkovsky—that "like Brakhage and Hans-Jürgen Syberberg, he seems as conservative as he is avant-garde" ("Between Two Worlds," 75). Something similar could be said about Daney's militantly non-revolutionary Godard (and Miéville as well). The idea of Sonimage, and really the animating spirit behind the entire oeuvre of Godard and Miéville, is that everyday life—domesticity, ebbs and flows between men and women, landscape, and the images of cinema and television that define so much of the contemporary everyday life—is the real stuff of art, and that a great deal of independence is needed if an artist is really to give life to this most important substance. This emphasis on reality is, of course, deeply Bazinian, which is hardly surprising given the enormous impact that the great critic had on the young Godard. The emphasis on independence is just as deeply Brakhagian. The American filmmaker is someone whose rewriting of cinematic language is very different from Godard and Miéville's but no less aesthetically and ethically ambitious, and while there is no real evidence of direct influence (as is clearly the case with Bazin), Brakhage still offers an enlightening comparison, a way to see what is really going on chez Godard and Miéville.

This is, though, contrary to some fairly widespread assumptions about the avant-garde. Peter Wollen's 1975 essay "The Two Avant-Gardes" remains quite influential in scholarly understanding of marginal film practice. He wrote there that "in Europe today there are two avant-gardes. The first can be identified loosely with the Co-op movement. The second would include filmmakers such as Godard, Straub and Huillet, Hanoun, Jansco" (*Readings and Writings*, 92). No doubt that this is still a valuable essay, in no small part because of the detail in which it evokes the trans-Atlantic component of the avant-garde; Wollen writes at one point that "I think the absence of any avant-garde of the Godard type in North America could ultimately prove a severe limitation on the development of the New American Cinema itself" (*Readings and Writings*, 93). But it is problematic in no small part because of these sort of comparisons, this sense that an "avant-garde of the Godard type" means a filmmaking practice that is explicitly, didactically political. And while that sort of near-didacticism may have seemed to be the most important aspect of Godard's work in 1975, when he was just coming out of his Groupe Dziga Vertov period and just joining up with Miéville, that kind of politics (post-1968, Mao-inflected leftism) would not interest him for much longer. What was emerging through the 1970s chez Godard (and this is true of Straub–Huillet too, with short films like 1982's *En rachâchant* or 1989's *Cézanne*) was a practice that was very much in the world, in a Bazinian way, but that also aspired to a kind of interiority that was not all that far away from what was going on in the New American Cinema (both in psychodramas and in more abstract works that sought to evoke interior states, such as what Brakhage referred to as "closed-eye vision"). Godard and Miéville are important because (like Straub–Huillet) their work challenges easy divisions between the personal and the social. That is a political act, but it is a poetic act as well.

What I argue throughout this book is that what emerges from these acts is, basically, a Modernist poetics. Definitions of "Modernism" have long been thick on the ground, and I am particularly sympathetic to the definition offered by Douwe W. Fokkema and Elrud Ibsch in their book *Modernist Conjectures: A Mainstream in European Literature, 1910–1940* (1987). In that book's first pages, they write simply, "The Modernist does not commit himself. He considers, and is critical" (3), and that is an excellent way of thinking of the broad intellectual position of Godard and Miéville. Later on, they observe how "the syntactic code of Modernism is no more than a one-sided emphasis on particular syntagmatic options—a particular selection from among the many syntagmatic possibilities, which in general are provided by the linguistic system and only rarely are newly invented" (34). This is a quite precise evocation of just where this critical consideration leads Godard and Miéville: to reconsider the forms they are working in—be they feature narrative or documentary cinema—rather than reinvent them wholesale. This is quite consistent with Daney's notion of "Le paradoxe de Godard" inasmuch as Godard and Miéville's connection to Modernism has them hanging onto what Daney calls "the rules of the game," the contours of narrative or documentary cinema, in much the same way that a Modernist like James Joyce continues to hang on to the skeleton of the nineteenth-century novel (at least until *Finnegans Wake*, a maddening work whose importance in twentieth-century literary history makes a good analogy for some of the films I discuss in Chapter 5).

This book's overall argument is equally informed by the complementary perspective of Fredric Jameson, and specifically by his analysis of *Passion* (1982), which could be used to explain all of the work that Godard and Miéville have done together. In his 1995 book *The Geopolitical Aesthetic: Cinema and Space in the World System*, he writes of *Passion* that "what is Modernist about this film is not the way in which it finds its narrative—story and history all wrapped up in one—if indeed it ever does, but rather its obsessive search for one, its lucid awareness of what it lacks, the convulsive effort of so many broken pieces to add up to something" (164). This obsessive search for a story, for a grand narrative that will explain the late capitalist world of Western Europe, is indeed a key concern for Godard and Miéville. Furthermore, they are always conducting that search through fragments: combinations of stills, interviews, and abandoned documentaries in *Ici et ailleurs*; jumpy, slowed-down visual narratives in *Sauve qui peut (la vie)*; images of history, landscape, and literature in *Liberté et patrie*. In all of this work, Godard and Miéville are searching for images that retain the traces of the classical cinema or twentieth-century literature: aesthetic harmony, structural rigour, communication. But throughout their work, as with so much Modernist narrative or documentary cinema (such as that of Ingmar Bergman or Jean Rouch) and Modernist literature (such as James Joyce), we can see these older patterns starting to give way, hinting at a more chaotic, alienating world just behind, one that the engaged and sometimes tortured artist is struggling to keep at bay. This is the situation that Jameson is evoking when he coins the term "survivor's Modernism," writing in a way that very clearly explains the work of Godard and Miéville that "[f]or Godard—surely as Postmodern *avant la lettre* as one might have wished in the heyday of auteurist high Modernism—has today in full Postmodernism become the ultimate survivor of the modern as such" (162). This is very close to Peter Harcourt's somewhat pithier description of Godard as "a cinematic Modernist in a Postmodern world" ("Analogical Thinking," 23). It is not at all clear that Jameson and Harcourt share a definition of postmodernism, a notoriously slipperly critical term. What they are both invoking, though, is the spectre of an aesthetic that moves beyond the already-critical tenants of modernism. What they are both invoking is the spectacle of alienation and disengagement. Godard and Miéville's work, like that of Straub–Huillet, is too easily classified as postmodernist in this sense because of the intensity of its difficulty and the seeming totality of its refusal of film language. This is really only true of their very late work, of the shorts they made in the 1990s and 2000s (as I argue in Chapter 5). Most of Godard and Miéville's work together, like the films of Stan Brakhage, shows that this sort of radical reinvention is the price that must be paid for retaining a belief in the most important elements of cinematic expression, and for continuing to believe in the ability of moving images to shed light upon contemporary existence.

Peripheria is, then, a very good name for a company defined by the "Sonimage practice." The work that Godard and Miéville have done together has always been about developing the periphery: both geographical (Grenoble/Rolle as opposed to Paris) and aesthetic (video and poetic/essayistic strategies as opposed to conventional narrative). Throughout their work together, they have sought to refine rather than struggle against marginality. Despite their interest in emerging technology, Godard and Miéville are not avant-garde in the literal sense of being on the front line, moving their chosen art form forward. Indeed, very much the opposite is actually the case. Colin MacCabe writes of their shared work, their atelier, that "[o]ver the past twenty-five years, Godard has constructed his own arrière-boutique in the small Swiss village of Rolle, but he has constructed it with a woman, and it is unthinkable without her" (*Portrait of the Artist*, 241). This image of the "*arrière boutique*," an image that MacCabe borrows from Montaigne's legendary backroom, identifies the key tension at the heart of Godard and Miéville. They are among the cinema's most radical filmmakers, but this does not fully emerge until their withdrawal from the world that they seek to interpret. They are always trying to get at the roots of their art form and the roots of European life, but they are not revolutionary. Following Serge Daney's formulation, there is nothing revolutionary about Godard and Miéville. They are troubled by the absence of rules. In leaving Paris, and in leaving the film industry, they in essence sought more deeply seeded rules to which they might be true: the rules of ethics over those of politics, the rules of aesthetics over popular or critical success.

Chapter 2
ABANDONMENTS

Antoine de Baecque notes in *Godard: biographie* that "Godard always has a project underway." He seems to admire this, and goes on to say that "works in progress, or even already abandoned, form for Godard the next film, which, once it's made, retains their traces" (561; m.t.). He was echoing a point made by Michael Witt in his 1998 dissertation on Sonimage; quoting Godard's *Introduction à une veritable histoire du cinéma*, Witt notes that "Godard claims to have embarked on dozens of unfinished projects between 1972 and 1978 for which only a handful of shots were completed, although traces of his abandoned projects invariably reappear in reworked and displaced form in subsequent works" (1). This book concentrates on the actual films, but I agree with de Baecque and Witt that traces of these abandoned projects are visible throughout Godard and Miéville's work. Sometimes they act as period dividers, most true of *Moi Je* and *The Story*, which signal the beginning and the end of the couple's interest in television and video. Sometimes they are summaries of overall concerns, most true of *One P.M.* and of the work in Quebec and Mozambique, all of which explicitly deal with mass-media communication and its troubled mechanics in a way that is very much of a piece with work in television and film that they did in the 1970s. But all are important for understanding Godard and Miéville's work together because all of these abandoned projects that I discuss here (and there are other projects that Godard abandoned that I do not cover) engage with the thematic and formal problems that give their shared oeuvre shape: the search for a form that moves beyond the fiction/documentary split, a concern with the process and difficulties of communication, and a desire to move out of Paris and make cinema in and about more marginal communities, places, and forms: African Americans, Quebec's Abitibi region, home movies, the San Francisco–based Zoetrope Studios, Mozambique, Switzerland. That sounds like something of a dog's breakfast, but in fact that little roll call could serve as a metaphor for what Godard and Miéville understood as "peripheral," a concept that was, as I explained in Chapter 1, "Introduction," something that they understood in a diverse way and has always been key to their shared practice.

I have tried to organize this discussion more or less chronologically, with the belief that the development of these abandoned projects, taken as a whole, echo the development of the films that the couple have actually made. In this "ghost work," we see remnants of the "New Wave Godard" as he searches for a new practice in the wake of 1968, then a passionate interest in using video to analyze the way electronic communication has transformed modern consciousness, followed by a restless internationalism, and concluded with a tentative return to the world of feature filmmaking. That is not exactly the trajectory of the actually finished work of Godard and Miéville, but it is quite close. Looking at these "ghost projects" together offers a surprisingly precise framework for their collaboration.

ONE A.M. / ONE P.M.

About half an hour into *One P.M.*, a 1971 version of an aborted film that Godard had tried to make in and around Berkeley with D. A. Pennebaker behind the camera, there is a scene with a group of black musicians playing together in the middle of the street. Within a few constantly moving shots, they alternate between jazz jamming, some Islamic singing ("Bismillah! Rahman u raheem! As salaam u alikum!"), some playful crooning ("Black magic ... black maaaagic ..."), and more militant slogans ("Calling all black people, calling all black people.... We're going to break into the Bank of America! We're going to break down the Statue of White Liberty!"). As the camera gets closer and closer to the musicians, the sequence eventually drifts into an utterly mesmerizing series of slightly blurry close-ups and extreme-close-ups and zooms, with one of the musicians chanting over and over, "Communicate! Communicate! Communicate!" The image goes completely white at one point, as Pennebaker zooms into the cloudy sky, but his camera drifts back out onto the faces of musicians and eventually winds up more or less where it began, settling on a medium shot of Godard (a shot cut off more or less at the waist), watching the session from a distance, smoking. This film fragment, never finished, edited by Pennebaker a few years later, and never really accepted by Godard, serves as a pithy summary of what would become "Godard and Miéville." This is what the two were looking for: communication, and more specifically, a kind of communication that could only be cinematic, a kind of communication with limitations, layered complexities, rhythms, and symmetries that could be realized only through the combination of sound with moving images.

This film was supposed to be called *One A.M.* or *One American Movie*. It was commissioned in New York as part of WNET's "Public Broadcasting Laboratory," the television station's experimental program that Richard Brody calls "the precursor to PBS" (342). The film was, ostensibly, meant to be a portrait of America—mostly Berkeley, although they also shot footage in New York and in Newark, New Jersey—on the verge of revolution. Godard seemed to have been thinking that he would do for the Berkeley/NYC of 1968 what he had done for the Paris of May 1968 with his *Cinétracts*. "Godard, who had arrived a little early for the revolution, did not finish *One American Movie*" is Richard Brody's sardonic assessment of the project (342). Instead, Pennebaker edited the footage they shot into a film called *One P.M.*, sometimes also known with the subtitle *One Pennebaker Movie* or *One Parallel Movie* (this also explained by de Baecque, 437–40). *One P.M.* could thus very easily be considered a "lost film," but this sequence I discuss here is key for understanding the way Godard's work was changing, and changing in the direction of what he would soon start doing with Miéville.

That is true of a few other sequences in the film, such as an early shot where Rip Torn recites, and sometimes screams, a countercultural monologue as a tape recorder plays the same lines, and does it as he rides up an elevator in a construction site. Pennebaker's camera shoots out of the skeletal building, ascending from darkness and right up to the top of the city, only to have Torn walk around the top floor, then get back into the elevator and ride right back down, all in one shot. These moments of abstraction—musicians lost in improvisation, lunatic actors in construction sites—crystallized a then-emergent aesthetic and political project, one based in an impatience with both narrative and linearity in general, a politics sympathetic to revolutionary idealism but able to present its excesses with a healthy dose of irony, and a visual sensibility richly attuned to the ecstatic possibilities of photographic realism. Those close-ups of the musicians in the street, especially those of the goateed flute player, have the feel of the sublime because of the way that they fully capture a sensual, overwhelming moment; much the same is true of the image of a dark city shot from a cage-like elevator fifteen stories up. In the 1970s, Godard and Miéville started to make work that sought a new language of film, one that (following Bazin in the 1950s) was rooted in a rigorous approach to realist aesthetics, but one that also (anticipating Daney in the 1980s) sought a cinema that "wants cinema to be something else, it even longs for the horizon where cinema risks being absorbed by dint of metamorphosis, it opens up its focus into the unknown" ("The Godard Paradox," 68). We can see the earliest glint of that cinema in these moments of *One P.M.*

QUEBEC

Godard's interest in Quebec is surprisingly substantial. The first instance that I know of regarding his concern for Quebec cinema is in the very long interview he gave to Jacques Bontemps, Jean-Louis Comolli, Michel Delahaye, and Jean Narboni of the *Cahiers du cinéma* in 1967 (it was published in number 194) titled "Lutter sur deux fronts."[1] He stated there that:

> The Canadian cinema is interesting as an example. The National Film Board is an impressive film factory, more so than Hollywood today. It's a great set-up. But what's the pay-off? Zero. There's nothing to see for it. The films just aren't coming out. What Daniel Johnson ought to do is nationalize all the cinemas in Quebec. But he won't do it. The best he's capable of is seeing that de Gaulle gets a welcome in the metro screens. So, over there as well, cinema is subject to a special brand of imperialism, just like everywhere else. (*Jean-Luc Godard par Jean-Luc Godard* t.1, 318 / "Struggling on Two Fronts," 294)

This demonstrates a remarkably detailed knowledge of Quebec politics. Not only was Godard aware of de Gaulle's 1967 visit to Montreal (where he famously shouted "*Vive le Québec libre!*" as he addressed a crowd from the balcony of Montreal city hall), but he also seems to know about Daniel Johnson Sr.,[2] at that time the Premier of Quebec as a member of the Union Nationale, a more-or-less nationalist party. Johnson famously chafed against Ottawa and suggested that Quebec should consider separation if it could not improve its position within the Canadian confederation; he was Premier during de Gaulle's 1967 visit to Quebec. His party had a generally conservative social policy and a generally classical-liberal approach to economic policy (hence the reluctance to nationalize Quebec's cinemas). And, of course, Godard is keenly aware of and impressed by the work of the National Film Board of Canada (NFB), and, more startlingly, he was fully aware of the fact that very few Canadians actually get to see very many of its extraordinary films.

Godard also signalled his interest in Quebec in his 1968 film *Le gai savoir*, where he signalled a number of other important interests as well. At one point in that film, the screen goes black and Léaud says that "[h]ere, the image is missing.

The English-Canadian police gouged out the eyes of the cameraman who was filming the faces and landscapes of Free Quebec." This not only ironically echoes General de Gaulle's famous words, but also bitterly evokes the spectre of the RCMP (which are not exactly the English-Canadian police but which are, after all, *Royal*), who were famous adversaries of some of the more militant formations of Quebec separatism. *Le gai savoir* is important as a sort of "transitional work," a work positioned between the Godard of the 1960s and the Godard of "Godard and Miéville." Colin MacCabe has also made this case, writing that "[i]n its concern to understand the language of cinema by taking it back to its component parts, and in its funding and subsequent rejection by television, *Le gai savoir* can be taken as a model for all the subsequent Dziga Vertov group films" (*Portrait of the Artist*, 204). MacCabe has written elsewhere that "it is Godard who has single-handedly developed an essay style beginning with *Le gai savoir*, 1968, and further developed in the television work with Miéville, which is now instantly recognisable" ("The Commerce of Cinema," 97).

The film stars Jean-Pierre Léaud and Juliet Berto, who read their lines to each other on a dark sound stage, the background entirely black. There are cutaways to images (sometimes in incredibly vivid colour) of consumer culture, mass media, urban life, and so on, but the film single-mindedly returns to Léaud and Berto in this "limbo-lit" space. In this way, it strongly recalls the visual schema of Godard and Miéville's first film together, *Numéro deux* (1975), which returns again and again to images of Godard in a very dark studio, surrounded by his machines, sometimes musing and sometimes brooding. Like some parts of *One P.M.*, *Le gai savoir* strongly anticipates the concerns—both aesthetic and political—that Godard and Miéville would investigate together: the changing nature of the European left, the ravages of capitalist modernity on the relationships between men and women, and the play between film and television. It seems to me a very important work in no small part because the "old Godard" of the New Wave really is falling away here, and a more politically voracious and technologically flexible Godard is emerging.

Godard went to Quebec shortly after the *Cahiers du cinéma* interview quoted above and shortly after making *Le gai savoir* (which, Brody says, he "shot in December 1967 and January 1968 ... but he did not finish it until later in the year, after May 1968" [317]). Brody connects his experiences in Quebec with his aborted passage through the United States. This was when he started but abandoned *One P.M.* (1972). Describing Godard's departure following the shooting of *One A.M.*, Brody writes:

> He abandoned the United States for several days in November, travelling to Montreal with [his then-wife Anne] Wiazemsky and the French producer Claude Nedjar (whom they had met by chance in New York) for the Festival of Political Cinema. Wiazemsky later recalled that both she and Godard were "seduced" by the Canadian landscape and wanted to return to Quebec. When they got back to Paris, she suggested that Godard make a film in Canada. Nedjar, who had a connection with media executives in Rouyn-Noranda in rural Quebec [in the northwestern region known as Abitibi], proposed an ambitious scheme: that Godard put together a ten-part television series there in collaboration with a group of leftist filmmakers who the director had met at the Montreal Festival....
>
> The ten-part project was to begin with documentary material: Godard intended to film discussions with local workers and students and to develop a fiction film from that research. Working with a group of politically active video-makers from the area, Godard recorded a large amount of video footage, but according to Anne Wiazemsky, he was unclear about what he wanted to do.... Godard quickly lost interest in the project and told her simply "we're going home." It was a fittingly inconclusive end to a year of frenzied, unfocused activity, which was only to escalate. (343–44)

Julie Perron's film *Mai en décembre: Godard en Abitibi* (2000), made for the National Film Board of Canada, interviews a number of these filmmakers and video makers, such as Alain Laury, Pierre David, and André Dudemaine (who was a student at the time), as well as the local community organizer Louise Bédard. The film also reproduces one of the broadcasts Godard did on the local television station CKRN; because the video images were basically illegible, Perron reconstructs the broadcast using still photos and the audio track (which was still in decent condition). Michel Larouche tells this story somewhat differently than Brody does, arguing that the shortness of the visit was not because of Godard's flightiness but because of his frustration with the local situation:

> 1968 was "The Godard Affair," as we call it in Quebec.... For about three weeks, four television broadcasts were completed (of a half-hour for the first three and one hour for the last one), and they were very low-quality, the staff technicians having refused to help (the recordings made by a recorder weren't transferred, but were simply re-filmed to be broadcast, and this produced a practically illegible image). For this reason, and for obvious ideological reasons, the project was very controversial and provoked violent reactions in the community. As for Godard, he only stayed three days. (160; m.t.)

Pierre David describes the experience of the broadcasts along these lines as well, recalling in *Mai en décembre* how in Abitibi, the status of professional television technician was as prestigious as that of notary or a lawyer, and having an iconoclast like Godard proposing such experiments as filming someone on the toilet was, to these skilled technicians, a sacrilege. Just as sacrilegious, really, was Godard's budding Brechtianism. During that CKRN broadcast, he moved behind the camera and started talking to the operator, saying that he had just as much of a right to participate in the discussion and pointing out that even if he questioned him directly, he still would not answer. A desire to move fluidly between the spaces in front of and behind the camera was the essence of the self-conscious cinema that Godard had been trying to develop though the 1960s. That interest in "behind the camera" would also become important for the films and television series that he would produce with Miéville a few years later. Explaining the genesis of Godard and Miéville's 1976 series *Six fois deux: Sur et sous la communication*, Michael Witt writes that:

> In a sense, this series could be considered to be a partial realisation of a project Godard had been working on since 1968, tentatively entitled "Communications." This was supposed to be a group film of 24 hours, which would examine various means of communications (you can see more of this in the events documented in Julie Perron's film *Mai en décembre: Godard en Abitibi*, which is in part a detailed piece of research on this ongoing project). ("Paroles non-éternelles," 260)

There really can be little doubt that this Quebec experience greatly influenced Godard's thinking on communication and set the stage for his work with Miéville; it is also a preview of the limitations he would face. For while Nedjar's suggestion that Godard, in Brody's retelling, "put together a ten-part television series there in collaboration with a group of leftist filmmakers" does sound like a blueprint for the two twelve-part television series that he did go on to make, the unexpected response of the local technicians, and the degree to which that response would be discouraging, were also shades of things to come. Godard clearly identified strongly with Quebec culture; that is borne out not only by Wiazemsky recalling how they were seduced by the landscape, but by statements that Godard made later. He returned to Montreal in 1978 to give a series of lectures on the history of cinema at Montreal's Concordia University; these were published in 1980 as the book *Introduction à une véritable histoire du cinema*, which formed the basis for his massive film project *Histoire(s) du cinéma* (1988–2004). Godard writes in that book that "Canadians are exiles too; they just don't know it. That's where their problems come from, and thus, maybe especially Quebec, they're not at all exiles from Europe in my opinion, they're exiles from America. I myself being an exile from France" (54; m.t.).

This sense of commonality based on exile from a bordering, semi-imperial power, an experience that Pierre Trudeau famously likened to sleeping next to an elephant, was clearly meaningful for Godard, and I return to it when I discuss Sonimage's presence in Africa.

Pierre Vallières has written about a Québécois kind of exile as well, although in different terms. He recalls of his father that "he was still working from 4:00 in the afternoon until 5:00 in the morning. I almost never saw him any more, for on weekends I would often 'go into exile' in [the Montreal suburb of] Longueuil. I would sit down at the foot of the Quai Saint-Alexandre and plunge my dreams into the depths of the river. I would stay there for hours at a time, lost in silent meditation" (*Nègres blancs d'Amérique*, 129 / *White Niggers of America*, 123). Godard arrived in Quebec in 1968, which is the same year that Vallières published his celebrated and incendiary autobiography *Nègres blancs d'Amérique*. This is a useful text through which to read "L'affaire Godard" inasmuch as it was very widely read in Quebec at the time of its release (it was published in France the next year, in 1969, and translated into English in 1971 as *White Niggers of America*) and also because it speaks not only in anti-Anglophone terms (although God knows it does that) but also speaks more broadly against various forms of the local elite.

This latter tendency is what marks its Fanonian roots; Frantz Fanon's 1961 book *Les damnés de la terre* was unsparing in its critique not only of colonizers but also of the local bourgeoisie that took their place, a class that Fanon saw as irredeemably mediocre. He alluded there to "[t]his bourgeoisie, expressing its mediocrity in its profits, its achievements, and in its thought tries to hide this mediocrity by buildings which have prestige value at the individual level, by chromium plating on big American cars, by holidays on the Riviera and weekends in neon-lit nightclubs" (*Les damnés de la terre*, 217 / *The Wretched of the Earth*, 177). Here is Vallières writing about the Parti socialiste du Québec: "At most it has served as a vehicle for illusions and has encouraged the development of organizations harmful to the workers of Quebec, such as the FTQ [Fédération des travailleurs du Québec], which is only a screen for American big-business style unions" (*Nègres blancs*, 238 / *White Niggers*, 214). This spectre of a local elite beholden to American culture, to the prestige of material comfort, a comfort seemingly gained at the expense of the masses, was clearly part of the conflict that Godard had inserted himself into. I am not trying to posit *Nègres blancs d'Amérique* as closely observed sociology; it is certainly far from that. It was, though, a very popular text (if perhaps more discussed than read), one that identified a growing impatience on the part of the Quebec left with the local bourgeoisie, an impatience that many Quebec leftists had inherited from anti-colonial movements around the world.

That said, another part of the dynamic that led to the failure of his Quebec project is clearly connected to Godard's status as a filmmaker from France, and this is also anticipated by *Nègres blancs d'Amérique*. Vallières spent some time in France, and it is an understatement to say that he did not see it as any kind of *mère patrie*. "The three months I spent in Paris were a veritable hell," he wrote. "I looked around in various places for a revolutionary organization disposed to utilize my energy. I did not find one. I encountered dozens of men who talked revolution, but not a single revolutionary organization" (*Nègres blancs*, 198 / *White Niggers*, 187). Godard must have seemed like just such a man, a famous European speaking constantly of revolution but not very interested in (or really very good at) organizing groups of people to work together. That status of "bad at organizing things" probably seemed rather privileged for someone who was ostensibly a political filmmaker, a bit like the unspoken privilege that alienated and continues to alienate so many leftist academics (who also tend to be bad at organizing things) from activist movements of many stripes. That kind of culture clash, one to which Godard was very likely to be basically oblivious, could not have made his dealings with local militants any easier.

Godard came to Quebec again in March 1977 to accompany a retrospective of his films organized by Serge Losique, founder of the Montreal World Film Festival and of the Conservatoire d'art cinématographique de Montréal, which was a sort of cinematheque housed at Concordia University's downtown campus. Concordia has videos of the question-and-answer sessions from this retrospective grouped with the tapes of Godard's aforementioned 1978 classes there.[3] In the first of these sessions, an unseen questioner (who Losique identifies as "*un professeur du cinéma*"—it is Tom Waugh) asks why he has agreed to a retrospective that includes films he does not like any more. He also asks what Godard's goal is in making this intervention in the cultural and political life of Quebec. Godard hems and haws about being invited and just coming along as part of a course he is going to do on film and television history. Losique takes the microphone at that point and scolds Waugh for not knowing that it was he and not Godard who chose the films, and then says "*pour la seconde partie de votre question, c'est complètement stupide.*" Later on, someone asks Godard about his experience with community TV in the Lac-Saint-Jean area. Godard tries to correct the questioner and fumbles for the name Rouyn-Noranda, which is actually where he visited, and recalls that it never came to much, the attempt to bring video cameras down to a strike culminating in a big snowball fight.

MOI JE

Michael Temple writes that the aborted film project *Moi Je* is important as a work "marking a transition between two phases of Godard's professional life.... At this moment, a new cycle seemed to be already underway, with the shifting collaboration between Godard and Anne-Marie Miéville, who Godard had met during the shooting of *Tout va bien*" ("Inventer un film," 188; m.t.). Temple wrote this as the introduction to the film's proposal, which is reproduced in full in Nicole Brenez's book *Jean-Luc Godard: Documents*, published as the catalogue of the 2006 exhibit "Voyage(s) en utopie, Jean-Luc Godard, 1946–2006" at Paris's Centre Georges Pompidou. What appears in that proposal is fairly skeletal, but it does indeed give the sense that *Moi Je*, if it had been completed, would have given voice to Godard's emerging obsession with communication, an engagement that was indeed properly realized once he began collaborating fully with Miéville.

Excerpts of this proposal were first published as illustrations for the 1973 interview that Godard gave to *Cinéma Pratique*, and it is clear why he thought they would make a good companion piece to an interview with this specific magazine. As I mentioned in Chapter 1, this is an important document because it, like the *Moi Je* proposal, marks Godard's transition from the Groupe Dziga Vertov toward "Sonimage practice," his move away from a Maoist-inflected Parisian internationalism and toward an engagement with the domestic, with the local. As the images reproduced in *Cinéma Pratique* suggest, the proposal is made up in no small part of collages of text and image; some of these are storyboards with captions, but an equal number are assemblages of cut-outs from magazines and newspapers. This combination of continuity and montage is precisely the schema of the three more-or-less feature films that Godard and Miéville would make together in the 1970s: *Ici et ailleurs* (1974), *Numéro deux* (1975), and *Comment ça va?* (1976). All of this work has the vestiges of the feature-narrative. Although all three eschew classical editing patterns (there is nothing like shot/reverse-shot[4] in any of these films) the viewer's attention is often focused by a decoupage that maintains some semblance of continuity. In terms of narrative, all three have a roughly analogous relationship to classical form in that they have actors who play roles in a narrative, one that is not very linear and sometimes violates realist illusionism, but one that is nevertheless recognizable as a story.

Not that there is really much of a story here. The film was supposed to be in two parts: "Moi, je suis un homme politique" and "Moi, je suis un machine." The creative tension between politics and technology was becoming a central concern for Godard during the 1960s and 1970s, and it is a veritable obsession for Godard–Miéville in the 1970s. The proposal sketches out a number of sequences that would involve a kind of exposition of the functioning of power and economics in everyday life; the sequences outlined for the second part are more tightly focused on body parts, machines, and the systems that they share (sequence 6 and 7, for instance, are broken into four parts: *machine sémantique, machine financière, machine culturelle,* and *machine* [230]). What seems to be really driving the project is a desire to explore the possibilities of video, and more precisely, the cultural and political significance of this then-emerging technology. Summing up the second part of *Moi Je*, Godard writes: "For me, using video today, four years after May '68, while Hanoi is being bombed … it's not a joke, but I am having fun using it" (240; m.t.). Godard could see, from a very early stage, that video promised a new way to make images, a way that would allow that image maker to intervene in the communications process in ways that were previously near impossible. *Moi Je* makes it clear for the first time that this technology that would define Godard–Miéville in the 1970s was more than just a nice gadget that allowed them to shoot cheaply. During this charged period, video provided a new way to be political. The proposal for *Moi Je*, skeletal though it is, is a sketch of what that kind of political activity might look like.

THE STORY

A very different impulse was at work in the project that Godard initiated with the partial sponsorship of Francis Ford Coppola. This was to be known as *The Story*, and it exists, like *Moi Je*, as a sort of semi-scenario that combines photocopied, cut-out magazine and newspaper images with typewritten text. Although it has never been published on its own, parts of it are easily available; a fairly lengthy (although not complete) version is reprinted in the first volume of Alain Bergala's *Jean-Luc Godard par Jean-Luc Godard* (418–41), and a more abridged (and fairly cryptic) English version is reprinted in Colin MacCabe's 1980 book *Godard: Images, Sounds, Politics* (163–68).

As its title suggests, *The Story* is far more straightforwardly narrative than anything Godard and Miéville had been doing in the 1970s. It tells a slightly convoluted but basically linear story about a blacklisted star named Frankie, a film critic named Roberto, and his wife Diana, who teaches video and screenwriting at the "University of San Diego." At this time, Jean-Pierre Gorin was teaching screenwriting at the University of California San Diego, and was sharing a beachfront apartment with Ira Schneider, who was visiting professor of video there.[5] We can see strong elements of the crime film and the Mafioso picture in the proposal; the story starts in Las Vegas and features the character

"Mario P, a writer famous for his books on the Mafia and gambling" (422). This combination of classical Hollywood and cinephilia strongly recalls the New Wave, and so it is no surprise that the film was supported in large part by the New Wave's most famous American student, Francis Ford Coppola. The inclusion of "Mario P" can be read only as some sort of wink to this benefactor, whose most famous film was, at that time, *The Godfather*, based on the novel of the same name by Mario Puzo.

Godard came to Coppola through the efforts of Tom Luddy, one of world cinema's great men behind the curtain. Luddy told Brad Stevens in a 2007 interview that "I arranged for Zoetrope to produce with JLG a film about Bugsy Siegel, entitled 'The Story.' We paid JLG in advance, and he took up residence at Zoetrope, did a treatment, had some meetings with actors, and went to Las Vegas with Francis Ford Coppola and me." Luddy has, as I mentioned in Note 5 of Chapter 1, been a sort of "American connection" for Godard; Stevens opens that article on Luddy and Godard by saying that "[a]side from a brief involvement with *Bonnie and Clyde* (eventually directed by Arthur Penn, 1967), there is no area of Jean-Luc Godard's North American career in which Tom Luddy does not figure." Luddy worked in 16 mm film distribution in the 1960s (he started out working for Brandon Films but also wrote the first catalogue for New Yorker Films, which distributed some Godard work), booked Godard and Gorin on two speaking tours of American campuses, and helped with some logistics on the shooting of *One A.M.* (he briefly appears in *One P.M.*). Luddy also programmed a then-complete Godard retrospective for the Pacific Film Archive in 1968, and he served as director of that institution from 1972 to 1980. That was roughly the point at which he began working with Francis Ford Coppola's Zoetrope Studios, and in 1979, Luddy took charge of special projects for Zoetrope.

By and large, this meant internationalizing the Zoetrope operation; in 1980, he supervised the Coppola-supported US release of Hans-Jürgen Syberberg's seven-hour *Hitler, ein Film aus Deutschland* (which Zoetrope released as *Our Hitler: A Film from Germany*). Between 1981 and 1983, he oversaw the international release of the restored print of Abel Gance's *Napoléon* (1927). That epic was accompanied by large symphony orchestras, many of which were conducted by Carmine Coppolla, Francis Ford Coppola's father. Bringing Godard to California to work with Zoetrope was entirely consistent with what Coppola had hired Luddy to do. The fact that Coppola was, in the late 1970s, developing his "Silverfish," a mobile-shooting trailer kitted out with cutting-edge video equipment that made production more flexible by allowing Coppola to look at rough video images of what had just been shot on 35 mm. This was a further indication of the interests that Sonimage and Zoetrope shared during this period (although Luddy has clarified to me, in a phone conversation on May 6, 2011, that the equipment in the Silverfish bore little resemblance to what Godard and Miéville were then working with in Rolle).

The collaboration was not particularly fruitful. Godard tried to engage a number of Hollywood actors; he was especially interested in Robert de Niro and Diane Keaton, both of whom he met with. Neither of them was game, though (in part because of the lack of a conventional screenplay), and gradually the project collapsed. "He seemed to lose interest or confidence, and he backed off," is how Luddy explained it to Richard Brody (412). Coppola, however, had advanced funds for *The Story*, and Godard had in turn passed a fair bit of that money on to Jean-Pierre Beauviala to work on a new, lightweight camera that would, as I mentioned in Chapter 1 and will discuss momentarily, eventually be known as the Aaton 35-8 camera. As Luddy told Stevens, in order to fulfill his obligations, Godard ceded the American rights (for ten years) to the films that became *Sauve qui peut (la vie)* and *Passion*. These were released in the United States by New Yorker Films and United Artists Classics, respectively, but Coppola's name was prominent on the masthead ("Francis Ford Coppola Presents"). Although these films have little to do with the subject matter of *The Story*, both *Sauve qui peut (la vie)* and *Passion* are more or less narrative films (albeit highly unconventional ones) that feature bankable stars (Isabelle Huppert and Nathalie Baye in the former, and Huppert, Hannah Schygulla, and Michel Piccoli in the latter). That was the kind of film that Godard had tried to make in the United States, and when he failed to do that, he basically went back to France and reinvented himself. This he did through new collaborations with Miéville (in that case, *Ici et ailleurs*). That is what happened here as well, with Godard returning to Switzerland to make, with Miéville, *Sauve qui peut (la vie)*. Like *Moi Je*, then, *The Story* was a highly ambitious failure that nevertheless announced the next stage in Godard and Miéville's work together.

MOZAMBIQUE

But that "communication" stage was not quite finished yet. Shortly after his return from San Francisco, Godard and Miéville journeyed to Mozambique. In his *Introduction à une véritable histoire du cinéma*, Godard recalled how he felt a kinship with the Québécois because he was an exile from France. He also spoke of another small country that was, in the shadow of a larger country, trying to find its own identity, perhaps through cinema. "We've made an agreement, for example, with Mozambique to go and study what an image of television might be in a country that doesn't have television yet. Mozambique is a country that lives by getting half its electricity from South Africa, a country it's forced to cooperate with" (56; m.t.). Godard and Miéville's experience in Mozambique, a Lusophone African country that had only gained its independence from Portugal in 1975, marks the real end of the "communication" period of their work together. Here is how Godard describes how he and Miéville came to work there:

> In 1977, a company that produced and directed films as well as television broadcasts, Sonimage, began contact with representatives from the People's Republic of Mozambique through the mediation of a mutual friend, from an international conference in Geneva.
>
> Sonimage proposed that Mozambique should take advantage of the country's audio-visual situation to study television before it existed, before it flooded the entire social and geographical body of Mozambique (even in only twenty years).
>
> Study the image, the desire for images (the desire for memories, to show a memory, to make a mark, of departure or arrival, a line of contact, a moral/political guide, in the name of one goal: independence). (*Cahiers du cinéma* number 300, 73; m.t.)

One of the other aspirations of the project was to create an environment in Mozambique where communications media could be accessible to all, and not just to a professional elite. They wanted to keep television out of the hands of a class of relatively privileged technicians.

And to return to the language of Chapter 1, they wanted to bring the "Sonimage practice" to Africa. Godard and Miéville planned to call their first series *Naissance (de l'image) d'une nation*. Michael Witt writes that the project "aimed to employ a multiplicity of formats (Polaroid, still photography, video, and Super-8) to explore the opposition between a culture entirely lacking in media imagery (Mozambique) and a society awash in images and sounds (Western Europe, France in particular), with the aim of drawing lessons from the nascent Mozambiquan audio-visual infrastructure" (*On Communication*, 332). Godard and Miéville were to work alongside the Mozambique-born Brazilian filmmaker Ruy Guerra, who had been in Mozambique for some time and would soon direct, Manthia Diawara recalls (*African Cinema*, 96), the first feature film by a Mozambiquan filmmaker, *Mueda, Memoria e Massacre* (1979). This was a period of quite a lot of international interest in media making in

Mozambique, with Jean Rouch running a Super-8 workshop at the same time as Godard and Guerra were in the country. Rouch's Super-8 project was lead by a group affiliated with Université de Paris X—Nanterre, where Rouch was in charge of the Centre national de recherches scientifiques. This group (which included French cultural attaché to Mozambique, Jacques d'Arthuys, as well as filmmakers Miguel Alencar, Philippe Constantini, and Nadine Wannono) participated in a round-table discussion on their experiences using Super-8 in Mozambique that was animated by Jean-Pierre Oudart and Dominique Terres and published in *Cahiers du cinéma*; there, d'Arthuys marvels that "there are, in Mozambique, 52 theatres, which is a lot for Africa" (56; m.t.). The country had, for a brief period, the sense of being at the centre of a very experimental, fluid moment in the evolution of cinema, both from a social and a technical standpoint. Diawara clearly sees this as an exciting moment in world cinema, writing that "you had three very important filmmakers in one place trying to create new images of an independent country—a radical, Marxist country" ("Sonimage in Mozambique," 97).

One new thing that these filmmakers were trying to get cinema to do was reflect everyday life. The special issue of *Cahiers du cinéma* that Godard and Miéville edited (it was number 300 and came out in May 1979) devoted a very long section to their experience in Mozambique. Part of this is a semi-poetic description of the meetings they took and the people they met—that section has the singularly non-poetic title of "Rapport sur le voyage n° 2A de la Société Sonimage au Mozambique." But it also features still images of everyday life and of video cameras. On page 94, there is a photo of a Mozambican man with a video camera in the top half and a photo of a track meet in the bottom half; in between is the text "*Essai d'actualités mozambicaines.*" Pages 110 and 111 feature facing photographs of a Mozambican behind a video camera and three women staring directly at the camera, at the viewer of the photo; under the image of the man at the video camera is "*Le droit de regard,*" and below the three women is "*Le droit à la parole.*" An emphasis on the local coupled with a desire to show what is behind the camera as well as in front of it was, of course, an important part of what Godard was trying to do in Quebec. As we will see shortly, it was a central preoccupation of the films and television series he and Miéville were producing in the 1970s. So it is no surprise to see him emphasizing it here, as Godard and Miéville came to the end of their "communication" period.

The reason that I am relying so heavily in this part of the discussion on secondary material is that just as with his projected television series in Quebec, this series of "*actualités mozambicains*," this *Naissance (de l'image) d'une nation* was never actually produced. In his essay "Birth (of the Image) of a Nation: Jean-Luc Godard in Mozambique," Daniel Fairfax writes that the project "now exists for us, however, as a trace, or phantomic presence, of a work that never was to be, and yet, as I examine later, the work as it exists at this stage not only contains valuable insight into what the completed video could have been, but also merits being considered in its own right as a kind of film, made with the tools of photographs and texts" (57). Diawara writes that "Godard, like Rouch, came under attack because of the high cost of his projects. Before the year [1979] was over, Godard's video project was cancelled. Television arrived in Mozambique without him realizing his dream" (*African Cinema*, 100). Diawara argues elsewhere that part of the reason for the failure of the project was that it tended to emphasize the creation of infrastructure, or what Diawara calls *mise-en-scène* compared to actual media making. "They went there, not to make films for television, but to prepare the ground for television," he writes. "Maybe Godard was not even interested in producing the images as much as he was in trying to define these images, trying to lay the groundwork, preparing the kind of television they should construct given the world situation" ("Sonimage in Mozambique," 111). So, like the experience in Quebec, this Mozambique work exists only in fragments, in reconstructions, in memories.

But the Mozambique project should not be seen as some sort of aberration or eccentricity; it is entirely consistent with what Godard and Miéville were doing at this time, entirely consistent with the engagement with a critical regionalism that was, as outlined in Chapter 1, at the core of the Sonimage practice. Michael Witt has written of how "[d]ecentralisation is a central defining premise to the Sonimage practice: the relocation of Sonimage to Grenoble constituted first and foremost a move from Paris, a desire to resist the political and cultural hegemony of the capital" (*On Communication*, 3). Thus, it is not surprising that Godard went to Abitibi, as opposed to Montreal, to make his broadcasts, and it is clear that many of the same impulses drove him and Miéville to visit Mozambique. I disagree strongly with Brody's assessment that "the country's significance for him was unclear. He was not connected to it by language, history, or culture" (414). Godard and Miéville were connected to Mozambique by the same sense of exile that connected Godard to Quebec, and that had, as I discussed in Chapter 1, pushed him and Miéville away from Paris, first to Grenoble and then to the small Swiss town of Rolle. Mozambique is a small country, and as a former Portuguese colony and thus part of Lusophone Africa, it is lacking even the colonially influenced connections that the Commonwealth or *La Francophonie* can give to African countries. Furthermore, Portugal was, as I discuss below, an important part of *Comment ça va?*, the film that Godard and Miéville made in 1976. That work is ostensibly about the conscience of a reporter at a communist newspaper, and how such a newspaper should cover Portugal's 1974 revolution is a recurring argument. That revolution was, in many respects, what May 1968 had failed to become: a complete reconstruction of a society, a reconstruction that included a very rapid wave of decolonization. As we will see in Chapter 3, when I discuss *Comment ça va?*, the example of Portugal loomed large over the European left in the 1970s. The Mozambique project clearly progressed from that well-established interest, one that now moved from the colonial metropolis to the rapidly transforming post-colonial margins.

BEAUVIALA AND THE AATON 35-8[6]

The early part of Godard and Miéville's return to working on film (basically the 1980s) featured a collaboration with Jean-Pierre Beauviala on a new camera that was to be called the Aaton 35-8. Godard and Miéville's first period of work together had been defined by technical questions and by technical experimentation. As I mention in the Chapter 3, this seemed to begin with their move to Grenoble in 1973, a move that was ostensibly in order for them to be closer to Beauviala, whose company Aaton was making cutting-edge cinéma-vérité cameras in that French alpine town. Godard and Miéville's interest in technical experimentation really gathered speed during this Grenoble period mostly through video, and they purchased a great deal of then-cutting-edge video equipment and thought of their company Sonimage as a workshop (and they frequently used the word *atelier* to describe it). Beaviala's Aaton, with its combination of artisanal and aesthetic sensibilities and its non-metropolitan location, was for them the ideal model of the way they wanted to work.

Their return to shooting 35 mm film corresponded with a return to working with Beauviala, this time on a more technical level. Godard approached him to design and build, for the production of *Sauve qui peut (la vie)*, a camera that would be the size of a Super-8 home movie camera (Godard often spoke of his desire to fit it into the glovebox of a Toyota) but which would shoot 35 mm film with as much sensitivity and detail as a full-size Aaton. The camera was dubbed the 35-8, and Beauviala began work on it in 1979. One aspect of the creation of the camera that it is important to bear in mind is that Godard and Beauviala were not trying to create a portable camera as such. Godard was at pains to point this out to Jacques Drillon when he interviewed him about the release of *Prénom Carmen*. Drillon began the interview by asking what kind of camera they had shot the film with, saying that "[y]ou get the impression that it's really light, and yet it seems that it's never shoulder-mounted." Godard responded that it was:

> An Aaton 35/8 that I had asked Beauviala to get together. I wanted a little machine, one that had the manageability of an 8mm, with 35mm. That's what gives the impression that it's lightweight, because the camera we chose, it wasn't by accident if ... We had to be able to capture things, to try, to react quickly. You don't make the same films with a big Mitchell. Anyway, no doubt Troyat wrote with a big pen. And I didn't want a portable camera. We had done that, with the French New Wave, at the beginning when it was impossible. Now, everyone puts the camera on their shoulder, and so it's shaky, it's blurry, so OK. (54, ellipses in original; m.t.)

This hybrid "*petit appareil*" was supposed to debut with *Sauve qui peut (la vie)*, but Beauviala did not finish it in time. It was ostensibly ready for *Passion* (1982), a film that Godard made on his own, but as Antoine de Baecque notes in *Godard: biographie* (607–8), it was not very reliable, and it was particularly difficult to make it work properly in cold temperatures (an issue for the shots of *Passion* taken around a wintery Lac Léman). Its next run came during the shooting of *Prénom Carmen* (1983), and the camera did not work significantly better.

Godard made his displeasure with this situation quite clear in a discussion between Beauviala and Godard called "Genèse d'un caméra" and published in two parts in *Cahiers du cinéma* 348–49 and 350 (1983); the first part of the dialogue was translated in *Camera Obscura* 13–14 (1985). The second part of the discussion was joined by Romain Goupil (who had collaborated on some scripts with Godard and served as his assistant), Renato Berta (a Swiss cinematographer who had shot *Sauve qui peut (la vie)* with William Lubtchansky), Serge Toubiana, and Alain Bergala (both of the *Cahiers du cinéma*). Throughout both parts of the dialogue (which is reprinted in *Jean-Luc Godard par Jean-Luc Godard* t.1, 519–57), Godard is unambiguously annoyed and Beauviala quite defensive; reading the transcript, one gets the sense that the struggles over the camera had strained their relationship to the breaking point. Beauviala was, twenty years later, fairly philosophical about the experience and the discussion, telling Richard Brody that "[w]e were like an old couple, who needed to have a good shouting match" (453). The first part of the discussion concludes with a collage Godard made of a man looking through a film camera on the left and an image of a donkey on the right, with typewritten text that summarizes his feelings in a more melancholy way:

for this shot
you would have had
to been able to
put the 8/35
in the glove box of a Toyota
under the seat of a DC 9
and in the basket of a bike
before finally
discovering
without looking for it
in Tralee
in Ireland
like Cartier le Bresson,
at the right hour
minute,
second,
and frame.
But here you are:
the Aaton 35 has lost its 8
like a clarinet without its C note
and this shot is impossible
(Jean-Luc Godard par Jean-Luc Godard t.1, 538; m.t.)

The camera was used at the beginning of production on *Prénom Carmen* (the film's opening titles mention this, with a credit for "*Caméras: Aaton 35/8 Arriflex*"), but Brody recalls that upon encountering the camera on the shoot, "Godard reacted angrily, used Beauviala's camera for only a few shots, and then switched to a conventional Arriflex" (453).

The problems here are worth dwelling on because this experience of the 35-8 signals an end to Godard and Miéville as filmmakers who saw technical innovation as central to their work together. It is very hard to talk about the first films, videos, and television programs that the two made together—basically, the subject of Chapter 3—without talking about the kind of equipment they were purchasing and experimenting with. This work on the 35-8 clearly indicates that he had some hope of carrying that sense of experimentation into the next phase of their work together, into their return to making work on 35 mm film. But that did not come to pass, and indeed the kind of films that they made during the 1980s and a bit into the 1990s lack the sense of tinkering that defines their work of the 1970s. But in the place of that tinkerer's spirit is a kind of consolidation of their shared project. In the 1970s, they seemed to be moving outward, and exploring new technologies was part of that. In the 1980s, they start to go deeper.

700ᴱ ANNIVERSAIRE DE LA CONFÉDÉRATION HELVÉTIQUE

Chapter 5 of this book is devoted mostly to short- or medium-length films that Godard and Miéville made during the 1990s and 2000s. Several of these were done as commissions and often dealt with film history, but sometimes, as in the case of *Liberté et patrie* (2002), they explicitly engaged with Swiss history in a way that had been unusual for them. The genesis of this kind of work can be seen, at least in part, in a film that Godard had undertaken to make to honour the seven hundredth anniversary of the Swiss confederation. Antoine de Baecque puts the project in the context of Godard's desire to remain the "*cinéaste total*," who worked simultaneously on shorts, commissions, essay films and features, as he had tried to do in the 1980s and 1990s (703).

Godard was no stranger to heritage commissions. His short *Lettre à Freddy Buache* (1981) was made as part of a commission to celebrate the five hundredth anniversary of the city of Lausanne, seat of Godard and Miéville's home canton of Vaud. It is one of his most tender, lyrical films of the 1980s; Jacques Aumont writes that with the piece, "Godard shows us the world, its light, its colours; he looks at it with us, directly" (175; m.t.). While the *Lettre* certainly puts Lausanne in a good light, it is by no means a simple heritage piece, or even really a tribute; it is a sort of meditation on the relationship between the solitude of creative work, the fecund openness of the city, and the friendship that acts as the intermediary between these two forces. Buache seemed to hope that a similar kind of film would emerge from another ostensibly dry "work for hire."

Although modern Switzerland was born in 1848, with the political triumph of the radicals over the conservatives and the consequent ratification of the federal constitution, some vestige of the "*Confédération helvétique*" can be traced back to 1291. This is the year when the three "mountain communes" of Uri, Schwyz, and Nidwalden joined in a federation (known in French as the "*Confédération des III Cantons*") that was basically meant to ensure the free flow of goods across the alps (in contemporary Switzerland these three cantons are collectively known as "*La Suisse primitive*"). The year 1991 marked the seven hundredth anniversary of this first confederation and included the usual national-heritage-type celebrations. Part of this, as Buache recalls in his "Préambule" to Godard's "Confédération" proposal, was that in his capacity as curator of Lausanne's Cinémathèque Suisse, he was (as with the earlier Lausanne film) approached to commission a dozen twenty-six-minute shorts "*dans les trois [sic] langues nationales*"[7] that would commemorate the history of Swiss cinema. The films would then be deposited with the Cinémathèque. Buache specified that these were to be collage films, writing that they would be made "using only the original images, intertitles, and dialogue, without adding the slightest explanatory commentary" (343; m.t.). Godard was ostensibly commissioned to produce a film on the Lausanne-based production company Gamma Films, which, as Buache notes, had participated in films such as *Lola Montès* (1955); the project became known as *Les Années Gammas*. Buache does not give many details of the commissioning process or the reasons that Godard lost interest in the project, saying only, "He accepted, and then backed out" (343; m.t.).

The choice of Godard to work on a Lausanne-based company is not insignificant, especially from the perspective of the seven hundredth anniversary of the "*Confédération helvétique.*" Lausanne is the seat of the canton of Vaud, which is the *terre natale* of both Godard and Miéville; Vaud is also the location of their adopted home of Rolle. Vaud is not, however, part of "*La Suisse primitive,*" and was indeed a relative latecomer to the country. From the 1500s until 1798, it was a subject of the canton of Berne rather than a full member of the confederation. Vaud was reconstituted as the Canton de Léman during the period of the Napoleonic-ruled République helvétique, which lasted from 1798 to 1803. Upon the ouster of French forces and the return to the Confédération Suisse, it became the Canton de Vaud. Commissioning Godard to make a film about a Vaudois production company as part of a commemoration of this seven hundredth anniversary would be a bit like asking Guy Maddin to make a film about a Manitoba film company as part of the celebration of the hundred and fiftieth anniversary of Canadian confederation. There would be nothing wrong with that, but it would have the implicit effect of calling attention to the finer and more complicated points of Canadian history—such as the fact that Manitoba was constituted as a province not in the year of confederation (1867) but three years later (July 15, 1870), as a result of the Red River Rebellion of 1869.

The proposal, which took the form of a fourteen-page letter to Buache dated October 21, 1991 (and is reproduced in *Jean-Luc Godard: Documents*), is more engaged with Swiss and Vaudois culture than anything Godard had yet done, either with Miéville or alone. It gives a good sense of the ways in which his interests were shifting homeward. Godard's letter to Buache includes mention of "'Aline' and/or 'Jean-Luc Persécuté,' which I had offered for my mother's birthday before her accident—strange present" (350; m.t.). "Aline" and "Jean-Luc

Persécuté" are both short stories by French-speaking Switzerland's most celebrated writer, the Vaudois Charles-Ferdinand Ramuz. Godard and Miéville's 2002 short film *Liberté et patrie* is in a kind of dialogue with the 1911 Ramuz book *Aimé Pache, peintre vaudois*, which is about an artist who eventually returned to Vaud after making a career in Paris. The very title of that short film signals its connection to Vaud, as "*Liberté et patrie*," freedom and homeland, is the motto of Vaud and is printed on the top half of its cantonal flag. Godard also holds forth there on the ways the Swiss have let outsiders tell them who they are:

> Swiss identity, unlike that of other people, is not made by / or / via an image. The typical image of Switzerland—chocolate, mountains, watches, banks—is made by others, not by the Swiss. A history of Swiss cinema has to give the sense in certain chapters that Switzerland didn't forbid representation—like Israel—but that it has simply lacked images since its birth. (356; m.t.)

The ways in which images fail to illuminate power dynamics within and between cultures was particularly important for Godard and Miéville in the 1970s, and here we can see it not via revolutionary politics (as in *Ici et ailleurs* or *Comment ça va?*), nor via the ravages of a deracinated consumer capitalism (as in *Six fois deux*), but returned to the local, Swiss, Vaudois context that is the setting of so much of their later work together in the 1980s, especially *Sauve qui peut (la vie)* (1980), *Je vous salue, Marie* (1985), and *Soft and Hard* (1985). That is a good way of thinking of the best of their final work together: it merges a lot of the formal experiments of the 1970s with the subject matter of much of the 1980s work. Ironically, this handwritten, rambling proposal for a film that never even began production gives quite a vivid sense of how focused and cohesive Godard and Miéville's work has been over the course of four decades. Much the same could be said of all of these abandoned projects.

Chapter 3
COMMUNICATION

"Indeed, it is a re-emphasis on the image which marks both Ici et ailleurs *and the subsequent films, a concern to understand the workings of the image in our lives, the way in which the image enriches and impoverishes us. It is this emphasis rather than the sound of Maoism that determines the strategy of the later films. If Maoism finally produced a dominance of the political where the aim had been to subvert the political, Godard's programme is now to hold a variety of practices in balance, playing one against another through his own activity as an image-maker without awarding primacy to any of them."*
—Colin MacCabe, *Godard: Image, Sounds, Politics* (74)

"These were the years when Jean-Luc Godard and Anne-Marie Miéville dreamed of being the directors-hosts-technicians of a little local television channel, and imagined that video would become a real communications tool."
—Alain Bergala, "Ondes de choc d'un pari lointain" (44; m.t.)

MIÉVILLE'S *PAPA COMME MAMAN*

I made the case in Chapter 1 that Godard and Miéville's career can be broken into three distinct phases: Communication, Realization, and Reconsideration. These phases, of course, flow into one another and overlap. One way that the "Communication" phase (which is to say the period of the 1970s) is often explained is that it is Godard and Miéville's "Sonimage Period." During this period, they were co-owners of a company called Sonimage, based in Grenoble, France, making work that mixed film and video often of a non-standard length (such as *Ici et ailleurs*, which is fifty-six minutes). One can see this phase end when the couple moved to Rolle, Switzerland, and released *Sauve qui peut (la vie)*, which, as I discuss in the next chapter, was far closer to being a narrative-feature film and which seemed to mark a "return to cinema" that was concurrent with a departure from France.

One work that complicates this, though, is Miéville's forty-minute film *Papa comme maman* (1977). This is the work that straddles the "Communication" and "Realization" periods inasmuch as it is very much a film and video collage along the lines of work like *Ici et ailleurs* (1974), *Numéro deux* (1975), and *Comment ça va?* (1976), but also because it was made in Switzerland, not in France. Brody recalls how Godard and Miéville moved to the Swiss village of Rolle, in the canton of Vaud, "[i]n mid-1977" (398). The film's national pedigree is far from being incidental. The work was part of a series produced by Télévision Suisse Romande (TSR) called *Ecoutez Voir*. The series invited four prominent Swiss filmmakers—Alain Tanner, Loretta Verna, Francis Reusser, and Miéville—to make medium-length films that used either Super-8 film or lightweight video. This is how Tanner explained its genesis to Michael Tarantino for the British film magazine *Sight and Sound*: "It was Francis Reusser who started it. He was interested in three-quarter-inch video and Super-8 film. Then there was Loretta Verna plus Anne-Marie Miéville plus myself. We decided to try something together and approached Swiss TV to find out if they were interested. They *were* interested, not so much in what we wanted to show or make but in so far as the technique was concerned. They know that Super-8 film is out there somewhere and so is three-quarter-inch video, but they have no one who can really experiment with it" (41).

Miéville, who had been spending the decade experimenting with just such technology, must have seemed an obvious choice to participate. Miéville used both film and video for *Papa comme maman*, and she also drew on the computer-generated text that she and Godard had used to divide the sections of all of the work they did together in the 1970s. *Papa comme maman* is a Sonimage work, but one made on her own and for Swiss television. It comes, more or less, in between the two television series Godard and Miéville did for French television: *Six fois deux: Sur et sous la communication* was broadcast from July 25 to August 20, 1976; *Papa comme maman* was broadcast on November 18, 1977; and *France/tour/détour/deux/enfants* premiered in 1979.

TSR's description of the film (which is found, along with the film itself, at http://archives.tsr.ch/player/reflexion-mieville, or at http://goo.gl/lsO1F) emphasized the theme of child abuse, but that is actually a relatively small part of *Papa comme maman*. It is, to quote the computer-generated text that fills the screen a few minutes into the film, "some speculation on the function of the mother." It is not hard to see, though, why its engagement with child abuse would come to dominate someone's memories of the film. Its opening sequence consists Miéville's voice-over explaining how common a phenomenon child abuse is. She notes that in this otherwise civilized country, it kills more children than diseases such as tuberculosis and diabetes. Miéville's voice-over is accompanied by a montage of photographs of abused children, which look like the photos police take as evidence of a crime. These photos have a cold, unflinching quality to them; these close-ups of the bruised, cut, burned, and otherwise damaged bodies of small children are searing. But the voice-over also notes, "You never see someone's mother ... you never see an image of a mother beating her child; you don't find them anywhere." Miéville goes on to say that this will all serve her examination of motherhood by explaining its absence. The first part of this examination is about an absence of motherly affection, of love. But the second and much larger part is devoted to a literal absence of the mother who has died.

Part of this examination seems rather conventional. There are a number of interviews with both Olivia, a young woman who looks to be about sixteen years old, and her father who, as he notes, has raised her on his own since his wife died when Olivia was four. But even these dialogues are a bit "off." The first one, with one of the family's neighbours talking about the days just after the death of Olivia's mother, is an extreme long shot, sometimes called an establishing shot; the camera is set so far back that it is difficult to make out individual people. It is basically impossible to see who is speaking. The image is dominated, instead, by a Swiss alpine lake (it is a composition that strongly anticipates the singing sequence in Miéville's 1984 film, *How Can I Love*). This is followed by two interviews that are each based on a single *very* long take: one with the father, which is a close-up, but not anything like a typical documentary interview, and then with Olivia, which is almost an extreme close-up, so much so as to draw attention to itself as an awkward composition. These last about six minutes each, and while they are both broken up by some computer-generated text, in neither case does the camera move at all, and the unblinking quality of the imagery is something that is closely connected to video as a distinct form. You cannot have shots that go this long without a cut in any other medium besides video.

The film's key sequence comes at the end of this interview with Olivia, in the form of a montage that, like so much in this period of Godard and Miéville's work, is based on drawing attention to interstices between two images rather than trying to join them dialectically. This sequence begins with computer text that reads, "*Maman comme modèle*," and is a montage of Olivia explaining how she imagines her mother and the domestic chores of motherhood. Miéville says on voice-over, "we've seen this," and then replays a portion of the Olivia interview, with her talking about things such as how she had always wanted an example of how to live her life, or how a mother is someone who can guess what her children will do before they do it. This is followed by Miéville's voice-over saying, "but we haven't heard this," and then a cut to a close-up of some domestic labour with the relevant sounds—dishes clicking in the sink as hands wash them, a blade running along a carrot as a hand peels them, and so on. The meaning in the montage is generated by the disconnects, and Miéville indicates this first by avoiding simple sound–image connections: she always says we never *hear* something when referring to the image of housework, that we *see* this when referring to the interview with Olivia. The main disconnect, of course, is in the way that she demonstrates how little Olivia understands about the daily life of motherhood, how rose-coloured and partial her view is. This analysis is central to the approach of all of the work under discussion in this chapter—that montage is especially useful for showing what we do not see and what we do not understand. Indeed, this sequence is a kind of mini-manifesto for Godard and Miéville's approach to communication: it is the most vivid, communicative images that make clear how little we comprehend.

What I want to argue in this chapter, then, is that Godard and Miéville's earliest work together is defined by a rather tortured approach to a basic human activity: communication. Their work of the 1970s is in many ways their most formally ambitious and experimental: it freely mixes film, video, and still imagery. That formal ambition is matched by a desire to engage with major political issues of that decade: revolutionary movements in Palestine and Portugal, and the phenomenon of revolutionary memories fading into a consumerist-led suburban alienation. They explore these issues in a way that is genuinely essayistic in that it is tentative and searching. They really do make the most of the medium of video, which they gravitated toward because it promised a kind of flexibility that film was lacking. This is especially true of the ease with which video images can be mixed and text can be superimposed over images, formal gestures that recur throughout this work and come to form the heart of many of the analyses. This tentative, searching, uncommitted quality, so visible in *Papa comme maman*, is typically Modernist, and so this work is also important because it marks the passage from "Godard the Parisian *enfant terrible*" to "Godard and Miéville the brooding Modernists," a characterization that could describe the whole of their extremely varied career together. In the final analysis, these works are *essais* in the French sense of the word: attempts. They are important precursors to the more fully realized, and perhaps more coherent, work that Godard and Miéville did together in the 1980s and into the 1990s (which will be the subject of the next chapter). It is difficult to understand that work, though, without taking full account of these audio-visual experiments that preceded it.

ICI ET AILLEURS

We can certainly see the glints of the revolutionary idealism and formal open-mindedness that defines *One P.M.*, as well as the interest in the dialectic between communication and interpersonal relationships, in the first film that Godard and Miéville made together. Although it was actually the third Godard and Miéville film to be released, *Ici et ailleurs* was finished in 1974 from footage that was shot in 1970 but not released until 1976. It marks the transition out of Godard's Dziga Vertov period and into his collaboration with Miéville. It is the film that sees him moving from a period of restlessly internationalist collaboration with Jean-Pierre Gorin (among a few others) to the "Sonimage practice," devoted to settling out onto the margins and into a more long-term collaboration.

The film's opening voice-over (over images of computer-generated text and then text from what looks like a magazine page) has Godard saying, "in 1970, this film was called *Victory*; in 1974, this film was called *Ici et ailleurs*." Miéville's voice repeats that over images first of machine-gun-toting Palestinians and then of a family watching television. They are alluding to the fact that *Ici et ailleurs* began as *Jusqu'à la victoire* (*Méthodes de pensée et de travail de la révolution palestinienne*), a film that Godard and Gorin wanted to make about the Palestinian struggle. The two of them, along with cameraman Armand Marco, spent time in and around refugee camps on the border with both Israel and Jordan in 1969 and 1970. Citing an article in *L'Express*, Richard Brody recalls that "[b]etween November 1969 and August 1970, Godard travelled to the Middle East six times, not always with Gorin and Marco" (*Everything Is Cinema*, 352). They were there to fulfill a contract for Fatah, then the most powerful political wing of the PLO; de Baecque's *Godard: biographie* recalls that "contacted by the Arab League via Hany Jawhariyya, Fatah's 'official' filmmaker, Godard received an order in November 1969, in the amount of $6000, as well as, in due time, the ability to film under the protection of Fatah, who put guides and interpreters at their disposal" (469; m.t.).

From the very beginning of the project, though, there is a sense that the two were slightly overwhelmed by the complexity of the situation. In his introduction to the manifesto that Godard published in the semi-clandestine newspaper *El Fatah* (reproduced in *Jean-Luc Godard: Documents*), David Faroult recalls that "[t]here remained, from the political contacts they made on their first trip at the end of 1969, a sense of confusion as to the contradictions that divided the different groups" (136; m.t.). That manifesto is not especially revelatory; Godard repeats a lot of the formulations of his 1967 *Cahiers du cinéma* interview "Lutter sur deux fronts" (where he talked about Quebec), summarizing his overall aspiration as "*En littérature et en art, lutter sur deux fronts*" (138). The situation that the group found there was not conducive to these kinds of revolutionary slogans, and perhaps the key problem was that they came there not as documentarians but as political filmmakers. One of the Fatah members who guided and translated for them, Elias Sanbar, has recalled in a text published in the first issue of Serge Daney's journal *Trafic* how "Godard never stopped looking at his notes the entire time we were working" (111; m.t.). He also recalled there how they had some lightweight video gear, but Sanbar seems amazed that they were using it in a way that would, in essence, preview Godard and Miéville's use of the technology in the name of argument rather than mimesis, their desire not simply to document something but to create a sometimes artificial work of art that would illuminate part of the world:

> At first, I had the feeling that everything had been discussed, systematised, written and cut, that that film was a kind of series of empty compartments that it was our task to methodically fill. But I was wrong, as I had to admit upon our return from this meeting with the militiamen and the immediate screening, thanks to lightweight video gear, of the images that we had just "taken." A confrontation then began between the pre-written text and the images that had just been shot. It mostly led to some re-writing and a request to re-shoot the same scene, to the great surprise of the Palestinian interviewees. (111–12; m.t.)

Although he had long used the tools of mimetic documentary, the emergent technologies of direct cinema and then video, Godard's work has always stood very far from direct cinema; it would get even further once he began working with Miéville. Here is where we can see the Bazin connection. Bazin prized a certain kind of realist aesthetics, but he saw that as *an aesthetic*. This helps to explain why most of his favourite films were feature-narratives, not documentaries. His love of the films of Robert Flaherty may seem a rare exception, but it only reinforces the point and indeed helps us understand *Ici et ailleurs* even more clearly. Like Flaherty's *Nanook of the North* (1922) or *Man of Aran* (1934), *Ici et ailleurs* is, finally, a highly artificial work, one that uses some elements of documentary form for an entirely imaginative and argumentative end. Where *Ici et ailleurs* breaks from a film like *Man of Aran* is in the confrontation between the pre-written text and the images that Sanbar evokes. Flaherty was famous for smoothing over such confrontations, for making his images conform to his pre-established views of the nature of life in remote areas. For Godard and Miéville, that confrontation between script and images and the tension that it creates are not only not erased but are indeed at the very core of the film. That conflict is the real subject matter of *Ici et ailleurs*.

Of all of these testaments of the unmanageability of the Palestinian situation that Godard found in 1969 and 1970, my favourite is definitely found in the interview that Gorin gave to the American film journal *Jump Cut* in 1973. Their writer Christian Braad Thomsen asked:

> Q: You attempted to do an historical film on the Palestinian situation. What happened with the film?
>
> A: We've had this film on our backs for two years, and it has passed through four or five stages of cutting. One of the interesting things about the film is our impossibility to edit it, but I think we've found some kind of creative possibility to reflect on the impossibility of editing the material. We plan to make four or five films each lasting one and one-half hours out of the ten hours of material we have. They will be struggling films in the sense that we will honestly speak about the problems we have been facing in trying to film an historical process.
>
> Q: So these films will really be about the impossibility of finishing the film? (18)

Thomsen had no idea how right he was. Godard and Gorin basically abandoned *Jusqu'à la victoire*, with the footage sitting dormant for several years. When Godard and Miéville returned to it, and made it the "elsewhere" (*ailleurs*) half of their first collaboration *Ici et ailleurs*, it had become something very different. What emerged in 1974 was not a political film that a militant group or political party like the PLO or Fatah would have wanted to commission. Instead, it became a meditation on the difficulties of communication, on the dual promise that cinema makes to transport its viewer elsewhere and to illuminate the world that lies before her. Cinema is able to do neither of these things fully, as Godard and Miéville show us, and yet these images do contain kernels of meaning that are too powerful to ignore fully. This is a mixture, then, of a Bazinian approach to realism and a Modernist approach to communication, and that combination provides a good way of thinking about the work that they have done together.

The opening sequence of *Ici et ailleurs* is a montage of images of a Palestinian refugee camp, the training of militants, Palestinians (two of them teenagers) directly addressing the camera, and manipulated video images (including some computer-generated text). Godard and Miéville's voices alternate on the soundtrack, although there is also some semi-synchronous diegetic sound, sound that comes from the world of the film's narrative. While the film comes back repeatedly to several of these images—a young woman addressing the camera, a chroma-keyed video still of Golda Meir superimposed over a stylized graphic of an armed Palestinian—this is not really a dialectic strategy. The montage is too multiple, too quick. Godard and Miéville are not settling on any kind of thesis/antithesis, choosing instead to highlight the complexity of the situation, the "chunkiness" of its politics. It is also not dialectical because, rather than moving back and forth between two concepts by way of making an argument, the montage is actually moving us forward, through the Palestinian situation and on to France. This begins when, following some images of a Palestinian meeting and close-ups of a calculator, the film gives us very shaky hand-held footage of what looks to be a riot in a European street with Godard's voice-over saying "*révolution française et et et révolution arabe*," followed by an extreme close-up of the word "*ET*" or "AND" which appears to be taken from movie titles. Here AND elsewhere: French revolution AND Arab Revolution. In turn, this is followed by a shot with the camera placed very low to the ground (a low-angle shot) of machine-gun-toting Arabs walking over some rocks. Godard's voice-over is now saying "*révolution arabe et et et révolution française*"; the next image is again the word "*ET*." A series of similar tripartite montages involving disparate images combined with Godard's voice-over and the word "*ET*" follows, and some of these images are of a young French family. This is the family that the film shortly settles on.

Before settling on this "*Ici*" of French consumer society, though, Godard and Miéville present a series of montages that made the film famous, or perhaps infamous. I refer here to the juxtaposition of Golda Meir and Adolf Hitler, who first share the screen about eighteen minutes into the film. A photograph of Hitler takes up about three-quarters of the screen, while Meir's image occupies the upper-right-hand quadrant; on the voice-over in (untranslated) German, there is a song about Auschwitz. This is the sort of video mix of which Godard and Miéville were becoming enamoured, and their work of this period, especially *Numéro deux* and *Six fois deux: Sur et sous la* communication, is full of them. One of the reasons this technique seemed so appealing to them during this period (and, as we will see, again during the 1990s and 2000s) is because this kind of mixing, while not exactly unique to video, is specific to the medium because it can be done spontaneously or tentatively simply by using multiple sources and a switcher; doing such mixing on film would require elaborate optical printing and lab work. This kind of visual mixing speaks to the flexibility of video as a medium. For many practitioners, however, that sort of flexibility was most useful in the context of shooting—taking hours and hours of footage with relatively lightweight gear and little concern for the cost of the tape and having shots that can last much longer than any shot in film (a shot taken on film can rarely last more than a few minutes). For Godard and Miéville, that flexibility came in the post-production phase. Thus, it turned out to be quite logical that when Godard shot in the Palestinian camps, he did not do so as a documentarian looking for unexpected footage. He found the unexpected and the spontaneous at the editing desk, when he and Miéville assembled and combined the footage using what was then-emerging technologies such as video switchers. For Godard and Miéville, the medium-specificity of video was not primarily about a new kind of long take but about a new kind of montage; it was, as in Palestine, not about mimesis but about consideration. And in mixing images of Meir and Hitler, of Auschwitz and Israel, we can see Godard and Miéville poking toward the history of the Middle East conflict's European roots, but doing it tentatively, flexibly—video-ly.

Something similar is going on in the "slide show montage" that shortly follows the first Hitler-Meir appearance. This is a montage made up of three images projected side by side onto a black background; a hand changing the slides is dimly visible. On the left side are images first of Nixon, then of Moshe Dayan and Golda Meir, then Nixon again, and then Pinochet, Hitler, and Brezhnev; on the right are images first of Palestinian fighters, then of the Viet Cong, then images of unidentifiable protesters and soldiers; in the centre are images of jet fighters, then a tank. Finally, the film settles on a close-up of a slide of a group of men with their hands on their heads, with Godard speaking on the voice-over about how grouping images is a matter of arranging memories. This is followed by a much denser collection of slides—three images by three images, for nine in all—some of which are photos we have already seen (Hitler, Dayan), some of which are new (advertising images—a shot of a baby next to its parent). These "slide sequences" explicitly call back what Godard had said in his *Cinéma Pratique* interview: "I have the impression that from now on you can say: this film can be made with the help of slides, and projected that way. Others can be shot in video and, if you have to show it to everyone, can be kinescoped" (158; m.t.).

As I mentioned in Chapter 1, in that interview, Godard stated that the kind of political film that he would like to make would be essentially a home movie, and while part of this is thematic—as he said, it would be the kind of movie that would show his wife and kid what kind of person he was—part of the reason he saw home movies as potentially radical was technological. Like video, home movie and slides are available to just about anyone, and they are easy to use and to disseminate. And like video, this technical simplicity means that they can be used in a way that is tentative, flexible, nimble, and polemical. Indeed, Gorin recalled in a 1973 interview with Robert Phillip Kolker (where both Godard and Gorin dismissed the possibilities of video) that during the shooting of what was then to be *Jusqu'à la victoire*, "we discovered a doctor in the south of Jordan who was making films with stills. Each week he received some stills from Amman, from El Fatah, edited them, put black spaces into them, made his own commentary in front of the people. He was a real filmmaker. That's the possibility we have" (64). These slide combinations are giving a sense of the dense array of symbols that evoke some part of the conflict in the Middle East. Pavle Levi calls the sequence "a perceptually uncontainable barrage of multiple and thoroughly discontinuous pictures" and "a quantitative assault on perception (and, consequently, on cognition)" (52–53) The "slide sequence" is an expansion on the use of video to combine Hitler and Meir and the montage that combined film footage of Palestinian and French life, all of which gives the sense of the uncontainability of mass-media representation. All of this is so dense that it sometimes feels like a kind of image-based assault on a passive viewer. Some of *Ici et ailleurs* is film, some of it is kinescoped video, and some of it is still imagery, some from slides and some from a combination of film and video. In terms of the way that it uses shifting media to illustrate a dizzying array of political and cultural connections, it is a vivid if sometimes overwhelming realization of the idealism that Godard and Miéville had invested in low-end technology.

This is a highly unconventional approach to this kind of media, and sequences that use the technology in this way demand new ways of reading images. This is the point that Gilles Deleuze makes in *Cinéma 2: L'image-temps*, specifically as pertains the film's most controversial imagery:

> You can, of course, always object that the only interstices are between associated images. From this point of view, images like those which bring together Golda Meir and Hitler in *Ici et ailleurs* would be intolerable. But this is perhaps proof that we are not ready for a true "reading" of the visual image. For, in Godard's method, it is not a question of association. Given one image, another image has to be chosen which will induce an interstice *between* the two. This is not an operation of association, but of differentiation, as mathematicians say ... (*L'image-temps* 234 / *The Time-Image*, 178; translation altered slightly)

I agree that this is a matter of differentiation rather than simplistic association, and one reason that this is a logical way to read the images such as Meir–Hitler or Nixon–Dayan–Brezhnev is that the film's sound–image relationship also has little to do with simple association and is rather quite disjunctive. We can see this kind of sensibility being developed in sequences like the ones where Godard and Miéville critique the Palestine footage. Over images of a Fatah chief giving a speech outside Amman—and like most of the documentary footage, this image has synchronized sound as well—Miéville's voice-over points out that he speaks in the name of the people, but he is alone and far away from the crowd. "*Comme toujours, le théâtre*," she says right before cutting to the French family watching television. Over a close-up of a young Palestinian directly addressing the camera, Godard's voice-over mixes with Miéville's to tell us that this is a pregnant woman who is ready to give her son to the revolution. After she says that, Miéville's voice comes onto the soundtrack and says that what is most interesting is this: the screen goes black, and we hear Godard's voice instructing the woman to do that again but to hold her head a bit differently. Once the woman's face comes back, Miéville's voice-over points out that we never see who gives the orders. And "something else that's no good," she says, now speaking directly to Godard: you really chose an intellectual who was sympathetic to the Palestinian cause, was not really pregnant but agreed to play the role. As a bonus, she was young and pretty. You remained silent about this, Miéville says; these sorts of secrets quickly slip into fascism.

This is the sort of effect that Elisabeth Büttner seems to have in mind when she writes of how "[i]n *Ici et ailleurs* Godard makes productive use of the chasm between then and now" (81). One effect of a bifurcated soundtrack—one half synch sound, one half voice-over—is to reveal the image as a historical object, not a mere reflection of present reality. This sound–image relationship, which accounts for quite a bit of *Ici et ailleurs*, asks the viewer not merely to watch these images, but to witness them being read. The call for an image-reading process that makes montage an art of interstices rather than associations is loudest in the film's concluding montage, which has Miéville's voice describing what goes on "here" and "elsewhere," and Palestinians training for battle: "*Ici, une famille française qui regarde la télé*," she says over a shot of that French family in front of the TV. "*Ailleurs, images de la révolution palestinienne*," she then says, over a shot of young Palestinian men working an anti-aircraft gun. The point of this montage and juxtapositions like it is definitely not association. The meaning lies not in the synthesis of these two opposing images, but in the gap between them. This emphasis on gaps, and on the complexities and contradiction that are to be found in them, is the characterizing quality of *Ici et ailleurs*.

This has not prevented the film from being denounced as a work of anti-Semitic propaganda. Brody summarizes the outrage that greeted the film's 1976 release in France by writing that "[a] militant Zionist group, called Talion (An Eye for an Eye) planted a bomb in one of the two Paris theaters where it was showing. The bomb did not go off, but the owner cancelled the booking.... On the evening of October 12, a showing was interrupted by the same Zionist group, who broke a window, released mice in the theater, and left behind a gas canister with Hebrew printing on it" (378). Brody clearly disapproves, but he also writes that Godard was (with Miéville, presumably) egotistically clueless about the degree to which the film was "harmful to Israel and the well-being of Jews," writing that "his immersion in video equipment and theory had brought him unwittingly back to the sort of unworldly aestheticism with which he had charged himself and the rest of the New Wave" (ibid.). His overall assessment is that "[t]he self-critical motive that Godard asserted as the basis for *Ici et ailleurs* nonetheless resulted in a work of doctrinaire exhortation" (377).

But *Ici et ailleurs* was a very important film for Serge Daney, who had a much more nuanced sense of its form and politics. At first he was critical of the work, writing in his 1976 essay "Le Therrorisé (Pédagogie godardien),"[1] that:

> In *Ici et ailleurs*, for example, a "film" based on images brought back from Jordan (1970–5), it's clear that the film's self-interrogation (the way in which it dissociates "here" and "elsewhere," images and sounds, 1970 and 1975) is possible and intelligible only because, early on, the syntagm "Palestinian Revolution" can be taken for granted (something already-said-by-others, in this case by Al Fatah), something in relation to which Godard doesn't have to define himself personally (and say not just "I" but "I am on their side") or mark his position in the film. He doesn't have to make his position, his initial choice—for the Palestinians, against Israel—acceptable, convincing, or desirable. (*La rampe*, 88–89, slightly different in *Cahiers* version; "Theorize/Terrorize," 118)

Daney remained a student of the film, though, and became just the sort of advocate that it deserved: tentative, unsure, engaged, and mobile. Indeed, the film seemed to follow him all over France, Europe, and the world. He showed it as part of a "*Cahiers* à Nantes" program in 1977 (alongside Chantal Akerman's *Je tu il elle* [1976]), and as part of his report on that event, he wrote in *Cahiers* 275 how in the film, "one sound doesn't critique another ... but instead—and this is more important—permits it to be heard" (*La Maison cinéma* t.1, 402; m.t.). Reporting on a Dziga Vertov retrospective at the 1977 Edinburgh film festival, he suggested that Vertov's approach to montage engaged "*L'extrême hétérogénéité des images*" in a way that was close to what was going on in *Ici et ailleurs*. In 1978, he tried to show it as part of a "Semaine des *Cahiers*" in Damascus, but, reporting on that event in *Cahiers* 290, he recalled that it had been censored by the Syrian authorities because of its Nixon-Brezhnev juxtapositions (*La Maison cinéma* t.1, 420). In *Cahiers* 308, he named it as one of the key films of the 1970s, placing it alongside Robert Kramer's *Milestones* and Straub–Huillet's *Einleitung*: "Three films that question cinema's political effects. Propaganda (Godard), militancy (Kramer), political engagement (Straub). At the *Cahiers*, these films were often travelling companions, veritable thirst-quenchers" (*La Maison cinéma* t.1, 270; m.t.). And the next year, in *Cahiers* 323–24, he used it as an example of the power of direct cinema, calling it a "*film charnière*," a pivotal film, and quipping that "[i]t wouldn't have done the PLO much good as propaganda, but the *Cahiers* would have sent it on a world tour" (*La Maison cinéma* t.1, 372; m.t.). And quite a tour it was for the film.

Following this discourse, we can see Daney identifying very real shortcomings in the film's rigour, coming to recognize the way first its sound–image relationship and then its Vertovian approach to montage actually opens up its view of politics, and finally realizing how important it is for the ways that it irritates totalitarian governments and rebel groups alike. None of this is to dismiss Daney's entirely reasonable critique of the too-easy way that the film assumes the revolutionary quality of the Palestinian struggle (indeed, Daney seems to become aware of the uses and misuses of the Palestinian cause anew during his time in Damascus). But the film became a constant companion for him and the entire *Cahiers* group in no small part because of the way that it, like films by Straub–Huillet, offered an analysis of political engagement in a way that was unafraid to completely reconsider the aesthetics of cinema, starting with the very technological basis of film, with video and even slides freely coming into the mix.

Daney was right to see *Ici et ailleurs* as a pivotal film of the 1970s. Specifically, it marked a turn toward a combination of Bazinian and Modernist positions that had long been nascent in Godard's work and which was now, with Miéville in the mix, emerging fully. The skepticism that is so central to a Modernist aesthetic position, a skepticism specifically of art's ability to transparently communicate meaning, is of course front and centre in *Ici et ailleurs*, and it could be said to be the real subject of the film. But that does not make the mimetic quality of these images any less powerful. An obvious example of this would be the raw force of the recurring image of the burned corpse of a Palestinian man, but the simple medium shot of the French family sitting on the sofa watching television is just as expressive. Really, the case study in the mixture of long take and Modernist skepticism is the still three-minute-long shot of the five Palestinian militants sitting on the ground talking about tactical errors. The soundtrack is made up both of voices speaking Arabic and Godard asking Miéville what they are saying. The quality of this as a representation, a mediated retelling, is quite explicit. But at one point, Godard says that he remembers when they shot this sequence, and that three months later the entire group was dead (presumably at the hands of Jordanian troops, although Godard does not specify that in this sequence). Godard says: "*Ils parlent de leur propre mort*" (They are talking about their own death). It is in this long take with a bifurcated sound–image relationship that the opening words of Bazin's famous essay "L'ontologie de l'image photographique" (part of *Qu'est-ce que le cinéma*) become almost unbearably poignant: "If we were to psychoanalyze the visual arts, the practice of embalming might be seen as fundamental to their birth" (*Qu'est-ce que le cinéma*, 9 / *What Is Cinema*, 9). Godard and Miéville have embalmed these men, but they have done it in a way that is highly artificial and highly self-aware. They have shown themselves to be true students of André Bazin, that champion of long takes and deep focus images. Bazin argued that *Citizen Kane* was a great realization of the poetics of cinema, a masterpiece of artifice and Modernist playfulness if ever there was one. It is clearly this kind of Bazinianism that MacCabe had in mind when he argued for the important influence of the old *Cahiers* editor in Godard's work (as I mentioned in Chapter 1). All the work that Godard did with Miéville shows just how rich Bazin's poetics of cinema were, and this Bazinian Modernism, on view fully formed for the first time in *Ici et ailleurs*, is what unites the very different work they did together over four decades.

NUMÉRO DEUX

The first fully "Godard and Miéville" work to be actually released was *Numéro deux*. That was in 1975, the year after *Ici et ailleurs* was completed but a year before it was released. The title refers to its genesis. It had originally been commissioned as a sequel to Godard's first feature, *À bout de souffle* (1960) by Georges de Beauregard, who had produced that film. "There were only two things that he was sure would remain from the earlier film," Brody writes of Godard's limited attachment to the idea of the film as a sequel or remake. "Beauregard's participation and the budget (600,000 francs; $120,000)" (379).

Numéro deux bears no resemblance to *À bout de souffle*, but it is a film that, because of its combination of film and video and its engagement with the dialectic between political memory and intimate family life, bridges quite nicely the work Godard had been doing on his own and the work that he would go on to do with Miéville. Films like *Weekend* (1967) and especially *2 ou 3 choses je sais d'elle* (1967) were sharp indictments of the way in which consumer culture was creeping into French life, turning people into savages in the former film and prostitutes in the latter. As I discussed earlier, his films of the late 1960s, including his Groupe Dziga Vertov work and the other political projects he mounted (*Le gai savoir* [1968], *Letter to Jane* [1972], etc.), saw Godard turning more sharply toward the left and away from conventional narrative cinema. Laura Mulvey argues that many sequences of *Numéro deux* "mark a crucial shift in the terms of Godard's presentation of sexuality. For the first time the chickens have come home to roost. The problem of sexuality is not *wholly* signified by a woman; the problems of male sexuality, and the attendant undercurrents of misogyny and violence, come out into the open" (*Visual and Other Pleasures*, 59).

Furthermore, *Numéro deux* has flashes of narrative, and its fragmented story is quite close to the tales of the ravages of consumerism that Godard had been telling at the end of the 1960s. But there is also a very real skepticism toward narrative clarity here. That skepticism manifests itself via visual and structural "interruptions" of the film's narrative flow rather than an abandonment of that narrative altogether. This is a good way of summarizing Godard and Miéville's view of communication—it is still possible in late capitalism, but it is always partial, always interrupted, always incomplete. This is the classic Modernist position, this awareness of the inadequacies of communicative form coupled with an inability to abandon those forms entirely, and a redefinition of cinematic Modernism is, as we will see, a central part of the Godard–Miéville project.

Numéro deux is a difficult film to watch. This is not to say that it is unpleasant or disagreeable. But it is hard, in that the screen is almost always divided into two or more smaller screens with entirely different images, and some of these smaller screens have densely layered images. As Serge Le Peron wrote in the *Cahiers du cinéma* (which published a special section on the film in January 1976), "an image is always a second-degree image.... Here the images of family life are shown alongside images of Jean-Luc Godard; he can't superimpose these on the images of the family, and for good reason" (11; m.t.). That reason is that the figure of Godard stands apart from this family he and Miéville evoke, apart from the world of the film's narrative. That world is rendered via complex images that make frequent use of superimposition. Godard's world in the film, however, is far sparer. It is always evoked as a dark, cluttered studio, where some of the small monitors show some different perspectives. For example, in the opening image, we see Godard speaking, turned away from the film camera toward an off-screen video camera. A large monitor at the bottom right of the frame showing that video image of him speaking. The camera itself provides a sort of relentless stare. The soundtrack is generally (although not always) unified, but the visual field is relentlessly complex. Serge Daney sees this complexity as key to the sort of "pedagogical turn" that Godard was then beginning (as I mentioned in Chapter 1). Daney writes in his "Le Therrorisé" essay that "Godard's pedagogy consists in for ever coming back to images and sounds, pointing to them, matching them, commenting on them, putting images within images and sounds within sounds ..." ("Le Therrorisé," 37 / "Theorize / Terrorize," 120; emphasis his). Perhaps because of this desire to deal with the quotidian in a way that is rigorous enough to do justice to its complex interior politics and its connection to external cultural and technological shifts, the story the film tells is a relatively unhappy one. It focuses on a family where three generations live together: a lonely grandmother and a grandfather who clings to vague memories of political struggle, a husband who works as a labourer and whose militancy on the job is a contrast to his conventional approach to family life, a wife whose constipation is a transparent metaphor for the ravages that consumer capitalism visits on the body (the degree to which capitalism ravages the feminine body recurs, in a much more nuanced way, in *Sauve qui peut [la vie]*), and two kids who are gently curious about their world but who are nevertheless bombarded by images of mass culture.

Numéro deux is close to the strategies of Straub–Huillet, but it differs in important ways. Serge Toubiana wrote, in that *Cahiers du cinéma* special section on the film, that it asks, "is it possible to make a cinema for minorities that isn't ghettoised (Straub: 'I think that we also have to make films for minorities, because we hope that they will be, as Lenin says, tomorrow's majorities,' *Cahiers du cinéma* 260/261), is it thinkable to film 'minoritarily' about majorities or of majority matters (for Straub, that's Corneille, Bach, Brecht, Schoenberg: universal culture; for Godard, it's the family, the couple, TV or ads: daily life)?" (19; m.t.). That is a very chewy sentence, but it is getting at a key point in Godard and Miéville's cinema: they are trying to film "minoritarily," even when dealing with dominant culture. There is a *formal* element of this "minority" practice that is just as powerful as any political position expressed on the level of narrative, and that formal practice is clearly of a piece with Straub and Huillet. *Chronik der Anna Magdalena Bach* (1968) is basically about a high culture that is familiar and easily accessible to most educated Europeans and North Americans, but the relentlessness of its long takes and its precise *mise en scène* renders that deeply unfamiliar. Similarly, the domestic drama of *Numéro deux* seems familiar and accessible since such drama is a mainstay of the enormously widespread genre of melodrama. But the relentless layering of visuals, the moving back and forth between diegesis and studio, and the frequently arresting frankness about sexuality and bodily functions is equally effective in rendering this domesticity deeply unfamiliar, accessible only to the few who are willing to invest the commitment and seriousness to embrace a wholly different film language.

Images of the body are a recurring problem in the film. Some of this consideration of Godard and Miéville's has to do with sexuality, some of it has to do with children, and some of it, most startlingly, has to do with both. Early in the film, there is a sequence that features the family's young daughter directly addressing the camera in a medium close-up, saying how sometimes she thinks what mommy and daddy do is nice, and sometimes it is shit ("*caca*"). This image dissolves (in an awkward early-video-technology dissolve) back and forth over an image of the husband and wife having anal sex. There is a similar sequence a few minutes later, this time with the girl's face in a tighter close-up, and more superimposed over the image of anal sex. The voice-over is the husband talking about how his wife has had an affair, how he wanted to rape her, and how she let him "fuck her in the ass" (*"finalement je l'ai enculé"*). It is only afterwards that they realized that their daughter Vanessa was watching. Maybe that's just family life (*"les affaires de famille; c'est peut-être ça"*), the father concludes. Writing specifically about the Godard and Miéville's 1979 television series *France/tour/détour/deux/enfants* (on which more shortly), Brody has tried to explain the degree to which the intersections of childhood and sexuality are recurring in Godard and Miéville's work during this period. He recalls that there was a considerable amount of intellectual debate about children and sexuality in 1970s France, mentioning how in 1977 *Libération* "published a petition seeking to lower to age thirteen the legal right to consent to sex with adults. Among the eighty petitioners were [Jean-Paul] Sartre, Simon de Beauvoir, Louis Aragon, Roland Barthes, Gilles Deleuze, Félix Guattari, André Glucksmann, Dr. Bernard Kouchner [co-founder of Médecins Sans Frontières and French Minister of Foreign Affairs from 2007 to 2010], Phillipe Sollers, and Jack Lang [French Minister of Culture in the 1980s]" (407). Brody goes on to say most of the signatories "were mainly pro-pedophile in the same way that some among them had been pro-Maoist, advocates in theory of a perversion that they would not put into practice" (407).

But while Brody is arguing that this sense of perversion had a sort of insurgent edge that was consistent with the French intellectual left of the 1970s, *Numéro deux* uses it, by and large, as a signifier of alienation. The kids understand sex in a way that is consistent with these debates Brody is evoking, but that understanding is generally coupled with Godard and Miéville evoking joyless, mechanical sex. Brody writes how the second montage of Vanessa's face and anal sex "becomes almost a surrealist vision of dangerous sexual suggestiveness" (380). Part of this is clearly because the camera is *very* close to Vanessa's face, which fills the entire frame. Part of this surrealist quality also comes from the fairly grainy quality of the video and the somewhat ghostly appearance of the face as it is superimposed over video images of anal sex. The memories of that surrealist vision, and the sense of danger and pain, hangs heavy over what is by far the film's creepiest sequence, when the two children come into the parent's bedroom. The parents are lounging around, naked, as they explain sex to the kids. The camera is close to the bed but set a bit high, and the little boy is in the extreme foreground with only the back of his head visible. There is a sense of intimacy here, but it is visually awkward. The parents explain how sex is an expression of love, with the mother pointing to her labia and saying, "look, these are the lips, the lips of sex," and the father pointing to his penis and saying "and so you see this? Here's a kind of mouth, and with this mouth, we kiss the lips of the sex of the one we love." "Is it silent, then?" the little girl asks. This inquiry about silence makes the duality of domestic sexuality clear. The parents tell her that this is a way of talking, but there is clearly a different sort of silence here, too. It is the silence of loneliness, of disconnection, and of futility.

But lest the film seems to be a harsh rant against modernity, a sequence about halfway through the film makes the complexity of the family's relationship with mass media clear. A screen-within-a-screen shows a medium shot of father and son watching television; the boy is watching soccer, and his father complains that he wants to change the channel to a Russian film. Godard and Miéville then cut to a smaller screen-within-a-screen, and there is another medium shot of the grandfather and the young girl. The grandfather is listening to headphones, but he puts them on his granddaughter's ears; they then pass them back and forth between one another. Eventually, the girl's mother comes into frame, sits down, and starts to file her nails. The media is offering chances both for some old-fashioned international socialism (a working-class dad favouring a Soviet film over soccer) and for connection (passing headphones between generations). But the emergence of the constipated mother into the frame is a reminder of the real state of the domestic space. It is also a reminder of an earlier sequence where husband and wife sparred violently as she listened to a radio broadcast on those headphones. These images of togetherness combined with distance, intimacy combined with pain, are rendered in a way that both contains emotional affect and achieves some fairly intense *distanciation*. There is a way in which images like these have the feel of the home movie that Godard spoke about to *Cinéma Pratique*. Their quotidian subject matter, or at least the way in which media consumption is rendered quotidian by its presentation in a domestic context, would ordinarily approach the lyrical. But the screen-within-a-screen framing compromises this dramatically; the edges of the frame are constantly visible, constantly disrupting identification. This is the sort of "middle ground" that Godard and Miéville have sought throughout their work together. *Numéro deux*, like all of this work, makes it clear that moments of lyrical clarity *can* still be found in a domestic space. But those moments are always bracketed, the viewer is always separated from them. The emotional power of a quiet, suggestive image is present in sequences like these, but Godard and Miéville will not quite allow us to get there. Like good

Modernists, they want to believe in this sort of "domestic cinema," but they know that both "domestic" and "cinema" can no longer support their idealism.

It is this sense of idealism that has been lost, but what remains is a sense of engagement, despite an awareness of futility. Robin Wood writes of the film's closing images of Godard in the editing room that "finally we are left with Godard, who can't make the film he hoped for. Alone, in semi-darkness, head in hands, slumped on the table in front of multiple television sets he typifies the impotence of the one who wants to transform the world, yet is overwhelmed by his awareness of the hugeness of the obstacles" (23). This is the basic Modernist position, one defined by an awareness of the inadequacies of form and a consequent self-conscious approach toward them, but still containing a residue of belief in the abilities of those forms. Just about every serious critical study of Joyce agrees that he clings to the form of the novel in *Ulysses*. The work has characters, a linear narrative (it tracks two of those characters as they wander through Dublin), and moments of extremely vivid description. None of this is true of *Finnegans Wake*, which really is a very different kind of work in the way that it leaves the form of the realist novel behind entirely. *Ulysses* is thus very similar to the ways in which Godard clings to the feature film by still using characters, narrative, occasional moments of genuine lyricism, or communication. "The image seems," Wood goes on to write, "the logical culmination of Godard's whole development" (23). That is fair enough, but it is also an iconic image of what Godard and Miéville were, in the 1970s, struggling to become. Indeed, that sense that this final sequence is an icon of what Godard *and Miéville* were struggling to become is supported in no small part by the female voice-over that accompanies these images of Godard with his head on the desk. When the image of the woman pops up on the video screen just visible in the corner, Godard looks up at it wearily, and the voice-over intones, somewhat angrily, "So you became an accomplice. Worse. You became the organiser of the crime." The voice-over goes on to enumerate a series of dualities, finally explaining the title of the film: "Yesterday and today. Kids and parents. Today and tomorrow. Now and later. Number one and number two. Finally I find my place. Number three." As classical music comes up on the soundtrack, we hear Godard whisper, "and we say, it's getting late." Then the film ends, with tentative statements from both of the artists about the impossibility or futility of closure. Cinema, finally, is not about kids or parents, number one or *numéro deux*; cinema is about trying to find that third space to the side of binaries, but also about knowing that such a search is exhausting, and often ends with the artist giving up, head in hands, whispering about how it's getting late. Godard had now left behind an explicitly militant cinema when he had broken with Gorin and ended the Dziga Vertov experiment. He and Miéville were emerging as artists whose work would seek to intervene in the world, even if they were always aware that, in the end, they were *artists*, fundamentally separated from their subjects (their place was as number three) and really creatures of the studio.

COMMENT ÇA VA?

The third film that Godard and Miéville made together was *Comment ça va?*, finished in 1976 but not released theatrically until 1978. It moves even further toward narrative than *Numéro deux*, and so it is not hard to see it as part of their slow return to fiction filmmaking that would be solidified by *Sauve qui peut (la vie)* in 1980. But it retains the political commitments of *Ici et ailleurs* and *Numéro deux*, both ideologically and formally. For while the use of video and other media does not dominate the film in the way that it did in *Ici et ailleurs* and *Numéro deux*, *Comment ça va?* breaks with the visual conventions of narrative cinema in equally radical ways and shares with these other two works a desire to disrupt what Laura Mulvey calls (in her seminal 1975 essay "Visual Pleasure and Narrative Cinema") "the ease and plenitude of narrative fiction film" (*Visual and Other Pleasures*, 16). In that essay Mulvey is especially interested in the way that conventional cinema has represented the female body, and that poses a particularly interesting problem in *Comment ça va*, a film in which the body of Anne-Marie Miéville seems to be constantly on screen, but which is nevertheless quite rigorous in the way that it denies a voyeuristic identification on the part of the viewer. The connection to *Ici et ailleurs* and *Numéro deux* is political as well, and *Comment ça va?* is a sort of combination of their engagements: the interest in the contradictions of revolutionary struggle and the workings of mass-produced visual communication.

The film is dominated by the conceit that we hardly ever get to visually identify with the film's characters. The first images of *Comment ça va?* are some computer-generated text ("A film between the passive and the active"), a black screen, and a shot of the back of a cabbie's head taken from the passenger seat; the soundtrack is a montage of diegetic sound of people talking and non-diegetic voices commenting on what is being said. This sets the tone for the film's formal sensibility overall. Although there is a fictional world, a diegesis with sounds linked to images, most of those images frame people from the back or the side, making the identification that is so central to realist form across media basically impossible. This is not only a matter of camera position. The first sequences where the owner of a communist newspaper (Michel Marot) and Odette, a reporter who works for him (Miéville) interact with one another only allow us to see her from behind and him from a very sharp side angle, but they also completely eschew cutting within the scene. They are a series of single takes, interrupted by cutaways to him working among the printing presses, but retuning to the exact same set-up for another long look at the same tableau. Godard and Miéville use this tableau-montage dialectic throughout the film, and it is just as important a part of what they are trying to accomplish as their use of odd angles. As in *Ici et ailleurs* especially, *Comment ça va?* is forcing the viewer to adapt a new strategy for reading images, for comprehending a visual narrative. For, as with *Numéro deux*, *Comment ça va?* is a feature-narrative film in the sense that it has characters (only two, but characters nonetheless) and a story (a minimalist one about a reporter arguing with her boss about how the left should use the mass media, but a story nonetheless). But it does not, of course, *look* like a feature film. Again, the position here is a Modernist one, evincing extreme skepticism as to the viability of the conventions of its form and yet unable to let go of them fully.

This Modernist practice, visually embodied by camera angles, editing patterns, and narrative structures, has strong echoes in the film's politics. The ostensible topic of the argument here is how to represent the 1974 revolution in Portugal (known as the Revolução dos Cravos, the Carnation Revolution). In a sequence that very strongly recalls the analysis of *Ici et ailleurs*, Odette and the owner argue about how information goes through a typewriter. This is put over a montage of black-and-white footage of typewriters and still photographs of political protests, with Miéville's voice finally saying: "Dammit, the journalist's power is there and nowhere else; it isn't in either France or Portugal, but between the two." Alain Bergala argues that there is an aesthetic quality to this focus on "*entre les deux*," writing this (in *Cahiers du cinéma* 290–91) of the film's refusal to ever show us the face of Miéville's character: "Of the woman, whose face we never see, we can say that she is in some part between the spectator and the actor, in a position that recalls the analyst's, neither entirely *in* nor entirely *off*, at the same time both in the shot and yet beyond representation ..." (*Nul mieux que Godard*, 29; m.t.). What we have at the core of the narrative structure, then, is not so much a heroine or a guide with whom we can identify, but a signifier of uncertainty and complexity, of in between-ness.

This emphasis on interstitial-ness, as we saw above, was for Gilles Deleuze key to understanding *Ici et ailleurs*, and that was in no small part because the images of the revolution itself, of Palestine, were incomplete and, as the film made explicit, often misleading. What we had instead was, as in *Comment ça va?*, an examination of the way that image makers from the outside, from

France, construct these events for their own purposes. A big part of the analysis of *Ici et ailleurs* had to do with the need to recreate or repackage complex political struggles as something palatable. The film was showing this kind of repackaging partially as an indictment of *engagé* politicos like Godard, for whom a young and pretty intellectual was a good stand-in for a pregnant woman who would give up her unborn son to the revolution. Rather than present images of Palestine (which it did) or invite viewers to read those images (which it also did), *Ici et ailleurs* used those images as a means to critique the power of the image makers. The fact that it did all of these at the same time is a testament to its self-interrogating Modernist standpoint. *Comment ça va?* is staging a very similar kind of interrogation, trying to get *in between* images of Portugal and France to understand the real power of the press, jointly embodied by Odette/Miéville the reporter and the left-wing owner. Jean-Paul Fargier wrote of the film that "if certain Communist Party intellectuals maintain a kind of affection for *Comment ça va?*, isn't that because the film seems to produce a kind of *forum effect*? [*effet de tribune*]" (35; m.t.; italics his).

What is being given a forum here is the way that the left deals with power, and so it is no small wonder that French Communists were fond of it. The film acknowledges the existence of the power of the media and refuses to allow leftists off the hook for that power's more unpleasant effects, since it is a communist newspaper owner, not the owner of *Le Figaro*, who is serving as Miéville's foil here. But the film is equally adamant about acknowledging the real power of European revolutionaries. Portugal's Revolução dos Cravos was enormously important for the European left, not only because it ended a very long period of fascist rule (Salazar's "Estado Novo" had begun in 1933), but also because it was initiated by the military, thus seeming to be a living example of a revolutionary alliance that cut across social barriers, with army officers, union leaders, students, and other activists all working together toward a common goal. It also had enormous international implications, signalling the end of Portugal's empire as most of its colonial possessions immediately became independent following the coup that toppled the Lisbon regime (many of the coup-plotting soldiers and officers had been radicalized by what they had seen and done in places like Angola and, of course, Mozambique). It was, in short, everything that May 1968 promised to be but was not: broad based, able to assume power, linked to an internationalist moment of decolonization, successful. For European leftists like Godard and Miéville, whose politics were forged in those flames of 1968, the stakes for understanding Portugal were very high indeed. It served as the ideal forum for a left that was struggling to redefine itself, and it also seemed to be a perfect forum for a political cinema that was in an equal state of upheaval and possibility, following the comparable letdown of experiments like the *Cinétracts* and the Groupe Dziga Vertov.

So just as *Comment ça va?* breaks with work like the *Cinétracts* or the Groupe Dziga Vertov to present, in a highly reworked form, an illusionist narrative, so it breaks with idealistic revolutionary posturing to engage with communist newspaper owners and actually existing governing alliances of students, workers, and military people. There can be no doubt that the film is critical of both of these systems. This narrative is extremely constricted at the level of both visuals and structure, and that narrative makes no bones about the compromised nature of media ownership or state building, even when they are in the hands of leftists. But again, the perspective here is one of skepticism, not rejection. These cinematic images of revolution and of argument need to be interrogated, but their connection to the material world, to actually existing political problems, cannot be fully dismissed. Like what we saw in *Ici et ailleurs* and *Numéro deux*, this is a classic Modernist position, one that has been filtered though the poetics of André Bazin.

SIX FOIS DEUX: SUR ET SOUS LA COMMUNICATION

That sense that the domestic and the political are inseparable in ways that are sometimes excruciatingly complex defines both of the television series that Godard and Miéville made in the 1970s. *Six fois deux: Sur et sous la communication (Six Times Two: On and Under Communication)* (1976) is the first of these, and so it would be easy to imagine that it sets the tone for the work that would follow. But this is deceptive. Some of Godard and Miéville's ongoing concerns, both aesthetic and ideological, are present here: the redefinition of the long take, the connection between film and television, the ways in which image culture and its attendant ideologies infuse modern domesticity, and so forth. But the vision here is a lot harsher and less open to complexity than the work that would follow. *Six fois deux: Sur et sous la communication* is a lot like *Ici et ailleurs* in that both works deal with film and television in the home and in the world, but neither work does this with the sense of aesthetic flexibility and intellectual curiosity that so characterizes their work together.

In many ways, this two-part series was the fullest realization of the regionalist aspirations that we discussed in Chapter 2. Michael Witt sees it this way, writing that "[b]oth series, but especially *Six fois deux*, seek to construct a 'softer' decentralised television practice, and to actively resist the centralised universalising homogenisation of broadcast television.... If broadcast television is characterised by the flooding of its territory from a central point (Sonimage use the terms 'arroser' and 'inonder'), then decentralised production constitutes a deliberate assault on the monolith from the margins" (*On Communication*, 81).

Six fois deux: Sur et sous la communication was broadcast from July 25 to August 29, 1976, and its form made certain demands on the way it was broadcast. Its title refers to the fact that it was broken into six episodes of two parts each, each one about fifty minutes long. The "A" part of each episode was "*sur*" or "on" communication and tended to be a precise examination of some aspects of the mechanics of communications; they follow, in many ways, Godard's statement in that *Cinéma Pratique* interview that he wanted to "explain, at every moment and from A to Z, how you make *Gone with the Wind*" (160; m.t.). The second or "B" part of these episodes tended to be more impressionistic portraits of people somehow engaged with visual communications, and often engaged with aspects of their everyday lives. To again invoke the *Cinéma Pratique* interview, we see Godard and Miéville trying to show how "the contradiction is that these films must be interesting enough for the problems of one family to be shown to the family next door" (159; m.t.). This seems like a fairly clear form of montage-inspired dialectics, but the cinephilic philosopher Gilles Deleuze disagreed vigorously with this proposition. In a sort of interview on the series published as "Trois questions sur *Six fois deux*," published in the *Cahiers du cinéma* in November 1976, there was the following exchange:

> But why are there always two with Godard? There have to be two for there to be three.... Fine, but what is the meaning of this two, this three?
>
> You're pretending; nobody knows better than you that it's not like that. Godard is not a dialectician. What counts with him is not two or three, or however many you like, it's AND, the conjunction of AND. Godard's use of AND is crucial. It's important because our entire way of thinking is modeled instead on the verb "to be," IS.... Of course, the AND is diversity, multiplicity, the destruction of identities. ("Trois questions sur *Six fois deux*," 11 / "Three Questions about '*Six fois deux*,'" 40)

We can hear clear echoes here of *Ici et ailleurs*, which so insisted on "*ET*" (AND) by repeatedly returning to a close-up image of the word. In *Cinéma 2: L'image-temps*, Deleuze argued for the strong connection between *Ici et ailleurs* and *Six fois deux: Sur et sous la communication*, seeing them both defined by an interest in the interstices, the gaps between images: "*Ici et ailleurs* marks a first peak in this reflection, which is afterwards transferred to television in *Six fois deux*" (*L'image-temps*, 234) / *The Time-Image*, 179). But we can also hear the concerns of the *Cinéma Pratique* interview echoing in Deleuze's analysis. It was there that Godard asserted that "you need two cameras together to really understand a character: their child and adult sides, their fascist and revolutionary sides, their voice that says yes and that little voice inside them that thinks no" (160; m.t.). Visually *Six fois deux: Sur et sous la communication* is all about combination, about layering: images atop images, characters divided by multiple cameras, reproduced, and mounted atop other characters, and so on. This may sound like dialectics at first, but as Deleuze well knows, it is something else. Really, it is something closer to palimpsest (writing on a sheet, or a screen, where the remnants of what had been there but erased are still visible). Deleuze repeats this formulation of *Six fois deux: Sur et sous la communication*'s emphasis on "and" in his *Cinéma 2: L'image-temps* (234), and he also expands there on Godard and Miéville's banishment of binary thought. Deleuze writes that "[t]he problem of the relation between images is no longer of knowing if it works or does not work, according to the requirements of the harmonics or of the resolved tunings, but of knowing '*Comment ça va?*'" (*L'image-temps*, 238 / *The Time-Image*, 183). Deleuze is playing here, of course, on the title of Godard and Miéville's 1976 film *Comment ça va?* The point he is trying to make throughout *L'image-temps* is that what was emerging in this period was a kind of cinema "which is capable of revealing to us the higher determination of thought, choice, this point deeper than any link with the world" (*L'image-temps* 232 / *The Time-Image*, 178). Godard and Miéville's work of this period—from *Ici et ailleurs* right though *Comment ça va?* and *Six fois deux: Sur et sous la communication*—is a great example of this sort of practice: an approach to cinema that is much more interested in representing thought than it is in representing some illusory version of the real world, as conventional narrative cinema so relentlessly tries to do.

This destruction of identity that Deleuze alludes to, then, is not solely a thematic matter. *Six fois deux: Sur et sous la communication*, like *France / tour / détour / deux / enfants*, is about the destruction of the identity of television itself. This is not a dialectical matter. *Six fois deux: Sur et sous la communication* does not exist in opposition to mainstream forms, but instead exists alongside it. By existing alongside, and essentially ignoring mainstream forms, the series presents television as an inherently complex form. It is not simply that television exists as "conventional commercial television" and "everything else." This was an insight offered by the North American avant-garde's complete reinvention of film language as well. By making films whose aesthetic was utterly distinct from mainstream forms, Stan Brakhage and his contemporaries (especially filmmakers like Michael Snow, Holls Frampton, or Joyce Wieland, who made very important films on her own as well as with the two of them) were emphasizing the AND of cinema. Godard and Miéville's reinvention of televisual language is comparably total. Deleuze sees this as a formal linguistic matter as well, saying in that *Cahiers du cinéma* dialogue that "children are provided with syntax in the same way that workers are given tools, to produce statements that conform to the dominant meaning.... Language is a system of orders, not a medium of information" ("Trois questions," 8 / "Three Questions," 37). *Six fois deux: Sur et sous la communication*, like *France/tour/détour/deux/enfants*, is speaking a televisual language that produces very different kinds of statements than dominant television.

One statement that the series makes is that it is essential, in an era where everyday life is dominated by visual images, to develop a critical stance toward these everyday images. It is not surprising, then, that the series was bookended with self-reflexive gestures. Episode 1A, "Y a personne" ("There's No One"), is a series of job interviews conducted by Godard at the Sonimage office. Episode 6A, "Avant et Après" ("Before and After"), is a kind of retrospective of the series, which mixes clips from earlier episodes and interviews with people who worked with Godard and Miéville, holding forth on their successes and failures and explaining formal and structural decisions that they made. The entire series is about making the work of image creation visible and subject to discussion and critique, and it is only logical to also include the images of *Six fois deux: Sur et sous la communication*. The series begins and ends with an examination of the work of making these images: job interviews in the production office conducted by one of the series' directors, discussions with technicians who worked on the series, clips of the programs themselves, and so forth. And that is the real topic of *Six fois deux: Sur et sous la communication*—work and the way mass-produced imagery obscures work.

The rest of the series wanders over various kinds of visual communication, although it pays special attention to advertising and news photography, which are recurring subjects of critique. These episodes, though, are paired with examinations of radically different forms of image making. One particularly good example of this pairing is Episode 3A and 3B, "Photos et CIE" and "Marcel," respectively. "Photos et CIE" is an examination of the way that mass-media images, especially news and advertising photographs, are constructed and operate on an ideological level. In both its interest in the psychological effects of the mass media and its status as a didactic visual essay, it shares a lot with *Le gai savoir*. "Marcel" is a portrait of a passionate home movie maker. "Photos et CIE" is typical of the "A" portions of the series inasmuch as it uses a great deal of visual effects—wipes, superimpositions, writing on the screen, etc.—to make its arguments about visual mechanics. It is mostly made up of a series of close-ups or extreme close-ups of magazine and newspaper images, which are made the subjects of examination or critique by writing directly over them or through montage. The episode also features long interviews with practitioners. The first of these is a French photographer whose voice is inserted over his photograph of an execution. This part of the episode, both visually and ideologically, strongly recalls similar critiques in Godard's *Le gai savoir*, Godard and Gorin's 1972 essay film *Letter to Jane* (which was almost entirely made up of a single image, a photograph of Jane Fonda meeting some Viet Cong, and Godard and Gorin's voices talking about that photograph), and the "*ailleurs*" portion of Godard and Miéville's *Ici et ailleurs*. "Photos et CIE," is also notable for its use of writing over the image (mostly single words that highlight what the photographer is saying: *rapide, lumière, moderne*), a video-enabled technique that Godard and Miéville used more and more during the 1970s. This first sequence of the episode is quite polyvocal; it combines, in a single shot, the voice of the photographer explaining his work, the voice of Godard and Miéville expressed though the writing on the image, and the voice of the photograph itself. That is true of the episode overall. One later sequence reproduces news footage of a press conference and uses writing directly on the image to bring out important points of contradiction, while another uses superimpositions and montages of political and advertising imagery to illustrate and sometimes contradict the voice-over of a woman talking about the ideology of American imperialism in Vietnam. There is also a long sequence that is a close-up of Godard flipping though a pile of magazines and speculating about the ideological significance of the imagery. A later extended interview, though, forgoes this kind of mass-produced imagery and is simply a shot of a British journalist who holds forth on the differences between professional and amateur photographers.

This interest in the split between the amateur and professional image maker is what most closely links the "A" and "B" episodes, although these two pieces come to some very different conclusions about the relationship between imagery and physical reality. Episode 3B, "Marcel," is mostly made up of interviews with a middle-aged watchmaker who enjoys making home movies of the Swiss landscape; at one point we see him seated at a desk, with a small 8 mm editing viewer, cutting out frames that he deems imperfect. But for all this attention to precision, artifice is far from the only goal in Marcel's work. As Godard interviews him (he is heard off-screen but never seen), he asks, "[w]hat you value in the cinema is that you see something again, pretty much exactly as you had seen it with your eyes?" Marcel responds by saying that "[t]he cinema restores everything that you've seen. I think that's great. My pleasure.

It's purely personal" (Touratier/Busto, 80; m.t.). Of course, this is not purely personal; it is the essence of André Bazin's conception of how cinema operates, how it "has an effect upon us of a natural phenomenon, like a flower or snowflake whose beauty is inseparable from its earthy origin" (*What Is Cinema?*, 7), to return to the passage from "L'ontologie de l'image photographique" that I quoted in Chapter 1. The key point in both conceptions of the cinema is the degree to which an aesthetic experience is inseparably connected to some part of physical reality, even as it alters that experience in order to heighten the aesthetic experience. Marcel's unselfconscious desire to both restore what he has seen and to manipulate the cinematic image literally a frame at a time neatly captures Bazin's understanding of cinema as aesthetic. It is therefore artificial (he is talking about the image's *beauty* after all) but distinctive as an aesthetic because of its special relationship to our senses, especially sight. Like Bazin, and Godard and Miéville, as well, Marcel understands very well that earthly origins are an inseparable *part* of the beauty of cinema, not the whole story.

About twenty minutes into "Marcel," there is a match-cut between Marcel working with his 8 mm footage to him at his workbench as he fixes a watch. A non-synchronous voice-over has him explaining how he does not want to be paid for his filmmaking activities, how he sees this as an escape from the grind of work. Godard's voice presses him a bit on this matter, but he is clear; work and art are fully separate for him. The match-cut, which so explicitly joins these two activities, tells a different story, and this really is the story the series is telling overall. Throughout *Six fois deux: Sur et sous la communication*'s "A" episodes, Godard and Miéville use drawing and writing directly onto the video images and similar effects, such as wipes or superimpositions, to isolate various parts of the image, focus the viewer's attention, and generally draw attention to the mechanics that are common to all manner of communications: professional, amateur, public, and private. At times, this visual commentary, this video écriture (*vidécriture?*) has a positively schematic quality. That is especially true of Episode 5A, "Nous trois" ("Us Three"). This is made up of images of the faces of a man and a woman, and on the soundtrack, they read letters they have written to each other. The content of the letters is a bit cryptic, although they are filled with references to police repression, torture, and isolation; the man seems to be writing from prison. A grid is often superimposed on the image, as are arrows that delineate directions for "*toi*" and "*moi*." Godard and Miéville are showing how the most emotionally charged form of communication imaginable, letters between separated lovers, exists in the material world of work, mechanics, and politics. This is possibly what Guy Hennebelle had in mind when he caustically criticized the series in the pages of *Écran*, writing that

Six fois deux: Sur et sous la communication seemed to be an embodiment of the problems of all of Godard's (and, he seems to mean, Miéville's) recent work, basically the work he had so far with Miéville.

> Since any technique harkens back to a philosophy, to what do the methods which Godard uses and abuses in almost all of his latest films refer? The answer is quite simple: to the narcissistic display of existential despair. Life is sad and the world is impossible to make rational sense of. Let's all cry. I would like to hear Godard's flatterers agree at least that this conception is antagonistic to Dziga Vertov's, with whose experience he claims great kinship and the relationship with whom he has willingly been credited. ("Un charabia indigeste," 57 / "Incoherent Gibberish," 9; translation altered slightly)

I detect here a hard-left rationalism at work, a desire to see a real political practice as something unsentimental, unsoiled by the bourgeois mushiness of emotion. But I am happy to answer Hennebelle's challenge there—sort of. The vision of *Six fois deux: Sur et sous la communication*, like that of the three features that preceded it, is antagonistic to that of the films of the Groupe Dziga Vertov. Unlike those films, which are a lot more hard-headed and a lot more uncompromising in their declaration of a new, ciné-revolutionary political practice, *Six fois deux: Sur et sous la communication* is a tentative, searching examination of the ways that ideology—capitalism and consumerism especially—define the rhythms of every day. As opposed to the 1969 films *British Sounds* or *Vent d'est*, which both offer unyieldingly didactic indictments of reactionary politics, *Six fois deux: Sur et sous la communication* moves more slowly and comes to more conflicted conclusions about the relationship between communications and politics. "If there is a certain didacticism, it's one of meaning, not of knowledge," writes Frédérique de Goëje (52; m.t.). Meaning, rather than information, is the name of the game here; the series is trying to teach its viewers about the *process* of communication, not about the specifics of some particular political situation.

Godard and Miéville are also trying to show that the material aspects of life (economic marginalization, commodity fetishization, and so on) are always more complicated than they at first appear, and also that these aspects always exist *alongside* the emotional and the sentimental, not merely in opposition to them. Marcel's love of moviemaking, to choose what is I think the best embodiment of the series' overall concerns, exists with (on and under, really) and not apart from his life as a watchmaker. The contention that life is sad and the world is impossible to make rational sense of can be expressed in a way that is gooey and maudlin, a way that says to the viewer: *pleurons* (let's cry). But that is not the only way it can be expressed, and it is not the way that Godard and Miéville are expressing it in *Six fois deux: Sur et sous la communication*. As Deleuze said to the *Cahiers du cinéma*, this is the discourse of *ET*; Godard, like Miéville, is not a dialectician. Love *and* politics, amateurs *and* professionals, work *and* art: these are the subjects of *Six fois deux: Sur et sous la communication*.

FRANCE / TOUR / DÉTOUR / DEUX / ENFANTS

Godard and Miéville's next television series—the twelve-part, six-hour *France/tour/détour/deux/enfants*—was the last work they would produce specifically for television for several years. It is in many ways a more marginal work than *Six fois deux: Sur et sous la communication*. Michael Witt summarizes the series' problems by writing: "Commissioned by the second French channel, Antenne 2, and made during 1977–78 in Rolle, the series was immediately shelved for almost two years" ("Going Through the Motions," 176). According to both Richard Brody and Antoine de Baecque, it premiered at the Rotterdam Film Festival in January 1979 (408 / *Godard: biographie* 554). Sally Shafto's filmography, which does not mention Rotterdam, pegs its premiere as the Venice Film Festival in August 1979, states that it was "Presented on Antenne 2 in April 1980 by Jean-Claude Phillipe in his Cine-Club" and also notes that it was "Filmed: In the house of William Lubtchansky in Paris in 1978" (359) (Lubtchansky had been the cinematographer on a number of Godard and Godard–Miéville films). Colin MacCabe says that the series was "made in Paris and Rolle" (*Portrait of the Artist*, 254), but it is not clear from this where it was shot and where it was finished. For the time being, I take this disagreement over pretty basic data on the series as further evidence of Antoine de Baecque's sense that Godard's archives are partial, unreliable, and mostly unavailable. Nevertheless, *France/tour/détour/deux/enfants* is unquestionably important as a kind of "transitional work," between the stages of Godard and Miéville's work that I am calling "Communication" and "Realization." As its hybrid television-theatrical history suggests, *France/tour/détour/deux/enfants* explores what can be done specifically with video and television, but it does so in a way that looks forward to specific parts of the feature narratives that define Godard and Miéville's work of the 1980s, especially *Sauve qui peut (la vie)*. That is especially true of the series' extensive use of slow motion, which is an important part of the aesthetic of *Sauve qui peut (la vie)*. Writing in *Cahiers du cinéma* 301, the year that the series was finally broadcast, Alain Bergala says that "Godard and Miéville's invention this time is to have found a new way for this machine to slow down imagery, using it like a poet or a painter" (*Nul mieux que Godard*, 33; m.t.).[2] Bergala also notes how much easier slow motion is to do with video than with film. One of the many reasons that *France/tour/ détour/deux/enfants* is important is because it shows us Godard and Miéville not only fully discovering their form—their machine, as Bergala writes—but also finding a way to balance the demands of poetic and commercial forms. *France/tour/détour/deux/enfants* is a conventional television series in the same way that *Sauve qui peut (la vie)* is a feature-narrative film. With both works, we see a typically Modernist impatience with convention and concomitant desire to integrate new formal elements (and slow motion is emblematic of this in both) that is still defined by a just-as-Modernist reluctance to abandon formal and structural conventions entirely.

The series is ostensibly about the life of the Virolleaud family, and it pays particular attention to the young girl Camille, and the intensity of that attention has raised a few eyebrows. Indeed, *France/tour/détour/deux/enfants* is engaged with the minutiae of the domestic every day in a way that might seem to call back to the 1973 series *An American Family*, which, like Allan King's 1969 film *A Married Couple*, was something of a sensation because of the way that cameras seemed to intrude into the most intimate moments of family life. *France/tour/détour/deux/enfants*'s first episode would seem to support this, and when I show that episode to contemporary Canadian undergraduates, their responses do indeed centre on sequences like the one where Godard and Miéville shoot Camille as she undresses and gets ready for bed. This is basically the first sequence of the first episode, and the fact that Godard and Miéville use slow motion for this sequence only draws our attention to the image's sensuality more vigorously. But sensual images are not the same as sexual images; that is usually the argument I offer to students who find the sequence creepy. This is an image of intimacy, but not of eroticism. Images of women undressing are obviously a very common visual motif in European painting; Degas's turn-of-the-century studies of "women at their toilette" are among literally countless examples. It is not hard to see this kind of imagery as defined by a voyeuristic and sexualized gaze. But such conventional imagery is defined by this kind of gendered power differential precisely because the of realist/ illusionist perspective that is being employed. The eye of the painter is seemingly omnipotent and thus gives the impression of ownership of what it surveys; this is the basic thesis of John Berger's seminal 1971 book *Ways of Seeing*. What is different with *France/tour/détour/deux/enfants* is precisely the lack of seemingly neutral omnipotence, the lack of illusionist realism. The slow-motion effect makes it explicit that Camille is being *visualized* by Godard and Miéville, not simply being presented or given over for easy consumption. There is no doubt that this image of Camille invokes the spectre of conventional European painting and its treatment of women, but, as so often with Godard and Miéville, it is the use of an aesthetic distinct to the twentieth-century medium of video (and not the medium of film, beginning it the late 1800s as it does) that makes this new. The slow-motion effect that Godard and Miéville are using here is specific to video; it is not that the image is being shot at a faster frame rate, but that it is being frozen and gradually advanced. It thus does not look smooth and lyrical; it looks jerky and highly artificial. I discuss this "video slow motion" again when I examine the film they made after this series, 1979's *Sauve qui peut (la vie)*.

Richard Brody, who interviewed Camille Virolleaud four times in 2001–2, follows a line that I see as perilously close to that of my students, though, recalling that "Camille was horrified at having to undress on camera, but did so and put on her nightgown, as rapidly as possible" (400–401). This is for Brody a jumping-off point for his previously mentioned discussion of the arguments about pedophilia as the last gasp of an anti-authoritarian May 1968 politics (see *Everything Is Cinema*, 405–8). Virolleaud published a short text in the *Cahiers du cinéma* in 2003, and to read that is to get the sense of a very shy young woman who was a lot less preoccupied with issues of personal modesty than Brody suggests. When the series was screened in the village of Lussas for its twenty-fifth anniversary, Camille Virolleaud attended and watched helplessly as the question period moderated by Alain Bergala began and two men argued about whether she had been exploited, utterly unaware that she was sitting right behind them. Once she managed to get the microphone and identify herself, the tone of her recollections shifts completely, and she mostly recalls the feelings of catharsis that came from meeting and talking with people during the festival. She concludes her text by saying that "I had the delicious feeling of having finally digested something that had been with me for a really long time" (67; m.t.). The anxiety that she recalls in the most detail in this text has to do with the ridiculously open-ended questions that Godard asked her as part of the shooting—how do you know you exist, why do you think you are not paid to go to school, and so on—because she had tried "to find 'the' right answer to his questions, with the idea that questions, like in school, could only have one right answer" (67; m.t.).

And thus we arrive at the real core of the program and the way that it intersects with the rest of the work that Godard and Miéville had been doing during this period. Just as Deleuze had seen *Six fois deux: Sur et sous la communication* as defined by an ethic of "*ET*" / "AND," defined by what he identified as "diversity, multiplicity, the destruction of identities," *France / tour / détour / deux / enfants* is a series defined by an interest in the open ended. If *Six fois deux:*

Sur et sous la communication was defined by an ethic of the palimpsest, then *France/tour/détour/deux/enfants* is defined by a correspondingly elliptical ethic. The questions not only do not have a single correct answer, but most of the questions that we hear Godard pose off-screen to a flummoxed Camille do not have any answers. When Godard asks Camille questions such as who is sitting in her bed in her nightgown, whether an image in a mirror really has an existence, and so on, it is not part of an argument that he is advancing in a linear way. It becomes part of the show's recurring pattern of goofy question and inability to answer. It links up with images in later episodes such as where Godard (as always, from off-screen) asks Camille, now outside her schoolhouse and looking both shy and annoyed, whether she thinks of herself as a home or as a school. The camera position in these sequences is more or less that of identical close-ups, and the camera is always still. There is a kind of constancy here that, across the entire series, becomes almost trance-like, an effect that is supported by Godard and Miéville's frequent use of slow motion in other sequences. Constance Penley writes of these dialogues with Camille that "[w]hat is taking place here is not really an 'interview' or a 'conversation,' it is more like an Augustinian dialogue, full of puns, tricks and seemingly nonsensical questions that turn into logical traps" ("Les Enfants de la Patrie," 38). I am not sure I agree with the invocation of the Augustinian dialogues as such, although this does help us to see that Godard and Miéville are posing these questions as semi-abstract, highly aestheticized ritual (Catholicism may be a lifelong fascination for the two, but the fact that they both come from the protestant Swiss canton of Vaud makes this feel ironic). They are presenting the questions as a means to achieve visual and structural harmony and rhythm. Small wonder, then, that the titles that open each episode announce the beginning of a new "movement." The music of *France/tour/détour/deux/enfants* is, in essence, a meditation on the shy, sad mysteries of childhood.

In discussion of the series, it is something of a ritual to mention how it is ostensibly based on the 1877 French children's textbook, *Le tour de la France par deux enfants*, by G. Bruno (the *nom de plume* of Augustine Fouillée).[3] Penley is atypical, though, in specifying the nature of the connection. She opens her essay on the series by describing the book and its story of two young kids travelling across France as something that is both pedagogical and patriotic: "As they go from province to province, they learn about farming, printing, making wallpaper, embroidery, cheesemaking, winemaking, crystal and glass, photography, barrel making, basket weaving, and fishing.... Little homilies sprinkled throughout the book inculcate the values of 'Devoir et Patrie': cleanliness, work, godliness, education, devotion to parents and country" ("Les Enfants de la Patrie," 33). This is undoubtedly a fair assessment of the book, which is quite didactic, but it is hard to see from this what could have possibly attracted Godard and Miéville to it. The answer is in that "province to province" part of Penley's description, for *Le tour de la France par deux enfants* is quite a study in regionalism. When the two kids find themselves in the Rhône valley, they are confronted by a hotelier speaking in a patois that they find completely incomprehensible. When seven-year-old Julien asks why this is, his fourteen-year-old brother, André, responds that while part of it is that not everyone has been to school, "in a few years it won't be that way anymore, and all of France will know how to speak the national language" (164; m.t.). As I mentioned in Chapter 1, centralization has, since the Revolution, been a characterizing aspect of French governance, and the groups that have chafed against this have generally done so in the name of cultural or linguistic distinctiveness. The book *Le tour de la France par deux enfants*, like a proper children's primer, makes gestures toward French patriotism, but the presence of a monolingual patois speaker is an invocation of what Michel de Certeau, in his *Une politique de la langue*, calls "*une France sauvage*" (146), and this is by no means a mainstream or even respectable way to present the country. That is not the case today, and it was certainly not the case in 1877, less than a decade after the Franco-Prussian war and a period of intense republican nationalism both because of the territory France lost during that conflict and the creation of the Third Republic in the wake of the postwar collapse of the Second French Empire.

The fact is that there is very little of this kind of de-centralized, regionalist consciousness explicitly present in *France/tour/détour/deux/enfants* (it was shot in Paris, after all), there are nevertheless important ideological connections between the book and what Godard and Miéville were doing during the 1970s. Regionalism is part of this; I have already discussed the degree to which Godard and Miéville were heavily invested in the idea of local television, a television that circumnavigated Paris and the other metropolises. While this idea never had much of a linguistic component, it was a significant challenge to French cultural and political orthodoxy and, I believe, an indication of the degree to which their world views had been influenced by their Swiss backgrounds. If I may be so bold, then, there is a certain kind of Swiss-style dissent at work in both *France/tour/détour/deux/enfants* and *Le tour de la France par deux enfants*. Both of these works follow their formats quite closely. Bruno's book really is a didactic textbook for French children in a way that is similar to how Godard and Miéville's series really is a work that belongs *on television*. *France/tour/détour/deux/enfants* follows certain conventions of broadcast television quite closely. The first sequence of every episode is more or less the same—shots of the two kids either working with sound gear or behind a video camera—and that sequence always has an emotional pop song on the soundtrack. Each episode concludes with a discussion with the series' *animateurs*, Betty Berr and Albert Dray, somewhat cryptically discussing what has gone on. Penley writes that these two "closely resemble television's ubiquitous announcers—smiling, plastic, more actor than journalist" ("Les Enfants de la Patrie," 39), although they are rather obvious stand-ins for Godard and Miéville themselves. There is a loose, wandering sensibility at work here, but one that holds very tightly to a central, if rather skeletal, core of structures. "Seminally Modernist" is one way to describe that paradoxical state of affairs; "very Swiss" would be another. Either assessment is appropriate when discussing pretty well all the work that Godard and Miéville have done together, whether they were living in Paris, Grenoble, or Rolle.

I am thus in full agreement with J. Hoberman's assessment of the series as a kind of linchpin of Godard and Miéville's work. Reporting for the *Village Voice* on the 1986 American Video Festival's retrospective of Godard and Miéville's videos, he wrote that:

> Showing these programs as projected video in a movie theater has the effect of turning extremely radical TV into marginalized movies. Still, in some ways, Godard's work is all one piece. Made between *Numéro deux* and his 1980 "comeback" *Every Man for Himself* [*Sauve qui peut (la vie)*], *Six Times Two* and *France/tour* at once elaborate *Numéro deux*'s juxtaposition of factory and landscape and anticipate the opposition of work and love explored in *Passion*. *France/tour* uses the analytic slo-mo that gave *Every Man for Himself* its original English title (*Slow Motion*), while the inspiration for *Hail Mary* might be found in *Six Times Two*'s interview with a schizophrenic woman who speculates on impregnation by the Holy Ghost. (*Vulgar Modernism*, 163)

This is the way to see these television programs, and *France/tour/détour/deux/enfants* especially: as experiments whose thematic and especially formal engagements set the stage for the feature-narrative films that Godard and Miéville made in the 1980s. I do not wish to give pride of place to this 1980s work simply because it is feature-narrative, or to consign the 1970s work to the status of "experiment" because a lot of it is of non-standard length (either a bit short or extremely long). But there is something tentative, and thus genuinely experimental, about this work I have classified under "communication." These 1970s works are genuine essays in that they are close to the French word *essayer*, or attempt. Sometimes this work is slightly incoherent. That is truest of *Six fois deux: Sur et sous la communication*, whose thematic range—while always based in an engagement with work, love, and art—does make it disjointed. Sometimes the work is startlingly vivid, having hit upon something genuinely transformative; that is truest of *Ici et ailleurs* (whose sound–image montage is remarkably complex and expressive), and of the sixth episode of *France/tour/détour/deux/enfants*, "Expression/français" (whose slow-motion imagery is exceptionally lyrical and mysterious). But overall, these works about "Communication" are genuine inquiries into a process central to the medium of cinema, and so they are naturally less assured and fully realized aesthetic objects than works like *Sauve qui peut (la vie)*, *Je vous salue, Marie*, *Le livre de Marie*, or *Soft and Hard*, which, I argue in Chapter 4, are the most sophisticated and ambitious works that Godard and Miéville did together. Understanding the collaboration that led to masterpieces like these naturally requires an examination of their earlier, developmental work. Godard and Miéville spent the 1970s getting their heads around the problems of communication. Once they moved past that and began to communicate ideas about something else—landscape, work, love, alienation, transcendence—their films moved onto a new level.

Chapter 4
REALIZATION

"Between the ages of 50 and 60, he once again gave the impression that anything is possible, worked with the maturity of lessons learned, and continued to experiment like a searching artist. Godard was living through what one critic, Frédéric Strauss, called his 'Golden Eighties.'"
—Antoine de Baecque, *Godard: biographie* (576; m.t.)

MIÉVILLE'S *HOW CAN I LOVE* AND *FAIRE LA FÊTE*

The "Realization" phase of Godard and Miéville's work together is marked by a shift from the experimental work of the "Communications" or Sonimage period toward narrative films. All of the films under discussion here—*Sauve qui peut (la vie)* (1980), *Prénom Carmen* (1983), *Je vous salue, Marie* (1985), *Le livre de Marie* (1985), *Détective* (1985)—are, more or less, narrative films in a way that films such as *Ici et ailleurs* or *Comment ça va?* really are not. There is a comparable gap between their earlier television work like *Six fois deux: Sur et sous la communication* (1976) and a program like *Soft and Hard* (1985), which is a much more lucid and accessible work than its precursor. Furthermore, the problems that are being played out in these works are less esoteric, although no less intellectually informed. Whereas the "Communications" films are all defined by various political engagements (the Palestinian struggle, the revolution in Portugal, a critique of the rise of television-led consumer capitalism), these "Realization" films are more closely engaged with interpersonal matters, specifically with the ways that men and women try (and often fail) to communicate and form intimate bonds. Of course, these kinds of considerations have political and philosophical meanings, and these works investigate these problems vigorously via indictments of capitalist-led alienation (*Sauve qui peut [la vie]*), meditation on theological problems (*Je vous salue, Marie* and *Le livre de Marie*), and a playful engagement with the philosophy of language (*Soft and Hard*). But viscerally emotional questions are front and centre (sometimes almost exclusively so, as in *Prénom Carmen* and *Détective*) in a way that they are not in the "Communications" period. One way to understand the thematic richness of this work, as well as the kind of aesthetic that Godard and Miéville were trying to develop, is to look at two short films that Miéville made by herself shortly after the beginning and just after the end of this period: *How Can I Love* (1983) and *Faire la fête* (1986).

How Can I Love is a minimalist study in failed communication, and a richly visual one at that. The film presents one woman awkwardly breaking up with five different men, of five different ages, and for very different reasons. The encounters between the woman and these men are all photographed in ways that give a sense of intimacy, if not of connection. Miéville opens the film with close-ups first of the woman and then of a man smoking in bed, and then cuts to a medium shot where the camera is set low, essentially next to the bed. But this medium shot has the man in bed and the woman in the foreground, basically out of focus; that is the set-up where they have a brief exchange about whether he really said that he did not love her. This is typical for the film, which is made up mostly of compositions like this one and comparably cryptic, awkwardly emotional dialogue. The exception to this tendency is the film's third sequence, which features a jarring cut to an extreme long shot of the woman in the mountains (an image that, as I mentioned earlier, looks very much like the mountain interview in her 1977 experimental television work, *Papa comme maman*), singing in English a song with the lyrics "How can I love a man / when I know he don't love me," complete with non-diegetic instrumental accompaniment. The music ends suddenly, though, when Miéville cuts to a shot of the woman walking down a mountain path. This is an odd sequence, one that pulls the viewer out of the soft-lit moodiness of the rest of the film. The alpine imagery looks a bit like something out of *Sauve qui peut (la vie)*, which, as I discuss below, makes extensive use of the Swiss landscape; really, though, the shot looks most like the comparably disruptive alpine interview in *Papa comme maman*, which I discussed in Chapter 3. What is worth noting here about the apparent disconnect between these two very different kinds of imagery is that they speak in a very visceral way and have a kind of affect that is uniquely cinematic, allowing the viewer to be either very close to a performer or to understand their connections to landscape. We see this tension in a key sequence in *Sauve qui peut (la vie)*, which I discuss below. In this short film, Miéville is exploring the same kind of tension—between intimacy and enormity, between intense emotional affect and kitsch—in a context that is shorn of the narrative or political elements of *Savue qui peut (la vie)*. It is a kind of distillation of that film, a riff on some of its key thematic and aesthetic tendencies.

Later on in this chapter, I recall how Laura Mulvey argues that *Prénom Carmen* "reveals the bare constitutive elements of his [Godard's] late cinema, all that remains when everything else is stripped away" ("The Hole and the Zero," 84). I think something very similar could be said about *Faire la fête*, certainly in terms of its connection to Godard and Miéville's mature cinema of the late 1970s to mid-1980s. *How Can I Love* is a thirteen-minute film, and it has a kind of spare precision that all of their films of this period seem to aspire toward. Its opening sequence is a series of cuts between two second-floor apartments, both above an unseen parade whose sounds are always audible. In one apartment, there is a woman who is at first by herself; she makes eye contact with, and eventually playful faces at, the small kids in the opposite apartment. Their young mother, however, looks at her disapprovingly, and this sense of unfriendliness recurs in the film's final scene, where the woman and the young mother are in line together at the supermarket. In this opening scene, though, Miéville uses long takes (a shot that lasts a long time without a cut) and has no camera movement; she alternates close-ups of the older woman and long shots (images where people are visible top to bottom, not to be confused with long takes) of the young family. The stillness of this imagery is a stark, evocative contrast with the clamour of the soundtrack's music and marching, one that calls forth the kind of turmoil of the film's long middle section. There, the older woman makes love with her boyfriend (we see them naked in the bed in a high-angle close-up) and then engages in long painful talk about whether to have children. The lighting in this sequence is much softer than the harsher natural light of the opening and closing sequences, although the pace of editing is slightly quicker and the camera generally closer to the actors. This opening sequence strongly calls to mind lyrical sequences in *Sauve qui peut (la vie)* shot in rural Switzerland (including footage of people playing Hornuss, a sport unique to the Swiss Jura that involves hurling a tiny disc at speeds that can approach 300 kph), or sequences in *Soft and Hard* where Godard and Miéville themselves are wandering around the shore of Lac Léman. The sensations of the local—the landscape, the sport, the festivities—are everywhere, even though inexpressible personal turmoil hovers suggestively over the imagery. This middle sequence, on the other hand, strongly calls to mind the long middle of *Soft and Hard*, where Godard and Miéville sit on the sofa and engage in a rambling and sometimes awkward dialogue, or sequences like the *plan-séquence* in *Détective*, where the middle-aged couple sits in the bathroom, sincerely trying to convince each other that there is something in their relationship worth saving. Miéville's editing in *Faire la fête* is steadier than the long takes that I am using as comparators here, but what we can see in all these examples is an attempt to use stillness, silence, and awkward conversation as a signifier of both longing *and* sensuality, of connection *and* alienation (between people as well as between people and their surroundings). These are problems with philosophical and political resonances, and sometimes such resonances are unfolded in considerable detail (as in *Sauve qui peut [la vie]* or *Soft and Hard*). All of the films of this period, though, are defined by an insistence on the difficulty of real connection, the pain that is inherent to the Western European experience. That is all that remains when the specific philosophical or political positions of Godard and Miéville's films of this period are stripped away, and that is what makes up the entirety of *Faire la fête*.

SAUVE QUI PEUT (LA VIE)

The popular discourse around *Savue qui peut (la vie)* (1979), especially in the United States, returns time and time again to the film's status as a comeback. Godard's presence as a guest on *The Dick Cavett Show* in 1980 gives a good sense of the degree to which it marked his return into the realm of multimedia celebrity. This 1980 interview is a real pleasure to watch.[1] It affords the opportunity to see Cavett's facial expressions alternate between flummoxed and slightly terrified, and his combination of wit and unapologetic cluelessness is, in my experience, without peer. "Much is made of your peculiar way of photographing a scene …," Cavett offers hesitantly, steering as close to formal analysis as he is capable of coming. "There are times when it looks like the camera got loose, and wandered away in the middle of a conversation." But as I return to the interview, I am forced to contain my sneeringly superior response, for their conversation opens with the following exchange:

> DICK CAVETT: Mr. Godard, the word "comeback" has been used about this film. By that I guess they mean that it may be the first of what you might call commercial feature that you've done in some time. Does that word "comeback" offend you?
>
> GODARD: In a sense, because I never went away. Maybe I was pushed away. I would rather say it's a reverse of comeback. What is it, come forth, go forth?
>
> CAVETT: Or continue?

This little bit of help with English in fact constitutes a real understanding of what this new phase of Godard's career represents. Not coming forth, and not really going forth either: for Godard and Miéville, the dawning of the 1980s was about *continuing*. That is very obviously true of *Savue qui peut (la vie)*, which is clear simply because of the fact that its central aesthetic eccentricity, slow motion, was used extensively, if slightly differently, in Godard and Miéville's 1979 television series *France/tour/détour/deux/enfants*. It is just as true of all the work that the two did together during these "golden eighties." I want to deal in this chapter with the period of Godard and Miéville's shared career that begins with 1979's *Sauve qui peut (la vie)* and ends with 1985's *Soft and Hard*. From the standpoint of formal and technical specifics, this is a remarkably diverse body of work, just as varying as the work they did together in the 1970s. It includes feature-narrative films, short- and medium-length videos, and short films.

This variability should not obscure the degree to which all of this work is part of a common vision. Throughout this period, which I am calling "Realization," we can see an ongoing engagement with problems of communication, which dominated their work in the 1970s, as well as a desire to reconcile this sort of broad philosophical engagement with the grittier realities of both domesticity and political action. What I want to argue here is that these films are equally invested in renewing both the basics of cinema as a medium and the concerns of political cinema and thus deserve a central place in the history of postwar European cinema and of global political art. Their work from the 1980s and 1990s continues the process that Godard and Miéville had begun by experimenting with video, with non-standard lengths, and with the contours of the feature-narrative film. It marks their movement from the stage of Modernist-inflected experimentation to a mature Modernist practice.

There are a number of important strains of the most splashily released of Godard and Miéville's films of the 1980s that might not be immediately evident, but which are important for placing them in the context of their work overall. *Sauve qui peut (la vie)* is certainly an autobiographical portrait of Godard inasmuch as its lead male character—named Paul Godard and played by Jacques Dutronc—is an unhappy television director with a lot of misgivings about his personal and professional life. Its other protagonist, a woman named Denise Rimbaud (played by Nathalie Baye) who leaves the metropolis (which appears to be Lausanne, which is where *Sauve qui peut (la vie)* was shot, although that is not explicit in the film itself) for rural Switzerland, has just as clearly autobiographical resonances. The film's most distinctive aesthetic eccentricity, the use of slow motion (it was released under the title *Slow Motion* in the United Kingdom), represents a continuation of the technique as it had been deployed in their TV series *France/tour/détour/deux/enfants*. Godard and Miéville are using a specifically televisual form of slow motion, and in *Sauve qui peut (la vie)*, as in *France/tour/détour/deux/enfants*, this has both aesthetic and analytical effects. The film's use of stars works in a similar way; the presence of Isabelle Huppert and Natalie Baye, two famous French actresses, is an example of the acceptance of some elements of commercial-narrative cinema, but their performances are deployed in such a way as to act as a critique of those same conventions. Acceptance of the star system coexisting with critique of capitalist culture, like aesthetic affect coexisting with analysis, are the sorts of paradoxes that define Modernism at its height, but they are also part of a dialectical strategy that defines the film overall. The analysis that results from these interlaced dialectics is that alternatives to advanced capitalist alienation are possible, but they are difficult, paradoxical, incomplete.

This is a more fleshed-out version of the conclusions that the Sonimage work tended to come to, so clearly embodied by the image of Godard with his head buried in his hands that concluded *Numéro deux*. *Sauve qui peut (la vie)* is a critique of Western European capitalist culture, but it is a Modernist one, a critique whose power is underwritten, rather than undercut, by the constantly questioning way in which it is mounted. Peter Harcourt has very neatly summed up the basic paradox that is at *Sauve qui peut (la vie)*'s heart, writing that "[i]t is a film that has been shaped to fit into the cinema Machine—that whole network of production, promotion, and exhibition which determines, more and more, what films get made and then which of those get seen. The anecdotal surface of the film is largely a ruse, as if to please or titillate the lumpen-bourgeoisie" ("Le Nouveau Godard," 27). I discuss below how I do not see the film as titillating at all (and indeed how it is a contrast in this way from the work Godard as done on his own), but I think that Harcourt, as always, is fundamentally correct. The ostensible narrative of the film is largely a ruse, a way for Godard and Miéville to reintegrate back into the machine of cinema, and to critique that machine from within. "I have simply tried to suggest that the film is both more interesting and more radical than it may seem," Harcourt also wrote in that article (27). He is quite right about that, and I believe that *Sauve qui peut (la vie)* is quite a bit more radical than the rest of its critical reception would suggest.

As I mentioned in the introduction to this chapter, this film was discussed by the press (both in French and English) as a sort of a comeback for Godard, which is to say a more accessible work than the avant-garde film/video/television work he had been doing. The reception did not start out this way, though. For although the film had a very high-profile premiere at the Cannes Film Festival, Jean Narboni reported from there that "[i]t's difficult to forget the journalists racing to recording studios and press rooms as soon as the film was over, finally freed from this agony and able to tell us how much they hated it" (8; m.t.). But Antoine de Baecque's biography, in a section called "Il faut sauver *Sauve qui peut* ...," recalls how one of the film's producers, Martine Marignac, put on a media blitz to try to repair the film's reception in the French press. It basically worked, and de Baecque notes in that section that "[b]etween the summer and fall of 1980, you can find almost 20 interviews in the French press: *Le Monde, Libération, Le Matin de Paris, Télérama, Le Nouvel Observateur, Le Figaro, L'Humanité-dimanche*, the *Cahiers du cinéma, Cinéma 80*, and even *France-Soir*" (588; m.t.). Summarizing the film's critical reception in the United States, Kristin Thompson sounds a very similar note; after citing coverage in the *Los Angeles Examiner, Rolling Stone*, and two articles in *New York Magazine*, she writes that "[j]ournalists and reviewers who had not seen a Godard work in nearly ten years responded with great warmth, acting as though their old favorite were returning from years of inactivity or confused wandering" (263). In the United States, there was a very good reason for this frenzied media activity: as we saw in Chapter 2, "Abandonments," the film, along with *Passion*, had been financed in part by Francis Ford Coppola, who had accepted the US rights to those films as a de facto repayment of money advanced for the aborted film project *The Story*. Coppola's company, American Zoetrope, which was in the late 1970s and 1980s still a prominent part of the US film industry, had a financial interest in seeing *Sauve qui peut (la vie)* do well, and de Baecque's biography recalls how Tom Luddy had sent a memo to Coppola (on October 15, 1980) reassuring him that Godard had taken to the American promotion of the film with gusto (589).

Another reason for this wider attention to *Save qui peut (la vie)* is clearly the fact that Godard and Miéville used well-known French stars, and therein lies one of the film's dialectical elements. The presence of Nathalie Baye and Isabelle Huppert clearly signals the film's status as "movie," as a work that is part of a commercial, consumption-oriented system of film production. At its core, the film is about the soul-killing quality of that system, about the integration into capitalism of the techniques of image making. This becomes most explicit toward the end of the film, during the sequence when Huppert's character, a prostitute called Isabelle Rivière, meets two executives in a high-end hotel room that seems to be doubling as their office. The two men are absurdly cold and mean spirited, treating Isabelle and a younger prostitute who is also there with complete contempt. But Godard and Miéville begin this sequence with a few long takes that introduce the situation, then cut to a shot of Baye's character, Denise Rimbaud, reading in bed followed by a shot of Lac Léman at sunset, and then return to the hotel, where we again see a series of long takes unfold as the executives berate and try to humiliate the women while they are having sex with them. It would be easy to treat this sequence as though it was just a series of images of degrading sex in a sterile, high-end hotel. In fact, it is more than that, acting as a painful invocation of a central tension in *Sauve qui peut (la vie)*: between quiet, gentle intimacy and retreat (embodied here by Baye in bed, crosscut with images of the softly lit lake) and a sleek modernity that degrades body and soul alike.

Throughout *Sauve qui peut (la vie)*, the degradation is explicitly gendered; for the most part, it is Paul Godard's soul that is being degraded and Isabelle Huppert's body. This is very clear in the hotel room sequence, whose images are brutal and rather self-flagellating—the older, fatter, nastier executive orders Huppert to lick him in various ways, synched up with other acts going on in the room, with an exactitude that strongly recalls the skills of a film director—even if their absurdity lends the scene an air of very black comedy. The images of the basically depopulated Swiss landscape, by contrast, are photographed in a way that is highly composed and picturesque. Wry, self-mocking humour thus lies just beneath both sets of imagery, but neither set of images is entirely defined by that humour; neither set is reduced to pure irony, to pure imagery. The Swiss landscape is genuinely lovely, and to combine it with a medium close-up of Baye in bed renders this element of the montage tender and intimate rather than cheesy, which is very close to the way that the landscape imagery operates in Miéville's *How Can I Love*. The sex scenes in the hotel are genuinely degrading for the women involved and difficult to watch because of that. This is likely the scene that led Constance Penley to write that "[f]requently works that are accused of being pornographic are redeemed by assigning them to the category of the erotic. *Sauve qui peut (la vie)*, if it were pornographic, could never find such redemption because it is deeply anti-erotic" ("Pornography, Eroticism," 16).

Rather than making this degradation titillating, Godard and Miéville take the edge off this element of the montage by allowing hints of the ridiculous to filter in. It becomes dark comedy, not erotica. That ridiculousness is emphasized by Huppert's performance style, which, especially in this sequence, presents her character Isabelle as utterly unflappable, even in the face of the most outrageously degrading commands from these caricatures of decadent capitalist excess. This is a variation on Godard's fascination with prostitution as a metaphor for capitalism, although the films he alone made on the topic are very different. The sturdy, composed sensibility that Huppert radiates in these sequences also links her to Baye's performance style with Denise. Godard and Miéville are using these two stars as dual icons of feminine toughness, but they are placing those icons in narrative situations that self-consciously clash with images of celebrity. Nathalie Baye is the quietly confused, bicycle-riding recluse; Isabelle Huppert is the abused prostitute. Both are thus marginal figures and could be seen as part of a gender-led critique of the costs of capitalist culture: capitalism pushes everything that is not defined by a masculine acquisitiveness to the edges of society. Godard and Miéville are, then, evoking the ravages of capitalist culture in explicitly gendered terms: women are never manipulators of capital or its power, and they can only be abused or exiled by it. In earlier films (such as 1962's *Vivre sa vie* or 1967's *2 ou 3 choses que je sais d'elle*), Godard had used prostitution as a metaphor for capitalism but did so in ways that were quasi-voyeuristic (and at the very least, quixotic). He had, in essence, talked a mean game about women being symbols of oppression. But with *Sauve qui peut (la vie)*, the shift is palpable; women are not so much sacrificed at the altar of capitalism as they are symbolic of capitalist culture's ethical emptiness. Thus, when I say they are "taking the edge off," I am trying to indicate the way in which they are relying on an intellectual and iconic approach to the representation of women, rather than a mimetic and visceral one.

For all of its video-led distancing, that is basically the strategy of *Numéro deux*. That work revised the gender politics of 1960s Godard by replacing sentimentality with a frank emphasis on abjection. However, it left voyeurism, or at the very least identification with the onscreen characters, more or less intact. *Sauve qui peut (la vie)* shifts away decisively from this identification-based strategy; the video screens may be gone, but there is nothing in this film that seems to be trying to give us a view into the "real life" of the characters of a filmmaker-constructed narrative world. The sequence with the hotel and the lake is thus also one of the best examples of the essentially iconic (as opposed to mimetic) approach that Godard and Miéville take not only to gender-led symbolic critique but also toward star performances. Baye and Huppert are not there to lead the viewer toward a simple, celebrity-based identification, or identification of any kind, but instead to encourage that viewer to see them as signifiers rather than characters, representations rather than imitations. Even though these performances are nuanced and at times highly demanding, Baye and Huppert are elements of a montage here. The combination of these very different star appearances, the combination of these very different icons, creates a portrait of the difficult, painful, and inherently variable struggle against the alienation of modernity.

There is an inherent tension in criticizing modernity via star performance, and this is part of what makes *Sauve qui peut (la vie)* typically Modernist, more so even than Godard and Miéville's films of the Sonimage period. A comparison with Samuel Beckett may clarify matters here; his evolution is a sort of a mirror image of the progression of Godard and Miéville's work from the Sonimage period to the 1990s. The kind of Modernist practice that

Beckett explored in his late career corresponds roughly to the earliest days of Godard and Miéville's collaboration. A theatre piece like *What Where* (1983) has roughly the same distance from, and lingering attachment to, the conventions of dramatic theatre that *Ici et ailleurs* has to those of feature film; Beckett's *Quad* pieces (I and II, both 1981), being works of rigid dance and movement made with a camera set about three metres above the dancers and in a single shot, are highly demanding but unthinkable outside of video in the way that is very similar to *Six fois deux: Sur et sous la communication*'s connection to televisual form. With this analogy in mind, then, I propose that *Sauve qui peut (la vie)* is Godard and Miéville's *Waiting for Godot* (1953). *Waiting for Godot* may not have featured big stars in 1953, but 35 years later, Hollywood director Mike Nichols staged it at Lincoln Center with Steve Martin and Robin Williams as Vladmir and Estragon. This eventuality only showed what was true of the play in 1953 and what is also true of *Sauve qui peut (la vie)*: that the denial of certain forms of narrative pleasure—clear linear progression, an ending that resolves central narrative questions (will Godot arrive? will Denise and Paul reconcile?)—does not place a work fully outside the realm of conventional forms.

Serge Daney could be writing about a young Beckett and the theatre when he writes that "[u]sing established norms as a starting point, Godard 'invented' (indeed cobbled together) the current shape of our perception of images and sounds. He has always been a little ahead of his time, but nothing had protected him from the average illusions of his day" ("Le paradoxe de Godard," 7 / "The Godard Paradox," 70). The way *Sauve qui peut (la vie)* uses star performances to find a state in between identification and iconography, in between critique and pleasure, is (like Beckett's use of theatrical conventions like clowning) a kind of "bricolage." It is a cobbled-together form of illusionist narrative. Godard and Miéville use the established norms of the commercial cinema as the starting place for their critique of the ravages of Western European capitalist culture. To see the beast you attack, you must be inside it but not consumed by it; that is what Godard and Miéville are showing through Huppert's stoic and vaguely ironic sensibility amid the madness of her life as a prostitute. A withdrawal from the metropolis must be coupled with an acceptance of loneliness and a pastoral sensibility that is always in danger of sliding into kitsch; this is what Godard and Miéville are showing through the images of Baye, alone amid the gorgeous mountains and lakes of the canton of Vaud.

This sense of *Sauve qui peut (la vie)* as engaged with the struggle against alienation and emptiness is close to Pascale Bonitzer's analysis that "[i]f the subject of *Sauve qui peut (la vie)* is movement, then its object is this nameless, shape-shifting, faceless terror" ("Peur et commerce," 6; m.t.). This invocation of a combination of movement and terror is especially instructive; Godard and Miéville are breaking apart movement both as an aesthetic gesture and as a means of understanding the play between the brutal and poetic elements of everyday life. The film's slow-motion sequences alternate between images of pure movement and banal violence and build toward a climax that is embodied by an image that completely blurs the two. This back and forth can be seen about twenty minutes into the film, when a slow-motion sequence of Denise riding her bike through the countryside is followed by a sequence that has her arriving in the city, parking her bike at the train station, and watching a young woman get hassled by two men and then struck by one of them in slow motion. This juxtaposition is typical of the overall use of slow motion; Godard and Miéville alternate between slow-motion images of violence and lyricism, suggesting as the film moves forward that the two sensations are inseparably connected. This is made manifest in the strangest, most overwhelming of the slow-motion sequences, about two-thirds of the way through the film. Paul Godard and Denise Rimbaud are sitting across from one another at a kitchen table, when suddenly Paul jumps across and throws Denise to the floor. As soon as he gets up, the film shifts to slow motion, but because of the odd angle of the shot—behind Paul, whose body partially obscures Denise's—it is very hard to see any facial expressions. The bits that are visible suggest a combination of pain and intense emotion, with one sensation flowing into the other. Sometimes it looks like they are fighting, while other times it looks like they are having sex.

The terror that Bonitzer alludes to is present in this image, and while that terror is not exactly faceless or anonymous, it is sudden, unmotivated, unexplained, and unexplainable. It is a violent motion, but also a very sensual one, with two bodies falling into one another in a way that makes them seem to combine as well as pull apart. At the end of the film, Godard and Miéville repeat this combination, but in two shots. When Paul Godard sees his estranged wife and daughter on the street, he embraces them warmly and playfully in slow motion and then asks his ex-wife if he can see them more often. When he pulls his ex-wife around in slow motion, it looks vaguely threatening for a moment, but when the image returns to normal speed, it looks playful. A few shots later, Paul Godard walks across the street and, in slow motion, is struck by a car; as he rolls over the car, he seems to fall gently, and allows his legs to go straight up into the air in a series of motions that can only be described as sensual. All of these images are undoubtedly of great aesthetic beauty, each being defined by an attention to camera position and colour that makes them feel vivid and artificial. They also display a delicacy that makes them seem genuinely mysterious.

But together, they are unfolding a dialectic between pain and happiness, all of it equally ineffable and fleeting. They are the abstract portions of the film's portrait of a Western European society where alternatives to the faceless forces of alienation are difficult to separate from the most visceral forms of pain that alienation is capable of inflicting.

The slow motion that Godard and Miéville are using here is a specifically televisual form of that effect, and it is a real advance over its use in *France/tour/détour/deux/enfants,* which had aired just before the filming of *Sauve qui peut (la vie).* The kind of slow motion that we see in both works is not the kind of slow motion that is typically used when shooting film—where footage is shot at a high frame rate and then projected at the normal speed. Rather, both *Sauve qui peut (la vie)* and *France/tour/détour/deux/enfants* freeze and then restart footage shot at the normal frame rate, and usually do this several times within a single shot. Like the fades and superimpositions that we discussed in Chapter 3, this is a sort of slow-motion effect that is very easily done in video but is quite a bit more complex to do in film with an optical printer. This sort of analytical ease was a big part of what had drawn Godard and Miéville to video in the first place. Godard and Miéville use this kind of slow motion throughout *France/tour/détour/deux/enfants,* slowing down important pieces of motion such as Camille getting dressed for bed. Indeed, the slow-motion image that opens Episode 3, where Camille runs down the street, starting well away from the camera but eventually coming into a close-up, strongly recalls the first slow-motion image of *Sauve qui peut (la vie).* That is in a sequence that starts with a head-on medium shot of Denise Rimbaud riding her bicycle, cuts to the words "*Sauve qui peut*" with the number "1" superimposed over the letters, and then cuts to a long shot of Rimbaud on her bike, with the verdant Swiss landscape in the background. It is a visually complex pair of images. In both shots of Denise, slow motion starts and stops. In the second shot, she eventually moves closer to the camera, but the limited depth of field means that the greenery in the background is a fully abstract blur of colour. The shot of Camille in *France/tour/détour/deux/enfants* is gentle and patiently lyrical, and the analytical qualities afforded by dissecting the movement offers the same invitation to dissect aspects of her everyday life as the scene in the bedroom, and other images like it, had.

"On numerous occasions in *France/tour/détour/deux/enfants,*" Michael Witt writes, "we are suddenly conscious that the human body, whether in isolation or viewed as part of a crowd, is being scrutinized in precisely the same way that particle motion is examined by a scientist through a microscope" ("Going through the Motions," 179). This is indeed what is going on in these sequences with Camille, but it is not what is happening in *Sauve qui peut (la vie)*. Rather than dissecting the movement of Denise Rimbaud on the bicycle, this televisual slow motion gives it a new rhythm, one that is slightly different: from Gabriel Yared's delicate, minimalist piano music on the soundtrack to the rhythms of her pushing the pedals. It also accentuates both the speed at which Denise is moving and the purity of the landscape because the image is shot with a telephoto lens and has relatively little depth of field. So, when the motion stops, we see Denise very sharply in focus but presented within a blurry, semi-abstract green background. Thus, there is both an analytical and an aesthetic component to the slow motion here, but the aesthetics are more highly composed and the analysis less didactic or pseudo-scientific than what we had in *France/tour/détour/deux/enfants*. Furthermore, the analysis that Godard and Miéville are offering in this scene poses, as they do throughout *Sauve qui peut (la vie)*, the idea that simplicity is basically an illusion. Leave the city to ride your bike if you want, but rather than uncomplicated ease and plenty, what actually defines the experience is syncopated rhythm and blurred sensations, as we see and hear in this image through the play of sound and image. *France/tour/détour/deux/enfants* used slow-motion images of a young girl to ask viewers to look anew at the domestic. *Sauve qui peut (la vie)* uses slow-motion images of a woman to actually do that looking and to offer an argument about what is to be found by that sort of contemplative introspection. "Even if the film doesn't speak of terrorism, it is placed on this level of violence without cause," writes Bonitzer ("Peur et commerce," 7; m.t.). Violence without cause is an aspect of capitalist culture that Godard and Miéville work hard to excavate in *Sauve qui peut (la vie)*; they also find moments of ineffable connection, and occasionally even of joy. The interdependence of these sensations, and that interdependence as a defining aspect of life *everywhere* in late-capitalist Western Europe, is nowhere clearer than in these slow-motion sequences.

Godard and Miéville are radically reordering the onscreen feminine presence in both works. In *France/tour/détour/deux/enfants*, that reordering is experimental in a very basic sense: it is in a closed-off space that they can control very tightly, and the imagery is making tentative statements about lyricism, the every day, and the ways in which the camera can objectify. In *Sauve qui peut (la vie)*, though, the experiment is over, and both the technique and the analysis is being sharpened, expanded, and fully realized. The imagery is giving us new ways to understand the onscreen body that is placed in a wild, uncontrollable landscape, new ways to look at women as they move through an unstable world.

As with *Passion* and *Je vous salue, Marie*, *Sauve qui peut (la vie)* has a short video companion, which serves as an opportunity for Godard to meditate on visual and thematic motifs as well as production problems. Alain Bergala wrote in rather sardonic terms about *Scénario vidéo de Sauve qui peut (la vie)*, which he saw when he was covering the release of the film for *Cahiers du cinéma*. He said there that "[w]hat is both quite troubling and quite fascinating about this videotape without a real destination is that it seems a bit 'too much,' making no room for any spectator, needing nobody for its existence both as an assessment and a challenge, in the manner of very old art (such as the statues in *Le Mépris*) or very modern art" ("Le juste milieu," 42; m.t.). This mixture of the very modern and the very old is the defining tension of Godard's next film, *Passion*, which has a comparably hermetic quality to it. But *Scénario vidéo de Sauve qui peut (la vie)* did have an intended audience, and a very precise one: the film's producers. Phillipe Dubois's introduction to the published transcript of Godard's voice-over for the piece notes that it was "first of all destined for producers and presented some ideas from the 'in progress' film" (117; m.t.). But I do not agree with Bergala's overall point here, that this piece is insular and somehow integrates the extreme hermetic tendencies of both classicism and Modernism. For while there are indeed traces of both in this video, there are elements of it that are as affecting on a purely visual level as moments of *Sauve qui peut (la vie)* itself. Early in the video, there are shots from different angles of a woman arranging a centrepiece on a table; the images are faded one on top of another (which are almost identical to the opening image of their 1985 television work *Soft and Hard*, which I discuss below), with Godard on the voice-over talking about the cross-fade as a device (later, he mixes these angles using a variety of video wipes that look awkwardly dated). The piece also has some richly colourful footage of a soccer match that uses the video-inflected slow-motion effect. The concluding sequence makes extensive use of the paintings of Edward Hopper, using shots of both *Gas* (1940) and *Night Hawks* (1942) while his voice-over discusses Wim Wenders shooting his new film (presumably *Hammett*, shot in San Francisco with support from Francis Ford Coppola). But this sequence concludes with a montage of fades between images of Isabelle Huppert and Hopper's *Eleven a.m.* (1926). This is all to say that the video may seem a bit much because of the complete lack of narrative and Godard's constant, cryptic voice-over, but it is really an elliptical meditation on some of the basic motifs—both visual and thematic—of the finished film. Of the video "scenarios" that Godard made during this period—*Scénario vidéo Sauve qui peut* (la vie), *Scénario du film Passion*, and *Petites notes à propos du film Je vous salue, Marie*—this is the one that most closely resembles an artist's sketch. It is clearly unfinished, but it is just as clearly worth talking about as an object unto itself.[2]

PRÉNOM CARMEN AND *DÉTECTIVE*

Godard and Miéville's 1983 film *Prénom Carmen* closes with a title card that reads "In memoriam small movies." Compared with *Sauve qui peut (la vie)*, Godard and Miéville's *Prénom Carmen* and *Détective* do indeed feel relatively minor, like interesting experiments in fairly specific problems of cinematic storytelling. They are not quite sketches in the model of *Scénario vidéo Sauve qui peut (la vie)*, but they are not far off of that. *Prénom Carmen* is doing more or less the same thing with the romance that *Détective* is doing with Hollywood cinema: following the basics of a popular form but making gestures that shift that form toward self-reflexivity. The fact that this self-reflexivity can be accomplished in both cases without abandoning these shells—*Prénom Carmen* is still recognizable as the Carmen narrative, and *Détective* is still recognizable as a hard-boiled crime film—points not only to Godard and Miéville's status as Modernists but also to their shared desire to revitalize popular forms, to create genuinely eccentric works of art that nevertheless reject hermetic or elitist strategies. That, finally, is what these two films share with *Sauve qui peut (la vie)*: an outward appearance of "difficulty" that is tempered somewhat by images of sensuality or visceral emotional affect. Youssef Ishaghpour also links these two films in his book *Cinéma contemporain: de ce côté du miroir*, writing that "*Prénom Carmen* is centred on the dissonance between direct cinema and the elaboration of The Image, as in the difference between pornography and Beethoven's quartets. In *Détective* the relation more closely resembles that between the stage and backstage" (146; m.t.). Like *Sauve qui peut (la vie)*, then, these two films are defined by a tension between high artifice and the pleasures of mimesis, between cinema as document and cinema as poetry or music.

In the opening of this chapter, I hinted at the problems that Godard and Miéville pose in terms of authorship. For Serge Daney, *Prénom Carmen* was important in large part because it presented a crisis for what had been loosely known as *cinéma d'auteur* (the rough equivalent to the North American notion of "arthouse cinema"). Part of this is because the film came out during a period when there was a veritable spate of cinematic Carmens, with films from Peter

Brook, Carlos Saura, and Francesco Rosi as well as Godard and Miéville interpreting the story. Reviewing the film for *Libération*, Daney wrote of how "the very notion of '*cinema d'auteur*' is in crisis" (*La Maison cinéma* t.2, 210; m.t.), echoing Ishaghpour's assessment of Godard's choice to cast himself as a mad filmmaker rotting away in a mental asylum as indicative of how "*le cinéma d'auteur est en danger*" (132). For him, *Prénom Carmen* was important in no small part because it showed that the popularity of the concept of the "auteur" had allowed filmmakers to make work that riffed eccentrically on other narratives but nevertheless had some possibility of widespread appeal:

> At the moment where the threat of a dichotomy between a popular-industrial cinema and a cultural-subsidised cinema, a dichotomy older than Herod, at the moment where the concept of the "auteur" has become a union complaint, at the moment where the defence of the gains of the New Wave takes on the sense of a noble lark, it's altogether heartening to find that filmmakers—like Godard, although he's not the only one—who first benefited from the label that they invented are also putting those benefits into play in the most modern (or Postmodern?) way possible. (*La Maison cinéma* t.2, 210–11; m.t.)

Among those benefits was the development of an audience for a specific filmmaker, and by the 1980s, that was definitely a benefit that had accrued to Godard (if not really to Miéville), especially in the wake of the relative success of *Sauve qui peut (la vie)*. That had not been entirely undone by the financial failure of *Passion*, which Godard made a year later. This joy in seeing a liberated and still genuinely curious filmmaker that defines Daney's experience of *Prénom Carmen* can be found in *Détective* as well. These are both films that revive older pop-narrative forms (the romance, the *film noir*) and make them both startlingly modern (especially because of the films' winking, ironic self-awareness) and just as startlingly visceral. Phil Powrie could well be talking about *Détective* when he says that "*Prénom Carmen*, like so many Godard films, is a self-referential, self-destructing machine, a collocation of cultural fragments which gesture at a myth and deconstruct it at the same time" (72).

Another aspect that complicates the authorship of *Prénom Carmen* is that it is based not on Bizet's 1875 opera *Carmen* (as were the other Carmens that came out during this period, along with Otto Preminger's 1954 adaptation of the Broadway musical *Carmen Jones*), but on the novella that the opera was based on, Prosper Mérimée's 1845 *Carmen*. Godard and Miéville emphasize this in the film by returning again and again to images of a string quartet playing *Beethoven*. Music is important in this film, but it does not follow that the only relevant musical comparison is that of Bizet. For *Prénom Carmen* is about the broadest themes of the *Carmen* narrative; the allure of the outlaw and the ways that passion can undo bourgeois respectability are the key concerns both of Mérimée's *Carmen* and of *Prénom Carmen*. When asked by *L'Avant-scène cinéma*'s Sylvie Steinebach if he meant to be provocative by not using the Bizet score, he snapped, "I could just as well have chosen Stevie Wonder" (5; m.t.), before dodging an actual answer via rambling philosophizing. Brody recalls how Godard told *Cinéma 84* that he wanted to use Beethoven's late quartets because he saw them as "fundamental music.... Music that is at the same time the practice and the theory of music" (Cited in *Everything Is Cinema*, 447). Here, Godard is echoing Theodore Adorno's sense of Beethoven's late quartets; in his 1937 essay fragment on those works, he wrote that "in the very late Beethoven the conventions find expression as the naked representation of themselves. This is the function of the often remarked-upon abbreviation of his style. It seeks not so much to free the musical language from mere phrases, as, rather, to free the mere phrase from the appearance of its subjective mastery. The mere phrase, unleashed and set free from the dynamics of the piece, speaks for itself" (*Essays on Music*, 566–67 / *Moments musicaux*, 16). *Prénom Carmen* is working in a similar way, trying in some ways to free film language from mere sequences, to take a "fundamental" approach to narrative cinema by unleashing images that can draw upon the visceral power of cinema, images that can in effect "speak for themselves."

This is all to say that *Prénom Carmen* is aspiring to abstraction, not adaptation, and we can see this most clearly in the images of a quartet playing those late Beethoven compositions. A particularly important example of such imagery is the lovely musical sequence at the beginning of the film. The camera is completely still, the lighting is very soft, and the camera is very close to one performer, with another performer's out-of-focus arm coming in and out of the foreground of the frame to the rhythm of one of the composition's leitmotifs. It is a visually complex, semi-musical composition that immediately brings to mind Straub–Huillet's very different but comparably evocative compositions in *Chronik der Anna Magdalena Bach* (1968). Specifically, it brings to mind Richard Roud's sense that Straub (again, seeming to mean Straub–Huillet) "makes no overt attempt to *express* the music; rather he lets it express itself" (77). That is clearly what is going on in this sequence with the string quartet (and other sequences like it in the film), and it is what is going on with Godard and Miéville's approach to the *Carmen* narrative as well.

While *Prénom Carmen*'s visual sensibilities are not as stark and spare as those of *Chronik der Anna Magdalena Bach*'s, the film is defined by a number of bare and expressive images that, through their deceptive simplicity, put into relief some key parts of the *Carmen* narrative. Perhaps the most visceral example of this is the scene in the film where Carmen goes into the shower, followed by Joseph, who then kisses her all over her body while he masturbates. This sequence opens with Beethoven on the soundtrack and a shot of Joseph in a hotel room pushing a bellboy out of the way as he tears off his shirt. The next shot is brief, but striking; a heavily shadowed and apparently nude Carmen (she is shot from the shoulders up) turns her head, brushes a bit of hair out of her face, and turns away. The centrepiece of the sequence, which lasts about thirty seconds, is a fixed-position long shot, with the camera pointing into the mirror above the sink, reflecting Carmen and Joseph in the shower in a medium-long shot (a medium-long shot, sometimes called a *plan américain*, is cut off more or less at the knees) that takes up about half the frame; the other half of the image is taken up with the bland geometry of the shower tiles. The Beethoven music remains on the soundtrack for about half of this image and then it suddenly cuts out, replaced by the sounds of the shower. The music resumes at the very end of the shot, just as Godard cuts to another image with no camera movement, a shot with the camera positioned high above the action (a high-angle shot) with Carmen lying down on the stark, white-tiled bathroom floor and slowly crawling into the frame and Joseph then crawling on top of her. The music continues to play as Carmen says, "You disgust me," and Joseph replies, "Me too." The music continues over the next shot in the sequence, with Joseph sitting naked on the bed and Carmen out of focus in the extreme foreground. Then the sequence ends as it began, with a close-up of Carmen, this time neutrally lit against a white background. This is a sort of retelling of a sequence that comes early in Merimée's *Carmen*, where Don José watches the women of Codova bathe:

> The moment the Angelus rings, darkness is supposed to have fallen. As the last stroke sounds, all the women disrobe and step into the water. Then there is laughing and screaming, and a wonderful clatter. The men on the upper quay watch the bathers, straining their eyes, and seeing very little. Yet the while uncertain outlines perceptible against the dark-blue waters of the stream stir the poetic mind, and the possessor of a little fancy finds it not difficult to imagine that Diana and her nymphs are bathing below, while he himself runs no risk of ending like Acteon. (*Carmen*, 19–20/ *Columba and Carmen*, 228–29)

The reference here is to the Greek hero Actaeon's seeing Diana bathing and Diana punishing him by forbidding him to reveal that he had seen her naked, under pain of being turned into a stag and killed by dogs. Carmen does not punish Joseph like that in either the film or the novella, but in both he suffers because of his unconsummated passion for her. Godard and Miéville latch on to this set of basic problems in the tale—voyeurism, sensuality, and feminine sexuality and power—and represent them in stark, minimalist cinematic terms. The *Angélus* becomes "fundamental music"; outdoor baths become dreary, solid-tiled showers; straining one's eyes to see naked nymphs becomes masturbation before a strong woman. All of this imagery is a series of shots with no camera movement, all but one of which have fairly harsh lighting. There are a few moments of lyricism—the close-ups that bookend the sequence, for instance—but overall, these are fairly austere tableaux, images that recall no filmmakers as strongly as Straub–Huillet. "The film seems to have been shot in an extremely simple manner," Roud writes of *Chronik der Anna Magdalena Bach*. "Straub [*sic*] has intensified the dynamics of the music by positively limiting the visual effects, and this contrast throws into brilliant perspective the complexity of the music" (77). Something very similar is going on here with Godard and Miéville's relationship with Merimée's narrative of *l'amour fou*, of the pleasures and costs of unbridled passion.

Prénom Carmen is cryptic and minimalist in a way that is no doubt different from Straub–Huillet. There are plenty of fixed-position long takes in the film, but none of them are as still or distancing as what we see in every Straub–Huillet film, definitely including *Chronik der Anna Magdalena Bach*. More importantly, perhaps, *Prénom Carmen* is much closer to allowing the narrative pleasure of the original text, while Straub–Huillet often abandon whatever pleasure is to be had from the original work in search of expressing something radically different, radically cinematic. That is much more often the case with the work based on literary sources than works (like *Chronik der Anna Magdalena Bach* or *Moses und Aaron*) that are based on musical works. The relationship between the film *Klassenverhältnisse* (*Class Relations*, 1984) and its source, Frantz Kafka's novella *Amerika*, is radically different than the relationship of Godard and Miéville's to Merimée's *Carmen*. On the surface, Godard and Miéville are much less faithful, since Straub–Huillet keep to the text of the *Amerika* very, *very* closely. But they are much closer inasmuch as, for Straub–Huillet, keeping to the text of the novel means having actors read the lines of their characters in completely flat voices, fully devoid of facial expression or meaningful bodily gestures. Straub–Huillet's task, one that Godard and Miéville have never been comfortable with, is to distance themselves fully from the logic of conventional film grammar. To return to Serge Daney's sense of the "Godard paradox," we can see in *Prénom Carmen* that "[t]here is nothing revolutionary about Godard, rather, he is more interested in radical reformism" ("Le paradoxe de Godard," 7 / "The Godard Paradox," 71). The film has characters that are not just "pure text" along the lines of those in *Chronik der Anna Magdalena Bach*, and, as a result, it has a narrative that, unlike that of *Klassenverhältnisse*, is possible not only to follow but to take a kind of conventional-narrative-cinema pleasure in. And Daney understood this quality of the *Carmen* narrative very well. Writing in *Libération* in 1984, he suggested that:

> If there's one quality that literary experts recognise in Merimée, it's sure the art of storytelling. Prosper is an effective narrator: no fat, just muscle and *yop la boum*.[3] Now, if there's one thing that we've looked for in vain (and looked since forever) from French cinema, it's surely that efficiency. (*La Maison cinéma* t.2, 536; m.t.)

Godard and Miéville recognize this part of Merimée as well, this sense of him as an essential storyteller. *Prénom Carmen* does not have a very clear narrative, but it does have a great deal of *yop la boum*, or yee-haw, and in many different forms. They are not seeking to abandon this part of Merimée; they are seeking to find a cinematic way of expressing it.

Thus, I am in agreement with the second half of Laura Mulvey's assessment that "[i]f, as it seemed to me, *Prénom Carmen* marks a moment of crisis in Godard's history, it also reveals the bare constitutive elements of his late cinema, all that remains when everything else is stripped away" ("The Hole and the Zero," 84). I think much the same could be said of *Détective* (1985), with the proviso that we are talking about the elements of Godard and Miéville's films from *Sauve qui peut (la vie)* forward. These bare constitutive elements include the presence of narrative and the parallel loading down of that narrative with serious art-historical or psychological weight, the use of painterly long takes, the judicious use of irony in both dialogue and performance style, and a preoccupation with the troubled relations between love and sexuality. In *Détective*, what weighs down the narrative is not the brooding psychological problems of *Sauve qui peut (la vie)*, nor the French literary culture that *Prénom Carmen* ransacks and rearranges. Rather, it is cinema that weighs down the narrative, and specifically, the memory of a commercial cinema that was still open and experimental in its form.

Détective concludes with all-caps red-and-white text that dedicates the film "A John Cassavetes Edgar G. Ulmer Clint Eastwood de Jean Luc Godard" (there are no commas or accents in the text). In his analysis of *Détective*, Peter Harcourt writes that "[t]he unselfconsciously complex yet popular film has virtually ceased to exist. This is why Godard feels an exile, why so many of his references invoke a world that is no longer there" ("Metaphysical Cinema," 9). That world could certainly be summarized by invoking these three slightly different kinds of independent filmmakers who remained attached to Hollywood.

All three made formally adventurous films, and for very little money, but none of them did so completely outside of a studio system. Ulmer is best known for *Detour* (1945), a *film noir* much beloved by the filmmakers of the French New Wave in no small part because of the fact that it was shot entirely on location, and shot *very* quickly and *very* cheaply. Cassavetes, like Eastwood, acted in many Hollywood films and had his own production company. Also like Eastwood, Cassavetes directed films for studios, such as *Love Streams* (1984) for Cannon (who would produce Godard's *King Lear* in 1987), *Gloria* (1980) for Columbia, and *Minnie and Moskowitz* (1971) for Universal—three films that are as different from each other as are Eastwood's *The Outlaw Josey Wales* (1976), *A Perfect World* (1993), and *Incivtus* (2009), all of which he directed for Warner Brothers. Like the "In memoriam small movies" that concludes *Prénom Carmen*, this text helps reinforce what we have already seen on the screen and what we can see in all of Godard and Miéville's films of the 1980s: that they are searching for a filmmaking practice that is both connected to familiar narratives and formal patterns and yet is in no way limited by them, searching for a cinema that is more fully itself. "*Détective* is pure cinema," writes Ishaghpour. "The logic of the object is no more; we have instead, against a collapsed world, the logic of style" (147; m.t.).

Again, that is a logic that Straub–Huillet followed with the greatest rigour, and as I tried to argue in Chapter 1, it is what Stan Brakhage was doing as well. *Détective* shows the degree to which Godard and Miéville have moved toward such radicalism without fully embracing it. We can see this in some part simply though the use of the crime film narrative shell. Ishaghpour sees this as a key to the film, writing that "[t]he 'policier' genre keeps up all the classical virtues—a beginning, middle and end—and in a time of chaos that tends to suppress story, characters, arguments, it re-establishes a little order" (144; m.t.). But rather than focusing on *Détective*'s status as a detective film, I think we can see this desire of Godard and Miéville to embrace a "pure cinema" without abandoning narrative most clearly by looking at the film's use of video. Video was, of course, a key component of Godard and Miéville's practice of the 1970s (as we saw in Chapter 3) and some of their uses of the media (especially in *France/tour/détour/deux/enfants*) moved close to a purely imagistic practice that Brakhage would have recognized. The 1980s is the period when Godard and Miéville moved away from that sort of experimentalism and back toward the mainstream, but they did so by incorporating some of these 1970s innovations. *Détective*'s first image is not film but video, a long take that is shot at a high angle and has Natalie Baye's character, Françoise, walking from one side of the frame to the other. Midway through the shot, it turns into the slow motion, only to go back into normal speed in the same shot (which we remember so well both from *France/tour/détour/deux/enfants* and *Sauve qui peut [la vie]*. The crucial difference in *Détective* is that this imagery is folded into a conventional narrative; the next shot it a very low-angle image of a Hi8 camera and a woman standing next to it (only her calves are visible), the street scene in the background placing them on a balcony. The voices of characters make it clear that this is all the surveillance part of an ongoing investigation by a hotel detective. When the film switches to video toward the end, it is because a boxer and his manager are being interviewed for television, and thus the effect is less visually disruptive than anything in these earlier Godard and Miéville works. But these two sequences share a highly complex soundtrack, one that combines both synchronous and non-synchronous sound with music to make an overwhelming sonic collage, especially true of the second sequence, the interview. Video is being used here in a way that parallels the film's use of the narrative and formal patterns of *film noir*. Godard and Miéville are deploying all of these cinematic elements in a way that makes the familiar strange, as good Modernists should, but which refuses to abandon the conventions of cinematic realism altogether.

This is most vivid in the sequence that directly precedes the video interview, where Françoise and her husband, Émile (played by Claude Brasseur), linger melancholically in their hotel room. The sequence in the shower, made up of only five shots, is just as affecting as the shower scene in *Prénom Carmen*, although far more tender. Indeed, the scene where the middle-aged couple mumbles through old arguments is quite touching, in no small part because of its cinematic simplicity. First, Françoise is in the frame alone against white tiles, then she is joined by a naked, dripping Émile. That sequence is followed by Émile drying himself, sitting alone on the tub and lamenting how he has become charmless. Eventually, he is joined and reassured by Françoise. It is only their voices on the soundtrack, punctuated by an extremely annoying hotel buzzer as their breakfast arrives. Godard and Miéville signal that this moment of tender lyricism is over when, in the last shot, the soundtrack fills with Françoise's screams and a cut to a close-up of a dead mouse that has been left in their breakfast spread. This is followed by a close-up of Émile pouring from a coffee pot, which turns out to be filled with blood. Ridiculously melodramatic music now fills the soundtrack but fades as the blood continues to come out of the white coffee pot. Seeing the blood, or the red paint, is a most Godardian ironic gesture; one of his most often-quoted sayings is that his films do not have a lot of blood, but a lot of red paint (he was talking about *Pierrot le fou*). The juxtaposition of sequences like these two shows the degree to which "Godard and Miéville" is fundamentally different from "Godard." For while Godard's films of the 1960s were playful and winking (we can certainly see that in different ways in films such as *À bout de souffle*, *Band à part*, *Pierrot le fou*, or *Weekend*), that sensibility more or less vanishes once he starts to work with Miéville. The difficulties men and women have communicating with one another, the difficulties they have maintaining real connections, become the recurring issues. Sometimes this is highly politicized (as in *Numéro deux*), but in both *Prénom Carmen* and *Détective*, we can see, as in *Sauve qui peut (la vie)*, the rendering of these difficulties in quieter and more purely emotional terms. These terms recall not so much the sharp political polemics of the Gorin-initiated film *Ici et ailleurs* but the awkward, lyrical silences of *How Can I Love*.

JE VOUS SALUE, MARIE AND *LE LIVRE DE MARIE*

In between *Prénom Carmen* and *Détective*, Godard and Miéville made two very different films, not quite together but sort of alongside one another. *Je vous salue, Marie* (released in English as *Hail Mary*) was a feature-length film written and directed by Godard, whereas *Le livre de Marie* was a short film (28 minutes), written and directed by Miéville. They were released together; the short film always preceded the feature. Both works are variations on the Marian narrative, but apart from that, they seem to share very little. Miéville's film is quiet, closely observed, and a bit sad, along the lines of *How Can I Love*; Godard's film is cryptic, pared down, and peppered both with tongue-in-cheek asides and images of intense visual power. These two films are in a kind of argument or dialogue with one another about the intense sadness of the Marian narrative, about how to film the ineffable, and about cinematic form (and specifically about artifice). All of these arguments are, finally, about Protestantism. In a way, this "Marie project" is Godard and Miéville's closest collaboration so far, the place where we can see two artists with highly distinct voices working toward some shared goal.

The complexity of these films was, upon their initial release in 1985, somewhat overshadowed by an international controversy surrounding the blasphemous quality of *Je vous salue, Marie*. Maryel Locke provides a useful overview of the hullabaloo in her contribution to the book about the film that she edited with Charles Warren (one that relies heavily on press materials produced by the films' US distributor, New Yorker Films). Locke summarizes the genuinely mixed quality of the *Je vous salue, Marie*'s reception among European Catholics when she recalls that while there were protests at Cannes and in Italy, "[o]ther European responses to *Hail Mary* began in a positive way, with the Catholic Cinema Office awarding a prize to the film at the Berlin Film Festival. The film was well received in Krakow, Poland. However, in Fulda, West Germany, the film was withdrawn when twenty people protested. In Athens, Greek Orthodox demonstrators forced the cancellation of the film in one theatre" (3). Discussions of this controversy invariably centre on the Catholic response, which was indeed both vocal and international. It is worth saying up front that I find the response by the Vatican nothing short of bizarre, and I am far from the only one who thinks this. Rev. André Dumas (former Dean of Paris's Faculté de théologie protestante) has written an invaluable article on the Protestant quality of Godard's 1980s films, and in that essay, he writes of *Je vous salue, Marie* that it is "to my mind the most rigorously theological film, possibly in the entire history of cinema, and thus I do not understand at all why it could shock the Vatican to the point of being roused" (91; m.t.). The feud with the Vatican only seems stranger in the light of Godard's letter of May 9, 1985, to Fr. Jean-Michel di Falco, then part of the Office catholique du cinéma, where he alluded to "the generosity of your reception of the film when it was distributed in France" and confirmed that "we are asking the Italian distributor, although we exercise no temporal powers over him, to stop the film screenings in and around the house of the Holy Father" (qtd. in Locke, 5–6).

This is all quite deceptive, for one of the most important aspects of *Je vous salue, Marie* is its attempt to engage with a Protestant view of the Marian narrative. That is also true of *Le livre de Marie*. Part of this engagement with Protestantism is theological, to be sure, but a big part of this is cultural as well. Colin MacCabe explains this in his Godard biography, writing that "[t]here are two points to be made about this concern with Catholicism. First, it is European culture and the European past which now obsess Godard, and that culture and that past are Catholic as well as Protestant. Second, however, Godard's interest in religion is profoundly Protestant. He has little interest in the content of religious beliefs—questions about that are brushed aside with some irritation. What is in question is belief itself, the faith that Luther defined and Calvin emphasised as the only essential element in one's relation to God" (317). Thus, in addition to this European sensibility, the Protestant quality of both *Je vous salue, Marie* and *Le livre de Marie* help to centre them in the Swiss canton of Vaud which, although almost completely Francophone, is also historically Protestant (and which borders the canton of Geneva, whose capital was the city-state that Calvin himself called home from 1536 to 1564). Freddy Buache argues that "*Prénom Carmen* is very much a French production. But *Je vous salue, Marie* is Swiss" (*Trente ans de cinéma suisse*, 119; m.t.). He was talking about more than money. Indeed, I think I am following the spirit of Buache's analysis when I say that *Prénom Carmen* and *Détective* are Parisian versions of popular forms and that *Je vous salue, Marie* is a Vaudois version of the Marian narrative. In a 1984 essay published in *L'Avant-scène cinéma* (just before the release of *Le livre de Marie* and *Je vous salue, Marie*), Buache argued that the 1980s marked Godard's emergence as "Un cinéaste vaudois" (that is the title of the article), and that in his films of this period, "a lyricism that is nourished by this place, where the calm of the garden reigns, envelops them; this calm has nothing to do with that of the glacial canton of Valais, where, during the construction of the Grand Dixence dam, Godard filmed, in the bustle of the worksite, *Opération béton*" (67; m.t.). Buache seems to be presenting the landscape of Vaud and its effects on Godard's films as being defined by stillness, simplicity, minimalism. However, Vaud is as far from the ornate glaciers of the Alps as it is from the bustle of Swiss industrialism. It is a minimalist place: I agree with Buache that the calm of the garden dominates, and there is skepticism toward earthly works and the ornate and a parallel emphasis on a faith in the revelatory possibilities of the everyday, natural world—what could be more Protestant? As MacCabe suggested, Luther's belief, spelled out in *Christian Liberty*, that "[t]he Word of God cannot be received and cherished by any works whatever but only by faith" (9), is basically the founding principle of Protestantism, and this is clearly visible in both *Je vous salue, Marie* and *Le livre de Marie*.

Godard and Miéville's "Marie project" realizes those Protestant principles in a way that is exceptional because of its explicitly religious quality, but otherwise, it is quite consistent in terms of its ethical and aesthetic commitments. One of the most important aesthetic connections that is emerging here, following on *Sauve qui peut (la vie)*, is that of Romanticism. The connections between Godard's work and German Romanticism is a major preoccupation of Daniel Morgan's 2013 book *Late Godard*, which focuses on work made by Godard alone, especially *Soigne ta droite* (1987), *Nouvelle vague* (1990), *Allemagne 90 neuf zero* (1991), and *Histoire(s) du cinéma* (although he also talks about *Prénom Carmen* and *Je vous salue, Marie*). For Morgan, the connection to Kant's explanations of the sublime is especially important, although he is also at pains to point out that "these films treat nature not as divorced from matters of history and politics but as thoroughly caught up in them, and caught up in a range of different ways" (72). Kathleen K. Rowe writes of Godard's connection to Romanticism that "[i]t's what allows the Swiss Protestant to peek leeringly out from under his more expansive and generous Gallic mask" (52). Writing specifically of *Je vous salue, Marie*, Youssef Ishaghpour writes that "[h]e has none of the 'protestant' asceticism of the Straubs" (295; m.t.). While I am happy to see criticism discussing the influence of Protestantism on Godard and Miéville's work, I disagree strongly with both Rowe's and Ishaghpour's statements. To be honest, I do not entirely understand what Rowe means, or why "Swiss-Protestant" equals "leering." André Dumas's article on Godard and

Protestantism also invokes Swiss culture, but it explains the connection in the opposite way, offering that Godard's work is defined by "irrespect," explaining that "[t]his 'irrespect' is more appealing than annoying, because Godard pays the price by remaining a small independent producer, a little Swiss shopkeeper" (88; m.t.). Dumas goes on say that "[a]s for independence, it consists not of capitalist accumulation, but of sobriety in search of serenity, and, along the way, acts of solidarity" (88; m.t.). That combination of sobriety and solidarity is a very precise summary of Godard and Miéville's work since the 1970s, defined by a combination of luminous images and political engagement as it is. I do think there is something not only Protestant but also very Swiss about this kind of sobriety, this kind of cool aloofness that is one of the positive aspects of a culture so defined by neutrality and isolationism. That sobriety is not finally so far from the kind of severe, ascetic quality of Protestant discourse that has also influenced Straub–Huillet (who are rooted in the religiously mixed region of Alsace). Perhaps what Ishaghpour means is that a shared search for a rigorous sobriety manifests itself in different ways for Godard–Miéville and Straub–Huillet, and I would agree with that.

Alain Bergala is much more provocative but ultimately more precise than any of these critics in his explanation of the Protestant qualities of *Je vous salue, Marie*. His essay "La passion du plan selon Godard" (originally written for *Revue Belge du cinéma* 22–23) suggests that Godard had made, "without knowing it ... a film about maternal incest." But Bergala goes on to write that:

> For his part, Jean-Joseph Goux recalls that in Christianity, the Virgin is, in the celestial bedchamber, the Mother *and* the Wife of Christ at the same time.... The Reformation, for its part, without taking on this radical patchwork, opposed the showiness of Catholic ritual with a purified and intellectualised liturgy, the ornamentation of the biggest Catholic churches with the most sober of cultural spaces, and has shown the greatest suspicion to the cult of the virgin. Godard, because of his Protestant origins, places himself somewhere between the prohibitions against representing the divine [*figurer la divinité*] (and specifically the Virgin) and the Catholic propensity to represent the Virgin (in order to sublimate incest). Godard places himself exactly between these two when he films the Virgin in *Je vous salue, Marie*. (*Nul comme Godard*, 90–91; m.t.)

This really is the key tension in both *Je vous salue Marie* and *Le livre de Marie*: between a desire to beautifully and lyrically represent the divine, and to recognize the ineffability of that divinity by withdrawing from form and adopting an approach that is purified and intellectualized, to paraphrase Bergala's summary of Protestant liturgy. This has thematic as well as formal components.

At the level of subject matter, both *Le livre de Marie* and *Je vous salue, Marie* are trying to present the Marian narrative in quotidian, almost banal terms. Godard's Marie is a teenager in small-town Switzerland, and the defining aspects of her life seem to be working at her father's gas station and playing basketball (in what seems like a fairly serious amateur league). Miéville's Marie is a young girl (she looks about 10 or 11) whose parents are in the process of divorcing. Neither Godard's nor Miéville's Marie is presented in a way that indicates any sense of divinity or that they are anything other than average Vaudoises. When her mother tells Miéville's Marie that she is splitting from her father and that she will only see him on weekends, pouts in just the way a pre-adolescent should, eventually standing on her head in defiance. Godard's film has an important scene where Marie and Joseph argue about why she will not allow him any intimacy; Joseph gets loudly frustrated, but Marie remains calm, insisting on the importance of silence, worrying that she will end up harming him, but finally calling him to account in harsh tones: "It's not your body; what disgusts me's that you don't believe." But in other places in both films, Marie can be seen as being possessed of a startling calm, a serenity that rises above the emotional turmoil of the every day. An early sequence in Miéville's film begins with the parents bickering at the dinner table; Marie interrupts this by cutting open an apple and putting an almond in the middle, imitating a school lesson about how the pupil floats in the middle of the eye. A very simple scene toward the end of *Je vous salue, Marie* takes place shortly after Marie gives birth. Joseph and the innkeeper's wife mill around the car, while the innkeeper helps Marie into the car with the baby. He asks if the baby will call Joseph dad, and Marie demurs, finally offering "*c'est la vie*" to his queries about the complex paternity at work here. Godard then cuts to a medium close-up of the baby on Marie's lap, as he tries, with limited success, to get his fist into his mouth. What joins all of these sequences is their sense that the Marian narrative is understandable in the terms not simply of the earthly and every day, but via very banal imagery. None of this imagery is about a Divine Mother providing an impossible ideal of womanly perfection; rather, it is all about showing Marie as the embodiment of a simple and very easily recognizable perseverance that confronts the pettiness of earthly relationships head-on. Sometimes this is foolish, such as when Miéville's adolescent Marie is standing on her head. Sometimes it has very serious theological imperatives, such as when Godard's young Marie admonishes Joseph in very specifically Protestant terms, reminding him, essentially, that it is by faith alone that he can do right.

In both films, the most startling images of "*Marie quotidienne*" come when she is made vulnerable before the camera, before the viewer. For Miéville, this is during a scene when Marie takes a bath with her mother. She playfully licks her like a cat, to her mother's delight, but then Marie hugs her mother and asks her to tell her about when she was little. Her mother is reluctant, saying that she always wants to hear stories about when she was little and lamenting, sadly, that it is difficult to recover the power, the force of that kind of love. Her mother gets out of the tub, and Miéville cuts to a shot of Marie in the corner of the tub (and of the frame as well), alone and looking sad. *Je vous salue, Marie,* concludes with a similar sequence that presents Marie as a worried, preoccupied mother. After a shot where a ten-year-old Christ stubbornly runs off into the woods, claiming he has to tend to his father's affairs (Joseph chases after him angrily), Godard shifts to a sequence where the angel Gabriel gets into Marie's car and yells, "*Je vous salue, Marie.*" Then, the scene shifts again to a series of close-ups of Marie in the car. In one fairly long take, she lights a cigarette, pulls her head back in a gesture of gentle exhaustion, and then takes out and applies some lipstick. Godard cuts to a few closer shots of her putting the lipstick on, and the last shot of the film is an extreme close-up of her red lips. These quiet, closely framed images in the car are in utter contradiction to what is on the soundtrack: choral music by Bach and a voice-over of Marie saying, "I am of the Virgin, and I didn't want this being. I left my mark on the soul of the one who helped me. That's all." The sequence is a remarkable combination of the banal and the divine, coupling acknowledgement of Marie's special status ("*Moi, je suis de la Vierge,*" the Bach music) with everyday indulgences (sneaking a cigarette in the car during a trying day). And like the tub sequence in *Le livre de Marie*, it is a quietly sad scene about loss and exhaustion. As she sees her parents divorce, Miéville's Marie is moving out of the blissful incomprehension of childhood and toward a genuinely earthly life that is open to both the pain and joy of family life. Peter Harcourt writes of this conclusion that "I am not sure how to interpret these final moments. It would appear, however, that, the divine task performed, both characters have been returned to carnality, to their physical life in the social world" ("Metaphysical Cinema," 6). A return to the social, and perhaps more importantly, the intimate (and all of the pain that this entails), is an important part of what Godard is evoking in this final sequence. That is a theme that runs throughout *Le livre de Marie*, as our young protagonist moves through the world and slowly comes to a deeper understanding, which is especially visible in a sequence on a train where she has a gently awkward encounter with a very rambly older man from their town. A central tenant of Christianity is, after all, that the fully human and fully divine Christ experienced this sort of earthly loss as he cried out, "My God, my God, why hast thou forsaken me?" (Matt. 27:46). These characters experience the same realization as their loved ones drift away, their world views expand, and their experiences are no less divine or transcendent because of this experience of loss or the banal moments of quiet enlightenment that they wander into.

This tension between the divine and the earthly is played out on the level of form as well. Placed next to each other, *Je vous salue, Marie* and *Le livre de Marie* constitute a kind of discussion about the ways to film the ineffable. About an hour into *Je vous salue, Marie*, Marie tosses and turns in her bed uncontrollably, seemingly in some kind of pain; this is crosscut with images of the wind blowing through the grass, followed by a montage of landscape imagery, including a shot of Lac Léman. Marie's voice is on soundtrack throughout, holding forth, sometimes quite profanely, on the relationship between her body, eternity, and the nature of a God who benefits from her suffering. In one of her interior monologues, Marie compares Him to a vampire: "God is a vampire who suffered me in him ... because I suffered and He didn't, and He profited from my pain" (Locke and Warren, 177). The last shots of the sequence are of Marie, naked in bed. The camera is at her feet in one shot, and the next is a close-up of her stomach as she breathes in and out. The final shot is a very long take of Marie in bed, blankets up to her chin, looking worried. The imagery and the text are strongly profane in both senses of the word. Marie sometimes speaks with a kind of absurd vulgarity: "*—on n'a pas besoin d'un trou de bouche pour manger, et d'un trou de cul pour avaler l'infini, il faut prendre le cul dans sa tête, puis avec le cul dans la tête, descendre au niveau du cul, et s'en aller, à gauche, oui à droite, pour monter plus loin*" (ibid., 224). The subtitles render this as "[y]ou don't need a mouthhole to eat with, and an asshole to swallow infinity. Your ass must go in your head, and so descend to ass level, then go left, or right to rise higher" (ibid., 176). But Godard also shows us, with steady editing and more-or-less static compositions, that Marie is possessed by a kind of pain and anxiety that is completely earthly and non-divine. Furthermore, this sequence repeats imagery from sequences earlier in the film that showed Marie writhing around in bed. The aesthetic of the film is, then, one based on reiteration, but not to the exclusion of narrative. The comparably central sequence in Miéville's film uses a static camera and cuts between medium or medium-long shots to a very similar effect. When Miéville's Marie listens to Mahler with her father, the sequence is made up of two very similar medium shots. A bit later in the film, when she dances by herself to Mahler, the aesthetic feels comparably still, even though Miéville cuts to different set-ups. She begins the sequence in the living room and then cuts to Marie dancing on a balcony overlooking Lac Léman, both shots with no camera movement, only to return to a series of closer, shorter shots in the living room where there is occasional, slight camera movement. There is a kind of blankness to the editing of this sequence. Marie dances frenetically, but the camera barely moves, and the editing passes from very long takes of Marie (one of which is against the stunning background of the lake) to a series of closer shots without anything more moderate in between them. As in Godard's sequence with Marie in bed, there is something about the stillness, about the steady but not disruptively artificial editing, and about the hints of repetition that gives the images a meditative rather than illusionist quality. This suggests that these images are trying to evoke something that cannot be represented and can only be suggested by an encouragement to discernment.

What I am evoking here is very close to Paul Schrader's sense of a "transcendental style," a formal pattern he saw as being very strongly present in the films of Robert Bresson. "Both Ozu and Bresson are formalists in the traditional religious manner," he wrote in his 1972 book *Transcendental Style in Film: Ozu, Bresson, Dreyer*. "They use form as the primary method of inducing belief" (61). Bresson is without question important for understanding both Godard and Miéville, especially this "Marie project." Bresson's book *Notes sur le cinématographe* seems to practically anticipate *Je vous salue, Marie*, especially in one of the later notes, where he describes the kind of modernism that we are seeing chez Godard and Miéville, especially in these "middle period" films:

> Proust says that Dostoyevsky is original in composition above all. It is an extraordinarily complex and close-meshed whole, purely inward, with currents and counter-currents like those of the seam a thing that is found also in Proust (in other ways so different) and whose equivalent would go well with a film. (*Notes sur le cinématographe*, 123 / *Notes on Cinematography*, 63)

Godard and Miéville are, in some ways, offering this kind of equivalent. Theirs is not a strategy that breaks radically from convention, just as neither Dostoyevsky nor Proust do. Instead, it gives us incredibly highly composed images that are joined together by an editing pattern that establishes a "closely meshed whole." It is this strategy, which accommodates meditation as well as narrative realism, that is significantly Bressonian. This is the style of Bresson films like *Un condamné à mort s'est échappé* (1956) or *Pickpocket* (1959). Both of these balance narratives with frequent shifts into rigorous, repetitive sequences, which are "original in composition above all," and thus stand, temporarily, outside the film's overall storyline and plunge the viewer into a more meditative state.

While Bresson and his poetics seem to me inarguably key to *Je vous salue, Marie*, the critiques of Schrader's position by Jonathan Rosenbaum and Kent Jones (both written for James Quandt's path-breaking 1998 anthology *Robert Bresson*) point to the real connection. Rosenbaum writes that "[d]espite Bresson's alleged and at times avowed Jansenism ... it seems to me that what his best films are doing has more to do with materialism than with the 'transcendental' qualities most critics have written about" ("The Last Filmmaker," 21). Jones echoes this by lamenting how in most writing on his films, "Bresson, associate of Cocteau and Kossowski and admirer of Godard, is defined as a Jansenist, an ascetic, an austere transcendentalist, or, worst of all, a Bressonian, rather than as one of the greatest of all Modernists. Meanwhile, if the severe pronouncements of avant-garde filmmakers like [Michael] Snow or [Hollis] Frampton are taken at face value, their work forms a counter-tradition that represents the true cinematic Modernism, in which narrative can have no part" (394). Of course, narrative of a sort is present in films by both Snow and Frampton (*Wavelength* is the story of a journey across a space; *Nostalgia* is the story of a journey through memory), but I do take Jones's point here. I think what he means is not narrative broadly defined but realist/illusionist, fictional narrative, which is basically the spine of conventional commercial cinema. What makes Bresson a materialist and a Modernist is fully present throughout the work of Godard and Miéville, and certainly in this "Marie project." Long takes that lead the viewer away from realist illusionism, but only do so intermittently; a narrative that is artificial and underdeveloped but still present and still carries a fair bit of the film's meaning; a relationship to the image that, through seemingly mimetic cinematic narrative or long takes, makes the viewer constantly aware of the push and pull between the material presence and physicality of what is on screen and the unrepresentable absence of its spiritual or ideological components: these are the defining aspects of Godard and Mieville's work together (especially in the 1980s, and especially in *Je vous salue, Marie*). They are also the defining aspects of an important strain of European filmmaking, one that is, following Rosenbaum, led most clearly by materialist concerns.

Laura Mulvey writes about the materialist aspect of *Je vous salue, Marie*'s importance, and what she has to say could very easily apply to *Le livre de Marie* as well: "In *Je vous salue, Marie*, Godard finds an apparently paradoxical means of restoring spirituality to realism, the unnatural nature of the virgin birth, but one that is also in keeping with the spiritual tradition of cinematic realism that links Dreyer, Rossellini, and Bresson to aspects of Godard and moments in Straub/Huillet" ("Marie/Eve," 40). What Mulvey is describing here is, really, a tradition of European cinematic Modernism, one that speaks in a kind of ciné-prose and exists alongside its more poetic variant in North America (where Michael Snow, Hollis Frampton, and Stan Brakhage are key figures). This is similar to the tension between Peter Wollen's "two avant-gardes," which I discussed in Chapter 1. *Je vous salue, Marie* and *Le livre de Marie* are the ultimate example of those two bicycles that Godard used to describe his experience working with Miéville; they are separate, but they are the same kind of machines, and they are headed down the same road. It is something of a back road, but it is one that has been taken by some of Europe's most important filmmakers. As we can see in these films of the "Marie project," it is one that goes by some of European culture's most breathtaking and evocative scenery.

The fact that I can describe these films in such informal terms attests to the way that Godard and Miéville were thinking about filmmaking at this stage in their career, in addition to explaining why they took an interest in the Marian narrative. Godard and Miéville had more or less left the essayistic form behind following their video and television work of the 1970s, but it is clear that the informality and intellectual openness of that kind of filmmaking continued to be attractive. In the *Nouvel Observateur* article that was covering the release of *Prénom Carmen*, Godard told Jacques Drillon that:

> What I'd like is for the people at IBM—I could tell them: "Look, I've got a book by Françoise Dolto on religion and psychoanalysis, I've got two characters, Joseph and Mary, I've got three Bach cantatas, a book by Heidegger. Make me a program which will arrange all that for me." But they can't, and so I've got to do it myself, and I don't want to spend twenty years on it! (54)[4]

Godard has famously quipped that "all you need for a movie is a gun and a girl," and that is a less frivolous view of filmmaking than it may at first seem. All he and Miéville needed for a movie in 1983 was a few cantatas and a feminist-theologian student of Jacques Lacan (the book by Heidegger they would save for their next work together). Indeed, all you really need is the introduction to that Lacanian's book. Richard Brody cites an interview that Godard gave in February 1983 to the magazine *Révolution* to the effect that he only really read the introduction. Sandra Laugier writes that "[t]he initial chapters in Dolto's book correspond exactly to the film's script. An early version or rough draft of the script, reproduced in the book *Godard par Godard*, includes passages that are exact quotations from *L'évangile au risque de la psychanalyse*" (29). That may be the case, but it is worth noting that the passages from *L'évangile au risque de la psychanalyse* that are quoted (by italicization) in the skeletal "*scénario*" that Godard wrote for *Je vous salue, Marie* are all found either in *L'évangile*'s introduction or within three pages of its first chapter, "La 'Sainte Famille,'" and that one of them is misquoted slightly (see *Godard par Godard* t.1., 590–92).

But despite my sense that Godard was only dipping in and out of her book, it is clear that one way to understand *Je vous salue, Marie* and *Le livre de Marie* is to see them as parallel attempts to explore the work of Françoise Dolto via the cinema. For Laugier, this is paramount; she writes that "[t]he desire to find the truth in Mary's story surely came to Godard from reading Françoise Dolto's 1977 book *L'évangile au risque de la psychanalyse*. Godard's continuous references to Dolto's book and work in *Hail Mary* have received very little critical attention despite the fact that they are obvious if not explicit." (29). Colin MacCabe writes in similar terms, saying of *Je vous salue, Marie* that "Godard's reliance on Dolto is very considerable, and her words punctuate Godard's own explanation of the film: 'This extraordinary couple help us to discover the depth of feelings in a meeting between an ordinary man and an ordinary woman'" (*Portrait of the Artist*, 290). The carnality of Mary and Joseph's relationship in *Je vous salue, Marie*, the way in which they are shown to have sexual desires, is a good example of Godard's desire to draw on Dolto's insistence on reading the gospel stories in terms of "*le couple*." Indeed, the close connection between later parts of the book and *Hail Mary*'s delicate balance of family life and theological meditation makes you wonder if Godard did not really read more of it than he was letting on to *Révolution*. Discussing the Gospel of Luke 1:26–38, Dolto told Séverin that "I see nothing basically objectionable in the fact that Jesus, as a man, was conceived as a result of the carnal union of Mary and Joseph! In point of fact, this carnal union is not what is responsible for making the fate of Jesus as a man the total incarnation of God" (*Jesus of Psychoanalysis*, 26 / *L'Évangile au risque*, 22–23). This is to say nothing of Miéville, who gives the impression of being generally less distracted and more willing to dig deeply into texts and ideas. I certainly get the impression that she read *L'Évangile au risque de la psychanalyse* all the way through. In a later chapter, Dolto and Séverin discuss the Gospel of Saint Mark 5:21–43, which begins with Christ healing a woman who had hemorrhaged for 12 years and ends with Him taking a dead twelve-year-old girl by the hand and telling her to get up. It is impossible not to think of *Le livre de Marie* and its narrative of a divorcing mother and a young girl slowly moving beyond the pangs of preadolescence into a fuller understanding of the world when Dolto tells Séverin that "[t]hey are both bound to their childhood bodies by a love tie that has not been broken. Christ breaks this tie and makes them autonomous. Having been freed—the little girl from being overvalued, the woman from being scorned—they blossom—capable at last, after twelve years, the one of walking alone, the other of living as a woman" (*Jesus of Psychoanalysis* 119 / *L'Évangile au risque* 116). This does give a different sense of the title than the one I began with when I first engaged with this film. It is only instinctive to assume that a little girl named Marie in a film released with *Je vous salue, Marie* must somehow represent the mother of God. But a hypothetical Biblical "Book of Mary" (which Miéville is *not* presenting as a Gospel according to Mary) could very well hold stories like the one in this short film. It is a story of awakening and healing told from a Marian perspective, a story of a couple with a complicated life together and a little girl moved by spiritual experiences to more fully enter into the world around her. Dolto is a committed Lacanian for sure, but she is often speaking in terms that offer a similarly Marian view of the Gospels, a view that seeks to restore the importance of the troubled, human, but immaculate figure who carried and nurtured and then had to learn to live without the Son.

This is all to say that Dolto's work was important at this stage of French intellectual history because of the way that it took a Lacanian approach to psychoanalysis beyond insular and ultimately circular debates about the development of consciousness and toward concerns that were both more immediate (family life) and more genuinely transcendent (the meaning of the Gospels). It thus offered a way for Godard and Miéville to genuinely move forward with their engagement with the icon of the family. In *Ici et ailleurs*, this engagement was sharply political and materialist—it was basically all about television and the Palestinians. In *Numéro deux*, the engagement with the family was sharply psychoanalytic—basically, it was all about bodies, sounds and screens. Dolto gave Godard and Miéville the tools to move to the next level of analysis, one that integrated the earlier two. *Je vous salue, Marie* and *Le livre de Marie* are about the material *and* about the bodily, but the two films also seek to engage what lies beyond both, the mystery of which lies in the fact that we cannot understand that "what lies beyond" except through our bodies that exist in a material world. That is the topic of *L'Évangile au risque de la psychanalyse*.

SOFT AND HARD

Raising money to finish *Je vous salue, Marie* was, as usual for Godard and Miéville, a difficult and complex process. As with *Sauve qui peut (la vie)*, part of the fundraising included the production of a short video, this time a twenty-minute piece called *Petites notes à propos du film Je vous salue, Marie*, which Godard produced in 1983. It shares a lot with *Scénario vidéo de Sauve qui peut (la vie)* in that it includes both outtakes and excerpts from the film itself, usually with Godard's voice commenting on them, along with images of him working in his studio. It is a bit more explicitly engaged with financial matters than *Sauve qui peut (la vie)*'s "video scenario," though. Toward the end of the video, there is a shot of Godard at his desk directly addressing the camera, saying, "we're asking you to participate, to produce with us," and that he is asking for no more and no less than they need: 300,000 Swiss francs. Bits and pieces of Godard and Miéville's next work together, *Soft and Hard*, hover over this little work, although that is not immediately apparent. *Petites notes à propos du film Je vous salue, Marie* is a video, as *Soft and Hard* would be. It has images of Miéville sitting around, talking, and such imagery accounts for no small part of *Soft and Hard*. *Petites notes à propos du film Je vous salue, Marie* has a shot of Myriem Roussel ironing, and a sequence where Miéville is ironing is key in *Soft and Hard*. And as Colin MacCabe recalls, "Godard's commitment to *Je vous salue, Marie* and his efforts to raise money reached as far as England" (*Portrait of the Artist*, 291), presumably via the circulation of these *Petites notes à propos du film Je vous salue, Marie*. MacCabe recalls agreeing to commission Godard and Miéville to make a film about Britain for the UK's Channel 4, ostensibly by way of supporting *Je vous salue, Marie*. What MacCabe describes sounds a lot like Godard's experience with Tom Luddy and Zoetrope Studios: "when Godard had received the money and finished *Je vous salue, Marie*, there followed a long period of procrastination, which resulted in Godard and Miéville making a documentary which reflected on their own lives in Rolle," and was not about Britain at all (*Portrait of the Artist*, 292).

All of this would seem to indicate the degree to which *Soft and Hard* could seem like a bit of an afterthought, a piece made on commission without a lot of commitment, done to raise money for a more important film and cobbled together from bits and pieces from that film's fundraising video. But that was simply not the case. Instead, *Soft and Hard* is among the most interesting works of this "Realization" period, a tentative but engaged essay on the possibilities of working and living together, and the connection of this kind of relationship to marginal places and landscapes. Godard and Miéville's films that follow this are of a distinctly different sort: they are mostly short films, ones that almost fully abandon narrative or realism in favour of more fragmented, and sometimes (although not always) more alienated strategies. These later shorts, while each accomplished and ambitious in their own ways, are nowhere near as ambitious, engaged and fully formed as masterpieces like *Sauve qui peut (la vie)*, or the "Marie project," or *Soft and Hard*. This is the last work that Godard and Miéville made as artists at the top of their craft—the last focused, fully realized, and optimistic work that they would make together.

The film opens with Godard and Miéville saying that "[w]e were still looking for the way to our language," and this sets the tone for the work that follows, however cryptically. Part of this tone setting occurs at the level of form; the sound/image/text relationship even in these first moments is layered and challenging. The screen is black with text in English in all caps: "Soft and Hard"/"Talk Between Two Friends"/"Hard and Soft"/"Two Friends," and so on. "Hard subject" comes on screen when Godard proclaims, "*l'époque du triomphe des télévisions privées*" ("the age of triumph for private televisions"). Godard starts his monologue over this text, and then we hear the same text, from the beginning and now in Miéville's voice, laid over Godard's as he continues to read. The piece has many instances of comparably layered and minimalist sound-image-text combinations. This opening sequence is also about setting the agenda in terms of a philosophical outlook as well as an overall structure. The first words on the soundtrack are clearly referring to Martin Heidegger's 1959 collection *Unterwegs zur Sprache*, which was translated into French in 1969 as *Acheminement vers la parole*. Two years before that translation, though, *Cahiers du cinéma* (in number 186) published Patrick Lévy's translation of an essay from that book, "Aus einem Gespräch von der Sprache" ("A Dialogue on Language"). That essay takes the form of a dialogue between "a Japanese" and "an Inquirer," wanders widely over aesthetics and philosophy (including Heidegger's own work), and deals a bit with cinema (specifically Kurosawa's 1950 film, *Rashomon*). The essay is clearly a major influence on *Soft and Hard*. Godard and Miéville are following both Heidegger's use of the philosophical dialogue and his desire to ruminate, however inconclusively, on the intersection between language, aesthetics, and knowledge.

The bulk of *Soft and Hard* is made up of a single twenty-seven-minute shot (interrupted by cutaways to television footage: sometimes adverts, sometimes bits of news) of Godard and Miéville sitting on the sofa, talking to each other, in a dialogue that is much like that of "Aus Einem Gespräch von der Sprache." Like Heidegger and his imaginary Japanese interlocutor, Godard and Miéville are talking about talking, with occasional reference to cinema, talking about the ways that communications (between two people, via the television, and everything in between) succeeds or fails. It is that failure of communication, or more precisely a lack of explicitness, that Lévy feels is the relevant connection between this Heidegger text and Godard's cinema. He writes in his translator's introduction: "Finally, the question is maybe this: can you conceive of a cinema that escapes objectification? ... Godard, when directing his actors, transforms them into objects in order to film in them that which escapes this objectification" (45; m.t.). Given that Lévy is writing in 1967, I am not quite sure which Godard film he has in mind here. Were he writing twenty years later, he could very easily be writing about images of sexuality in *Sauve qui peut (la vie)* or images of the divine in *Je vous salue, Marie*. He could also be writing about sequences in *Soft and Hard* such as where, toward the beginning of their dialogue, Godard and Miéville have the following exchange:

> G: That's probably the difference between you and me, regarding the image. What I really like in it is its inaccessibility, which is what bothers you…. Does one have to show things? You say I don't like TV because it doesn't show things, whereas you probably like it for the very same reasons….
>
> M: That's not it. Television never shows things, yet it makes you think that it never stops showing them, and this is what showing things is, and that there's no other way to show them. (Godard and Miéville, "*Soft and Hard*," 163–64 / Translation from the BFI's subtitles)

This exchange has strong echoes in Heidegger's imaginary Japanese friend's sense of the significance of gesture in Japanese Noh drama, and in *Rashomon* as well. Midway though their dialogue, "J" illustrates the gestural language of Japanese performance by holding up his hand. He and "The Inquirer" then have the following exchange:

> I: If we were to succeed in thinking of gesture in this sense, where would you then look for the essence of that gesture which you showed me?
>
> J: In a beholding that is itself invisible, and that, so gathered, bears itself to encounter emptiness in such a way that in and through it the mountains appear. (*Unterwegs zur Sprache*, 108 / *On the Way to Language*, 19)

The concern here with the unseen and its connection to visual arts (performance, cinema) is central to the fragment of the Heidegger dialogue that appeared in the *Cahiers du cinéma* (and it is a very small part of a fairly huge text). So I rush to make a similar point to the one that I made earlier about Robert Bresson. Both Jonathan Rosenbaum and Kent Jones have recently argued that Bresson's formal eccentricity is best understood not as a religious manifestation, but as a Modernist one (and thus goes some way toward explaining the representational strategies of *Je vous salue, Marie*). Here, however, the formal eccentricities of Japanese art that seem to fascinate Heidegger so much—especially this emphasis on gesture over mimesis and in the dialectic between what signs make invisible and the mountains that those same signs can summon—seem less connected to a sustained tradition of Japanese cultural production than they are to important elements of Modernism (and thus go some way toward explaining the concerns of *Soft and Hard*). During this part of her exchange with Godard, Miéville offers the example of "the image of an egg, apparently still but within which all sorts of things happen invisibly"

(Godard and Miéville, "*Soft and Hard*," 164 / BFI subtitles). This sort of invisibility, this interest in instances where representation fails, is entirely consistent with the concerns of late Modernism also quite consistent with the concerns of this Heidegger fragment.

This engagement with Modernism is signalled by the sequence that directly precedes the beginning of this dialogue, where Godard and Miéville ramble over the lakeside landscape and read from Hermann Broch's 1945 novel, *Der Tod des Vergil*. Broch was a German novelist important both for the development of European Modernism generally and to Godard specifically. Richard Brody seems to conflate Romanticism and Modernism when he writes that "[f]rom his father, Godard acquired a taste for German Romanticism, and as an adolescent, read works by Hermann Broch, Thomas Mann and Robert Musil" (6).[5] But these authors are (much like Stan Brakhage) Modernists of a distinctly Romantic stripe, and that is not a bad way of understanding Godard and Miéville as well. This is, more or less, Kathleen K. Rowe's argument about Godard's work of this period. She writes that "seeing Godard as a twentieth-century heir to the Romantic movement helps explain not only his ambivalence toward women, but also his retreat from politics, his representation of himself as an anti-hero of sorts, and the stance of ironic detachment evident in most of his work" (51). This sense of retreat from politics is, for both Godard and the Romantics, largely illusory. Retreat is clearly important for both the Rolle dwellers and those most famous lovers of the German mountains. Both are retreating as part of a project of radical transformation via an engagement with peripheral spaces, a project that is not synonymous with political transformation but is certainly not opposed to it. The sequence where *Der Tod des Vergil* is invoked is a good summary of Godard and Miéville Modernist-Romantic duality as it seeks to integrate visual images of peripheral landscape with a poetic text that is about that most Modernist of preoccupations: the inadequacies of art.

Following a shot where Miéville walks along the shore of Lac Léman, we cut to a shot of Godard and Miéville in their car, pulled over alongside a county road. Godard, who has a book in his hand, says "art's despair, that's what I was telling you about" (Godard and Miéville, "Soft and Hard," 162 / BFI subtitles). He then starts to read from *La Mort de Virgile*, Albert Kohn's translation of Broch's *Der Tod des Vergil*, which first appeared in 1952. Miéville wanders off, and we then fade in and out of shots of the camera panning across clouds (a shot that opens *Sauve qui peut [la vie]*), shots of the grass, and shots of the forest. Miéville's voice then comes on the soundtrack to continue the reading, and we have shots of her by the lake, the text "Death and Life," a shot of just the lake, the text "Soft and Hard," a shot of a small river, the text "Two Friends," and then a cut to the beginning of the aforementioned twenty-seven-minute shot of their dialogue on the sofa. Both Godard and Miéville read from a part of *Der Tod des Vergil* that shifts from incredibly dense prose into poetry (an important characteristic of the book) over the images of clouds, grass, and forest. The passage includes the following bit from Broch's book:

ihre Verzweiflung, ihr verzweifelter Versuch,
    aus vergänglichem Sein das Unvergängliche zu schaffen,
 	
    aus Worten, aus Tönen, aus Steinen, aus Farben,
    auf daß der gestalte Raum die Zeiten überdauere....
 	
und es enthüllt sich dem Menschen die Schönheit als Grausamkeit,
    als die wachsende Grausamkeit des ungezügelten Spiels, das
        im Sinnbild Unendlichkeitsgenuß verspricht,
 	
        erkenntnisverachtenden, genießerischen Genuß
            idischer Schein-Unendlichkeit
            und darob unbedenklich Leid und Tod zuzufügen vermag,
            da es im grenzentrückten Gebiet der Schönheit geschieht,
        nur dem Blick noch erreichbar, nur der Zeit noch erreichbar,
        aber nicht mehr der Menschlichkeit und der menschlichen Pflicht....
(*Der Tod des Vergil*, 116–17)
	... art's despair, its despairing attempt
	    to build up the imperishable from things that perish
	        from words, from sounds, from stones, from colors,
	        so that space, being formed, might outlast time....
	
	and thus beauty revealed itself to man as cruelty,
	        as the growing cruelty of the unbridled game
	            which promised the pleasure of infinity though the symbol,
	            the voluptuous, knowledge-disdaining pleasure
	                of an earthly sham-infinity,
	            hence thoughtlessly able to inflict sorrow and death,
	            as happened in the realm of beauty at the remote periphery,
	            accessible only to the glance, only to time,
	        but no longer available for humanity and the human task....
	(*The Death of Virgil*, 122–23)

When Godard reads it over images of the Vaudois landscape, it becomes:

> ... le désespoir de l'art est son essai désespéré de créer l'impérissable avec des choses périssables. Avec des mots, des sons, des pierres, des couleurs afin que l'espace mis en forme dure au-delà des âges.... À l'homme donc, la beauté se dévoile comme de la cruauté. La cruauté grandissante du jeu non réfréné qui promet dans le symbole une jouissance de fictive infinité terrestre qui peut sans hésiter infliger souffrance et mort puisque cela se passe dans le royaume de la beauté. *A la périphérie, à la périphérie lointaine, à la périphérie lointaine exclusivement accessible au regard exclusivement accessible au regard*, et par lui, accessible à la durée terrestre mais inaccessible à l'humanité, aux devoirs humains. (Godard and Miéville, "Soft and Hard," 164; emphasis mine)

As you can see here, it is Godard who emphasizes the passages about the "the realm of beauty at the remote periphery / accessible only to the glance," which is mentioned only once in the original text. So while this is a passage that is deeply pessimistic about the powers of art to create lasting, significant objects, to "build up the imperishable from things that perish," it nevertheless has vivid imagery that resonates strongly with Godard and Miéville's desire to transform their realm of beauty, the cinema, by immersing themselves fully in the remote periphery of Rolle, Switzerland. *Soft and Hard*'s formal strategy is comparable in some ways to that of *Der Tod des Vergil* inasmuch as both shift their modes of address without much warning: Godard and Miéville move from lyrical montages to long dialogues rendered in a single, twenty-seven-minute, fixed-position shot, and Broch moves between a prose style defined by incredibly long sentences that form incredibly long paragraphs and poetic digressions that are dense with vivid imagery.

But speaking, speaking *with* someone, and the difference between speaking and saying are the major concerns of Heidegger's *Unterwegs zur Sprache*, especially of its centrepiece essay "Der Weg zur Sprache." That essay, to my mind, has just as much influence on *Soft and Hard* as the fragment of "Aus einem Gespräch von der Sprache," which was translated in *Cahiers du cinéma*. In "Der Weg zur Sprache," Heidegger goes to great lengths to distinguish between "to speak to one another" and "to speak with one another," and this is the key dialectic in *Soft and Hard*. Heidegger writes that:

> To speak *to* one another means: to say something, show something to one another, and to entrust one another mutually to what is shown. To speak *with* one another means: to tell of something jointly, to show to one another what that which is claimed in the speaking says in the speaking, and what it, of itself, brings to light. (*Unterwegs zur Sprache*, 253 / *On the Way to Language*, 122)

The whole video, really, is an attempt to reconcile the gap here, to engage in a kind of communication where two people are speaking *to* and speaking *with* each other. Furthermore, this engagement with the philosophical resonances of language is a clear echo of their interest in Françoise Dolto, who writes that "[i]t is through language, in the widest meaning of the term—that is, every mode of meaningful expression—mimicry, gestures, tones of voice—that the child opens himself to its being as a human creature and makes its masculine or feminine desire specific" (*Jesus of Psychoanalysis*, 73 / *L'évangile au risque*, 69–70). Godard and Miéville clearly see language as utterly central to their shared task and struggle to tell of things jointly, to make their masculine or feminine desire specific as they explain the way that they approach representation, cinema, and the landscape that is all around them. But they also want to entrust each other with the different things that they show: their different backgrounds as filmmakers. Miéville recalls during the sofa dialogue that she started as a filmmaker by projecting her family's photos on the wall of her darkened bedroom, while Godard recalls that, for him, it was all about Henri Langlois and the Cinémathèque française of the 1950s, or their different ways of inhabiting their shared domestic space (a *plan-séquence* early in the piece has Godard playfully swinging a tennis racket while Miéville irons). Summarizing this essay, in italics no less, Heidegger writes in that same essay that "*Das Wesende der Sprache ist die Sage als die Zeige*" (254) / "*The essential being of language is Saying as Showing*" (123). A desire to *both* say and show, to communicate *both* in poetry and prose, *both* in photographic realism and high artifice: that is the project that Godard and Miéville have spent a career nurturing. *Soft and Hard* is a vision of what that sort of project could look like once it is fully freed from the conventions of narrative cinema. It is thus somewhat different from Serge Daney's sense of Godard as an innovator who loves the rules. But it serves as a kind of pure experiment, like something a pair of scientists might attempt if they were told to poke around in their lab together, to let their curiosity run wild. "Some of their assertions, such as those about projection / subject / subjugation, may not be substantial or sustainable in any kind of traditional theoretical or academic context," writes Rod Stoneman, who took over from MacCabe as Channel 4's commissioning editor for *Soft and Hard*. "But they do offer a brilliant and exemplary mode of thought, developing film as 'a form that thinks,' as Godard puts it in chapter 3A of *Histoire(s) du cinéma*" (33). *Soft and Hard* is thus the mirror image of *Prénom Carmen* or *Faire la fête*: works that reveals the highest and most fully realized aspirations of their work together when everything else has been stripped away.

Chapter 5
RECONSIDERATION

MIÉVILLE'S *APRÈS LA RÉCONCILIATION*

I call this discussion of the last part of Godard and Miéville's career "Reconsideration" because it seems haunted by uncertainty, by a vague sense that this project that they had shared for two decades—the 1970s and 1980s—was coming to an end. Part of this uncertainty is driven by extratextual concerns, specifically Miéville's growing interest in her own feature filmmaking and Godard's growing pessimism, in evidence both in his feature films (especially 1996's *For Ever Mozart* or 2001's *Éloge de l'amour*) and his massive *Histoire(s) du cinéma* project (1988–2004).

Of these feature films that Miéville began making after 1985's *Soft and Hard*, the one that most closely corresponds to the work that she and Godard had been doing together across three decades is *Après la réconciliation* (2000). The opening images of the film are domestic scenes shot on video, strongly recalling material from *France/tour/détour/deux/enfants* (1979). That many of these images switch back and forth from regular speed to the video-led slow motion (discussed in Chapter 4) also brings this tale of men and women failing to connect with one another very close to *Sauve qui peut (la vie)* (1979). Catherine Grant describes the opening as "a home-movie styled scénario-vidéo that acts as a teaser for the film that will follow" (115). The middle-aged couple at the centre of the film, played by Godard and Miéville themselves, have a troubled but strangely resilient relationship that is very similar to that of the middle-aged couple in *Détective*. The film also strongly recalls *Soft and Hard*. The bulk of *Après la réconciliation* is made up of a long sequence in a very nice house where Godard, Miéville, and a thirtyish woman named Cathos (Claude Perron) engage in long, philosophically inflected dialogues and strike the occasional ridiculous pose in long shot. Here, *Soft and Hard*'s tennis-playing

Godard is replaced by Claude Perron's spread-eagle dance moves. This is even preceded by an outdoor sequence where Miéville and Perron walk through the woods and talk about Heideggerian issues such as speech as object, recalling the sequence where Godard and Miéville read from Hermann Broch with the environs of Lac Léman as a backdrop. During a tracking shot that follows the couple as they walk, Miéville says, "We have placed ourselves upon the word, setting ourselves above it, instead of listening from it … (Miéville, *Après la réconciliation* 26/*Après* subtitles). This echoes a lot of what Heidegger has to say about understanding language *as* language, a concept that joins most of the essays contained in *Unterwegs zur Sprache*/*On the Way to Language*, a text that, as we saw in Chapter 4, is key to the concerns of *Soft and Hard*. *Après la réconciliation*'s credits end with a list of "*Auteurs cités*" that includes "M. Heidegger."

The way that Miéville mixes the concerns of the narrative and non-narrative films that she did with Godard, and does so in, more or less, the format of a narrative film, indicates the degree to which it is *she* (and not really Godard) who is the heir to the experiments that they had been conducting over the past decades. In his film *JLG/JLG: Autoportrait de décembre* (1995), Godard returned to concerns such as landscape and European philosophy, specifically to Heidegger. This film is a small masterpiece in its own way (its images both of domestic interiors and the landscape of Lac Léman are as subtle and beautiful as anything in his oeuvre), but it is insular to the point of being a semi-monastic meditation unlike any of the work that he did with Miéville. The other films that he has made on his own are, in the case of his essay films, comparably monastic. This is especially true of his *Histoire[s] du cinéma* series, which, as I explain shortly, I do not see as the masterpiece that so many have hailed it. His feature films, however, are possessed of a politics that is engaged and complex, but is quite divorced from the concerns of the 1970s and 1980s. *For Ever Mozart* (1996) is an alternately lyrical and stinging portrait of the Bosnian war, *Éloge de l'amour* (2001) is a lament for the decline of passion as a unifying philosophy, and *Film socialisme* (2010) is a sprawling and frequently quite beautiful portrait of the dream of European and Middle Eastern socialism. But all of these Godard-only feature films are thoroughly divorced from the delicate balancing of domestic struggles, landscape, and philosophical debate that defined his best work with Miéville.

I do think that this was a powerful combination: Godard and Miéville's mixture of domesticity, landscape, and philosophy in these films led to a recovery of the radicalism of both Modernism and Romanticism. It also helped to flesh out the ideas about gender, localism, and politics that were present in their earlier work together but which sometimes seemed a bit incoherent. The really late films of Godard (since 2000) are far more concerned with political and philosophical meditation, with occasional dashes of intimacy and place. As with a nice piece of fish that is rubbed only with salt, the effect is simultaneously overwhelming and a bit bland, with a strong aftertaste of lost possibilities. *Après la réconciliation*, though, is defined by just this three-way *combination* of domesticity, landscape, and philosophy; it has a formal pattern that both draws on earlier experimentation and tries very hard to hold to the contours of the feature-narrative film. It is therefore a thoroughly Modernist work that is defined by skepticism toward such contours but a reluctance to abandon them entirely, just as the work of the 1970s was trying to be and the work of the 1980s so spectacularly was. Looking at the film today, it is hard not to see it as a final effort in a great project in European cinema, one that was completed as other work—such as *The Old Place* (1998) or *Dans le noir du temps* (2002)—was being finished and indicating that this project had ended.

This sense of a project ending is certainly borne out by the films, videos, and television works that Godard and Miéville have done since the 1980s. The work that they have done together since *Soft and Hard* (1985) is mostly short and medium length. The shorts at the beginning of this period retain some of the politicized-Modernist projects that they began in the 1970s and brought to a peak in the 1980s. This is especially true of *Pour Thomas Wainggai, Indonésie* (1991), *Deux fois cinquante ans de cinéma français* (1995), and *Liberté et patrie* (2002). But what we mostly see in this period is that the overall concerns of their work together began to edge away from a committed, meditative Modernism and move toward a sometimes defeated, sometimes cynical, and rarely less than pessimistic form of postmodernism.

In Chapter 1, I mentioned how Peter Harcourt has argued that Godard is "a cinematic Modernist in a Postmodern world" ("Analogical Thinking," 23). I think that is most true of Godard and Miéville during this "Reconsideration" period, where we can see them slipping away from the philosophical concerns of Modernism and toward the language games of postmodernism (especially in the Museum of Modern Art–commissioned *The Old Place* [1998]), only to pick the project back up, suddenly, unexpectedly, with work such as *Pour Thomas Wainggai, Indonésie* (their contribution to the 1991 anthology film *Contre l'oubli*, commissioned by Amnesty International) or *Liberté et patrie* (commissioned for the 2002 Expo suisse nationale). It is work like *Pour Thomas Wainggai, Indonésie*, *Deux fois cinquante ans de cinéma français*, or *Liberté et patrie* that shows us that the proverbial battle has not been lost. But there is plenty of other work in this later period that indicates that some retrenchment was going on.

COMMERCIAL FILMS: *LE RAPPORT DARTY* AND PARISIENNE ADVERT

Godard's time making work for hire in the 1980s is not exactly a central part of the discourse around his films; Miéville's contribution to this work is completely absent from the little discussion that we do find. Some of this likely has to do with the inherently ephemeral nature of the television commercials, to say nothing of the sheer strangeness of an artist like Godard directing them. The critical discussion that these commercials have generated has thus unsurprisingly radiated the sense of being a bit flummoxed by the ad work. Furthermore, the "commercial film" that Godard and Miéville made together, 1989's *Le Rapport Darty*, is a genuinely singular piece of their oeuvre: commissioned by the department store Darty, gnomically cryptic even by Godardo-Miévillian standards, and now basically impossible to find and view. I do not want to make grand claims for the importance of rediscovering this work. The Parisienne commercial Godard and Miéville made together is wittily amusing and little more than that, and I am also basically in agreement with Thierry Jousse's assessment that "[f]inally, *Le Rapport Darty* seems more like the correspondence between the Marx Brothers and the Warner Brothers than an anthropological treatise" (98; m.t.). That does not mean, though, that there are not aspects of both *Le Rapport Darty* and the Parisienne advert that are worth talking about, which illuminate ongoing formal concerns that we have seen in Godard and Miéville's work since the 1970s.

That is especially true of *Le Rapport Darty*. This is neither a comedy nor an anthropological treatise. Strictly speaking, it is a commissioned film, one that the French department store Darty hoped would be a kind of video version of an annual report. In some ways, then, it was the very essence of the kind of work that was central to the original plan for Sonimage. As I discussed in Chapter 1, Colin MacCabe has recounted how Godard and Miéville wanted to "operate as though Sonimage was a handicraft industry with customers ordering video programmes for particular purposes" (*Images Sounds Politics*, 23). You could argue that Darty was simply a big customer placing just such an order. *Le Rapport Darty*, though, did not turn out to be a simple piece of work-for-hire. In a typically self-reflexive gesture, Godard and Miéville both talk in the film itself about how the company was not happy with the piece. As I discussed in Chapter 1, Nicole Brenez has written of how "the film has currently been banned by Darty, who refuse to allow it to be distributed or shown" ("The Forms of the Question," 177), although the film's text is reprinted in full in the second volume of *Jean-Luc Godard par Jean-Luc Godard* (185–89). What it is really an example of, then, is Antoine de Baecque's sense (also mentioned in Chapter 1) that when Godard works with other producers, "someone orders a film from him and he makes it like he wants to, with other people's money, within and against the system at the same time" (520; m.t.). There is no better example in the Godard and Miéville corpus of a work where we can see them working "both within and against the system."

Nearly impossible to see though it is, the film has nevertheless attracted some passionate critical defenders. Brenez writes that "[a]n essential essay on the relationship between the business and the image, *Le Rapport Darty* develops before our eyes the state of the film: it brings together, superimposes, and confuses all at the same time the project, the rejection of that project, the execution, the exegesis, the evidence of the fabrication, and the disintegration of the finished project" ("The Forms of the Question," 177). Douglas Morrey has written an entire essay on the film, "An Embarrassment of Richess," as part of a 2005 anthology called *Formless: Ways in and out of Form*, and writes there that "[w]hat Godard and Miéville succeed in doing, as so often in their television and video work, is in showing us a reality that is at once immediately familiar and unlike anything we have been shown before" (232). As with their video and television work, what defines their analysis of the strangeness of the modern familiar are video-specific variants of slow motion and montage.

There are parts of *Le Rapport Darty* that really are as visually rich and surprising as anything that the pair did in the 1970s. One recurring visual motif is a kind of frenzied montage that is, as I have been discussing, specific to the video control console. We see this kind of montage for the first time about ten minutes into the work, when a long shot of a loading dock (on one half, a man sweeps up; on the other, someone loads a tuck) and of a forklift moving boxes in a massive warehouse are juxtaposed via a very fast set of swerving wipes back and forth. Godard and Miéville do something similar, but with fades rather than wipes, as they show a meeting between Darty managers and floor staff (they quickly fade back and forth between a shot of a manager and one of a group of workers who move in slow motion). The effect is dizzyingly vertiginous as the two spaces combine with one another swimmingly. This is a vertigo that, while not exactly specific to video (it could be done on film with an optical printer, although it would be awkward), is very easily achieved with the flexible, relatively inexpensive video gear that defines Godard and Miéville's "Sonimage practice."

We saw this as early as *Ici et ailleurs* and then with a vengeance in *Six fois deux: Sur et sous la communication* (1976), which included a large number of such montages. Surely the most graphically striking example of this montage strategy is when Godard and Miéville juxtapose a shot that slowly tracks along a display floor for washing machines with a close-up of a man looking downward, opening and closing his eyes slowly and moving vaguely in the opposite direction of the tracking shot. The shot of the man is slowed down so much as to seem nearly still, and the shot of the washing machines is both deep and thus seems to signify material plenty but also genuinely striking because of the vertical lines of the ceiling that take up the top third of the frame. Unlike the other montages that I have mentioned, the two images are utterly distinct at the level of both graphics and motion, and so their combination via this fading back and forth is more disorienting still. The contemplative quality of both images—a steady tracking shot, a man looking still and pensive—is at odds with the disorienting effect of their juxtaposition. This is entirely consistent with Godard and Miéville's vision of consumer-capitalist-led culture, especially the vision that they offered in *Sauve qui peut (la vie)*. I argued in Chapter 4 that a big part of that film's analysis of culture is that to see the beast you attack and that you must be inside it but not consumed by it. Godard and Miéville illustrated this most vividly through Isabelle Huppert's stoic and vaguely ironic sensibility amid the madness of her life as a prostitute and Nathalie Baye's ability to couple her withdrawal from the metropolis with an acceptance of loneliness and a pastoral sensibility that is always in danger of sliding into kitsch. That kind of tension is basically a matter of accepting the coexistence of beauty and madness, of the banal and the magnificent. That is basically what is going on in sequences of *Le Rapport Darty*—like this one with the washing machines and the blinking man.

Jousse is correct to identify the film's primary debt to Marx and his brothers. It would be pointless to deny the overall tone of mockery, embodied in no small part by the fact that the voice-over claims that the film has actually been abandoned by its makers and is being completed by a robot named Nathanaël, a character voiced by Godard in a very silly robot-sounding voice. But it would be equally wrong-headed to ignore the multiple ways in which *Le rapport Darty* is linked to Godard and Miéville's overall project: on the level of form via the use of video-specific effects, on the level of institution-building via its status as a commissioned work-for-hire, and on the level of historical analysis via its searching but still critical indictment of consumer culture.

Given this ongoing critique of consumer culture, the presence of actual commercials in the Godard and Miéville corpus is, of course, counterintuitive. But Godard was no stranger to the form. In 1972, he shot a commercial for Schick aftershave lotion that was never aired (it is now available on YouTube). Although it was made seven years earlier, it looks like nothing so much as a scene out of *Sauve qui peut (la vie)*. In 1987–88 and again in 1990, Godard did a number of commercials for the blue jeans manufacturer M&F Girbaud. The irony of this once-committed Maoist's turn toward the "*film de pub*" attracted a lot of commentary, in no small part because the commercials had excerpts from works such as *Les fleurs du mal* on their soundtracks (these commercials are available on the DVD included with Brenez et al.'s book *Jean-Luc Godard: Documents*). H. A. Rodchenko both summed up and moved beyond this kind of chatter very nicely in his short *Film Comment* piece on the jeans commercials, writing that "[t]he French press seems not to know how to regard the Girbaud commercials, other than by trotting out one or the other of the usual personas—Godard as sellout (dragging poor Rimbaud and Baudelaire with him), Godard as genius. It might be more accurate to say that Godard is doing what he's always done: looking at the world around him" (4).

Something very similar could be said about the commercial that he and Miéville directed in 1992 for the cigarette company Parisienne. The piece is mostly made up of images of young people visible only from the waist down (even in high-angle shots, such as one where we see a barefoot jeans-wearer shuffle through a mass of cigarette boxes on the floor), and features an excerpt from Racine's *Bérénice* on the soundtrack ("Do you not hear, this cruel joy ..."). It is obviously shot in a mall (de Baecque's *Godard: biographie* states that it was filmed in a mall around Zurich's train station [705]), and it features images of basically banal youth culture (a guy skateboarding a slalom course around oversized cigarette boxes) as well as slightly more sinister tableaux (the last image is a close-up of a book that bears the title "Parisienne People"; a young woman ignites a lighter in front of it, and the reader slowly moves his cigarette toward the flame). Godard and Miéville are, basically, observing the world around them, the world of the train-station mall (a distinctly Western European site, without a very good North American equivalent), a place defined both by an atmosphere of chaotic youthful loafing and the vague sense that its vision of consumerism is slowly creeping into everything. The book that dominates the commercial's first and last shot looks exactly like the classic Gallimard/NRF paperback (as identifiable in the Francophone world as Penguin paperbacks are in the Anglophone). So, when its title becomes fully visible in the last image, the effect is jarring. I would not make extravagant claims for this sensation, and I certainly do not think that this commercial is some sort of attack from within on consumer culture. And yet, the way in which Godard and Miéville are using the form of the commercial to observe the world around them is making its contradictions visible as well; these boxes are fun to skateboard around, satisfying to slosh through, but a little weird in the way that they appear in places they really do not belong. As with so much of Godard and Miéville's work, montage is what makes this realization possible, and montage is more often than not the very basis of the commercial's aesthetic. Thus, Godard and Miéville's turn toward the form is not surprising at all. Like the video montages of *Le Rapport Darty*, there is a distinct sense that they were trying, in their later work, to condense some essential elements of their ongoing practice into a highly concentrated form. Much of the nuance of the longer work gets lost in that process. But much of its ambition remains visible.

ANTHOLOGY FILMS: *L'ENFANCE DE L'ART* AND *POUR THOMAS WAINGGAI, INDONÉSIE*

It is difficult to believe that *Pour Thomas Wainggai, Indonésie* (1991) was made only two years after *Le Rapport Darty*, so utterly different are its tone and scope. It is harder still to believe that it was made just a year after *L'Enfance de l'art* (1990), another anthology film whose shared non-profit pedigree (*Pour Thomas Wainggai, Indonésie* was made for Amnesty International, and *L'Enfance de l'art* for UNICEF) obscures its complete difference from the later work. Of all of Godard and Miéville's films and videos of this period, *Pour Thomas Wainggai, Indonésie* is the one that most clearly builds upon the concerns of their earlier work rather than just summarizing or meditating on it. Part of this has to do with formal concerns (the editing and composition are very subtle here, and strongly recall *Sauve qui peut [la vie]*), and part of it has to do with political matters (it is as engaged with political repression and its consequences as work such as *Ici et ailleurs* or *Comment ça va?*). *L'Enfance de l'art* is engaged with politics as well, and it is also formally eccentric, but it has the feeling of a sketch, or perhaps a rehearsal for later films that Godard made on his own (especially 1996's *For Ever Mozart*). Putting the two films side by side offers a good way of understanding the tensions at play in their work of the past twenty years or so.

L'Enfance de l'art was part of an anthology film called *Comment vont les enfants?*, produced in 1990 by UNICEF. The other filmmakers involved were Lino Brocka, Rolan Bykov, Euzan Palcy, Ciro Durán, and Jerry Lewis. The anthology was a collection of short sketches about the struggles of children worldwide, and the individual chapters deal with issues such as alcoholism, racial tension, poverty, and so on. The film opens with medium close-up of a young boy whose mother is reading aloud from Victor Hugo's *Les Misérables*. There are occasional sounds of jets, explosions, and gunshots off-screen that continue when Godard and Miéville cut to a close-up of the mother. The off-screen sounds of explosions and gunshots continue, although the film shifts to a series of shots, which more or less maintain classical-Hollywood continuity, of the mother, a few children, and some heavily armed young men wandering around a bombed-out area. The reading stops for a while, and then picks up again; at one point, the voice shifts to that of a young man as he writes on the back of images of the French revolutionary icon Marianne ("The most terrible / is ...") before he is shot.

Judging by the two texts that close the film, Godard and Miéville seem to have been given the "right not to go to war" file, although what they actually produced is quite far from the well-meaning liberal docudrama that is suggested by the anthology's topics that were taken from the 1989 UN Convention on the Rights of the Child, as the text in the film explains. The short is arch, ironic, and faintly ridiculous in the manner of earlier Godard films like *Alphaville: Une étrange aventure de Lemmy Caution* (1965) or segments of Miéville's *Après la réconciliation*. The way that it represents war strongly anticipates Godard's meditation on the war in Bosnia, 1996's *For Ever Mozart*. It is definitely an anomaly for Godard and Miéville, though. It is much more absurdist and self-aware than the narrative films that they made together in the 1980s, but it is more narrative than the essayistic, montage-based work that they did in the period under discussion in this chapter. As a series of gestures that convey the absurdity of war, it succeeds reasonably well; overall, though, it is neither especially sophisticated in terms of its aesthetic or political stance, nor is it particularly significant for understanding the work they have done together as a whole.

That is not true of *Pour Thomas Wainggai, Indonésie*, which was also part of anthology film, this one called *Contre l'oubli*, produced in 1991 by Amnesty International. This was a much larger project than *L'Enfance de l'art*, featuring no fewer than thirty-one filmmakers directing short segments, each one devoted to a single person who had suffered state-sponsored human rights abuse. Most of the contributors were French, and included Jane Birkin, Claire Denis, Raymond Depardon, Bertrand Tavernier, and Alain Resnais, as well as the Belgian filmmaker Chantal Akerman and the US expatriate Robert Kramer. Godard and Miéville's contribution, ostensibly about the Papuan independence leader Thomas Wainggai, is a meditation on the role of mass media in political action. Much of the piece's three minutes is given over to dark, carefully framed images of the inside of André Rousselet's office, images that look a bit like the office interiors of *Sauve qui peut (la vie)*. Rousselet was at that time the head of Canal+, the private French broadcaster, and we see him at his desk, writing a letter. The voice-over has him reading the letter he is writing to Indonesian President Suharto asking for Wainggai's release, protesting that he was arrested for sewing flags. As he reads, Godard and Miéville cut away to still images of Wainggai and Papuan daily life before coming back to Rousselet's dark office and returning to synchronous sound, as his secretary walks into the room and reminds him of a meeting. They follow this with another montage of still images, including an extreme close-up of a shot of Wainggai from the previous montage, before returning to a medium shot of Rousselet signing the letter and stating his name and title on the soundtrack.

This back and forth between images of powerful media people making futile gestures of opposition and photographs of oppressed political leaders that give no specific political information but that provide a simple, powerful record of their presence, their refusal to disappear completely, is not exactly political agitprop. Rather, it is an example of the sort of committed but realist politics that Godard and Miéville had adopted in the 1980s, politics that were some distance from the more fiery, Marxist-inflected rhetoric of Godard's Groupe Dziga Vertov days. A letter from a television executive is likely to have little effect, but that does not mean that the media has no role to play in political change. Indeed, what seems to keep the memory of Wainggai and his struggle alive in a climate of near-total repression on the part of the Indonesian government is precisely *imagery*. There may be no direct cause-and-effect relationship between Rousselet's letter and the release of a political prisoner like Wainggai, but that does not mean that they have nothing to do with one another. Very much the opposite is the case, as the montage of images tells us at the beginning of this piece. *Pour Thomas Wainggai, Indonésie* concludes with a shot of Rousselet reading the letter back to himself. Indonesian music comes up on the soundtrack and drowns his voice out, just as Godard and Miéville cut to the last image of the piece, a photograph of Indonesian women and girls. This complex mixture of sound and image evokes the degree to which mass-circulated imagery and Third World struggles are, in Europe, completely intertwined. The two present this as a simple fact rather than something to rebel against. Indeed, the closing credits simply state that the piece is by Jean-Luc Godard, Anne-Marie Miéville, and André Rousselet.

The tortured deliberations about the role of the media in covering political strife that was so central to *Comment ça va?* are thus basically absent here. That is not to say that Godard and Miéville have "sold out," or somehow compromised the principles that they laid out so forcefully in the 1970s. Rather, they have moved beyond the impasses that these principles inevitably created. *Comment ça va?*, in fine Modernist-leftist fashion, basically cried, "What is to be done?" *Pour Thomas Wainggai, Indonésie* responds: "Get on with the business of making struggle visible, in whatever incomplete, inadequate way you can." That is more Modernist than leftist, more Godard–Miéville of the 1980s than of the 1970s. But one could very easily say that it is a film that takes the politics of the 1970s and applies to them the aesthetic rigour and philosophical nuance of the 1980s. It is one of their few films of this period where their shared project is both clearly visible and just as clearly moving forward. That it is a mere three minutes long is an indication both of the diversity of the work Godard and Miéville have done together (some very long, some very short) and the value of looking closely at all of it (even though a lot of this shorter material remains difficult to see).

COMMISSIONED FILMS: *DEUX FOIS CINQUANTE ANS DE CINÉMA FRANÇAIS* AND *THE OLD PLACE*

Following these two anthology contributions, Godard and Miéville made two films that were closer to traditional commissions than the UNICEF/Amnesty project, but much less commercial than *Le Rapport Darty* and the Parisienne advert. Both *Deux fois cinquante ans de cinéma français* (1995) and *The Old Place* (1998) were, like *Soft and Hard*, helped along by Colin MacCabe. The former film was part of the British Film Institute's series of television programs (aired on Channel 4) celebrating the one hundredth anniversary of the Lumière Brothers' first projections; that series was called "The Century of Cinema." After a time running BFI's production unit, MacCabe was put in charge of their publishing and education units. He recalls, in his *Portrait of the Artist at Seventy*, that he had been given those jobs "with the aim of building the kind of education that Bazin had sketched out a generation earlier" (300). *The Old Place* was made for New York's Museum of Modern Art, with MacCabe and Mary Lea Bandy (Curator of MoMA's Department of Film) acting as executive producers. MacCabe was connected to the institution because he had helped organize a very successful 1992 MoMA retrospective of Godard's post-1975 work. These two films were ostensibly didactic projects, both being made for art-educational organizations; however, very little didacticism is visible in either one. *Deux fois cinquante ans de cinéma français* was made in the midst of Godard's massive *Histoire(s) du cinéma* project (1988–98), and it would be easy to assume that it has a comparably pessimistic and monastic quality. This is definitely not the case. I am in agreement with Jonathan Rosenbaum's assessment that "[t]he fragmented style and narrative of *2x50 Years* is markedly different from that of his eight-part magnum opus *Histoire(s) du cinéma*," although I disagree with his next assertion, that "the philosophical underpinnings are very much the same" (39). Overall, *Deux fois cinquante ans de cinéma français* seems to me closer to the intellectual ambitions of *Soft and Hard* than to those of *Histoire(s) du cinéma*. On the other hand, *The Old Place* strikes me as quite consistent with the *Histoire(s) du cinema* project, even though it is about painting rather than cinema. It is deeply pessimistic, so much so that it has largely abandoned the belief in art as communication and is instead mostly about playing language games, both at the level of film language and spoken language. Prioritizing game playing over communication is, of course, what Jean-François Lyotard saw as typically postmodern; the third chapter of his 1979 work, *La condition postmoderne*, is entitled "La methode: les jeux de langage." Like the tension between *L'Enfance de l'art* and *Pour Thomas Wainggai, Indonésie*, the split between these two commissioned "history films" shows us that the project that Godard and Miéville had been developing all these years was still hanging on as the 1990s moved forward, but it was clearly starting to wane.

It would be very easy to see *Deux fois cinquante ans de cinéma français* as a kind of less important adjunct to *Histoire(s) du cinéma*, but I believe that it is much less self-important or tortured than that sprawling series that has attracted so much recent critical acclaim. It is precisely the fact that *Deux fois cinquante ans de cinéma français* has a sense of humour that makes it a more serious film. Overall, it has a distinctly ironic edge that gives its critique of the slow death *of film culture* (less so of film itself) a sense of sad inevitability, a state of affairs that is being presented by two artists sophisticated enough to laugh easily at their own excesses. Talking about Miéville's 1997 feature *Nous sommes tout encore ici* and Godard's 1996 feature *For Ever Mozart*, MacCabe wrote that "I told Godard that I found Miéville's film much better thought through than his own effort. Reading the treatment of *For Ever Mozart*, you could see a companion piece to *Nouvelle Vague* (1990) and *Hélas pour moi* (1993), where the complexity and range of material was, among other things, an indication of a lack of interest in the feature film as a form" (*Portrait of the Artist*, 307). Something very similar could be said in comparing Godard and Miéville's *Deux fois cinquante ans de cinéma français* and Godard's *Histoire(s) du cinéma*. I find *their* film much better thought through than Godard's own, very similar effort, which seems to me to indicate a lack of interest not only in the feature film as a form but in the hybrid essay film as well. That is a form that is present in each phase of their work together. We see it at the beginning in the 1970s (*Ici et ailleurs*) and at the high point of their feature work together in the 1980s (*Soft and Hard*). This last period of collaboration is, as we have seen in this chapter, by and large defined by this kind of work.

I do not wish to mount a full-scale critique of *Histoire(s) du cinéma*, only to say that to see it is to get inside the mind of an artist who is, finally, deeply dissatisfied with what cinema can accomplish. We certainly see this in Godard's brooding voice-overs that lament cinema's failure to fully confront the way in which Auschwitz transformed the world, but I think we can see it through the basic elements of the work's aesthetic, which immerse the viewer in a soup of cinematic imagery, one that makes understanding an utterly daunting task.

(As an appendix to her 2006 monograph on the work, Céline Scemama has catalogued each film that Godard references, a list that runs to ten pages and 419 films.) I am thus in full agreement with Colin MacCabe's assessment that "[i]t is not possible to find a comparison to Godard's *Histoire(s)* in cinema or television, but there is good reason to compare it to James Joyce's *Finnegans Wake*" (*A Portrait of the Artist*, 315). And while I take MacCabe's point about both *Histoire(s) du cinéma* and *Finnegans Wake* taking all of history as their subject matter and using montage as their basic aesthetic, I want to weep when I compare either one to vivid, fluent miracles of expression such as *Sauve qui peut (la vie)* or *Ulysses*; *Je vous salue, Marie* or *Dubliners*; *Ici et ailleurs* or *A Portrait of the Artist as a Young Man*.

I would not put *Deux fois cinquante ans de cinéma français* on the same level as any of these, but the piece is a sharp, incisive critique both of the state of film culture in France and of the current state of dialogue, of communication. After a poetic introduction, with Miéville's voice over images of magic lanterns and early cinema, the film opens with Godard interviewing Michel Piccoli at a hotel café. Godard mentions to him that he is president of a newly formed commission to celebrate the first screenings of the Lumière Brothers, and Godard proceeds to interrogate him. "Why celebrate the cinema?" Godard asks. "Isn't it celebrated enough already?"[1] A lot of this conversation, where Godard becomes increasingly insistent about the exact meaning of "*célébrer*," is made up of a single, unmoving shot over Godard's shoulder, with Piccoli in a kind of awkward medium shot (which is also seriously backlit, with Piccoli looking a little dark and a bright window set just on the left side of the image) which has him alternating between making quizzical facial expressions and struggling, mostly without success, to get a word in edgewise. That shot lasts almost seven minutes; Godard and Miéville cut away briefly to a shot of what looks like a Méliès film as Godard talks about what he is trying to do with *Histoire(s) du cinéma*. They then return to a very similar shot, this time just of Piccoli with the camera set a little bit closer to him, but just as awkwardly framed and lit. Apart from a few brief cutaways to silent films and photographs, this shot lasts nearly ten minutes.

At the level of form, this second sequence thus strongly recalls the long dialogue-on-the-sofa sequence of *Soft and Hard*; the uniquely unblinking gaze of the video camera is interrupted only by occasional insertion of found images (in *Soft and Hard* television news footage, in *Deux fois cinquante ans de cinéma français* images of early cinema). The crucial difference is that the sequence in *Soft and Hard* is a genuine conversation between Godard and Miéville, whereas this sequence with Piccoli is a caricature of such a dialogue, an image of a patient, patrician senior statesman being cornered by a slightly obnoxious cinephile. This sense of caricature is consistent with the film's sense of both of film culture and historical memory. The scene that follows this cup of coffee has Piccoli in the kitchen, gently interrogating a young, *L'Équipe*-reading busboy about the history of films, photographs, and cartoons, with occasional fades and cutaways to images of turn-of-the-century colour photographs and animation cels. The busboy's surly responses indicate an unapologetic ignorance. The film is peppered with sequences like this, with Piccoli in his hotel room asking everyone who comes in (mostly young maids and bellhops) about film history and getting responses based only in the most banal and disposable pop culture: "But I know Arnold Schwarzenegger.... But I know Madonna," the maid offers gently (she also notes that the only cinema in town closed before she was born). To Piccoli's question about Jacques Becker, a bellhop aggressively responds, "Boris, not Jacques, *Boris* Becker. Boom boom! He's a really good server!" When asked about his own cinematic preferences, the bellhop squeals gleefully, "Oh, yeah, the super-violents! They're pure butchery!" This dialogue on the state of cinema is just as monological as the bit between Godard and Piccoli, just as devoid of real engagement.

As much as a report on the state of cinema, then, *Deux fois cinquante ans de cinéma français* is in equal part a callback to the work Godard and Miéville did in the 1970s, a report on the state of knowledge and communication. The report is pessimistic in some ways, but just as in the 1970s, their analysis is not one-sided. Godard and Miéville's decision to use mostly production stills rather than film clips (which are almost absent from the work once it leaves the hotel café) is illustrative. For while these production stills clearly signify death at some level (they are motion pictures that no longer move), their stillness signifies a contemplative spirit in equal measure. Something similar occurs with a number of sequences shot by Godard and Miéville themselves. This is most true of a very delicate long take of the young maid who is cleaning Piccoli's bathtub. Godard and Miéville frame her in a close-up, her eyes gazing downward and bathed in gentle light against an off-white background. Piccoli's voice is on the soundtrack, rattling off the names of French film actors. Part of the significance here is clearly that she does not recognize the names (Odile Versois, Nadia Sibirskaia, Jules Berry, and Odette Joyeux are the first four), and thus does not say anything. But she is framed to very self-consciously suggest the Pietà (even though she is gazing to the right, a reversal of the Virgin Mary's typically leftward glance); she is bathed in soft light, in a close-up cut off just below her shoulders, and her downward gaze indicates nothing so much as mourning.

What, exactly, is she mourning here? The death of an art form, one whose vocation for photographic realism Godard's mentor André Bazin saw as essentially spiritual? That is clearly part of what the image is evoking, given that

Godard and Miéville place this Pietà in an explicitly metacinematic context both through Piccoli's voice-over and because of the still images that follow it. Thus, it is hard not to see this image and think of Bazin essays like "L'ontologie de l'image photographique," where he writes that "[w]e no longer believe in the ontological identity of model and portrait, but we recognize that the latter helps us to remember the former and thus to rescue it from a second death, spiritual this time" (*Qu'est-ce que le cinéma?*, 10 / *What Is Cinema?*, 4).

Godard and Miéville spent the 1970s making work that both rejected a simple ontological connection between image and subject and tried to use cinema (film, video, television) to save various kinds of subjects (women, revolutionary politicos, image makers) from a kind of political death. In this 1970s work, they evoked that death through images of violence, alienation, political frustration, or consumerist objectification, as we saw in *Ici et ailleurs*, *Numéro deux*, *Comment ça va?*, and *Six fois deux: Sur et sous la communication*, respectively. In *Deux fois cinquante ans de cinéma français*, they are suggesting death through images of casual ignorance and indifference. But rather than images of failed Palestinian uprisings or disconnected suburban families, it is these production stills to which they return, to which the maid in Piccoli's hotel room seems to be gazing down at both lovingly and mournfully. These photographs, shorn of their ontological relationship to cinema by virtue of their stillness, nevertheless rescue that medium from a second, more spiritual death.

Laurent Roth argues that *Deux fois cinquante ans de cinéma français* is both melancholic and monumental, which I think is correct, but I disagree with his assessment that the film is also "*résolument muséographique et fétichiste*." Roth believes that "Godard [sic] is trying to be the first spectator—and a jealous, exclusive one—of the films that make up his imaginary museum" (85; m.t.). Godard and Miéville are not "exclusive" in this film; they are lonely. Far from being jealous lovers of cinema, they are seeking more companionship. This search for solidarity as acted out by Piccoli is basically unsuccessful. When they do manage to find such solidarity, such companionship, is actually when the film switches back to a first-person perspective, and they offer their montage of critics. They identify fifteen writers, and Godard and Miéville take turns reading a bit of their writing over a series of superimposed images: images of the texts, of the faces of the writers themselves, and sometimes of what they were writing about. As I mentioned in Chapter 1, this roll call is made up of Denis Diderot, Eugène Fromentin, Elie Faure, Georges Sadoul, Jean Epstein, Jean-Georges Auriol, André Malraux, Jean Cocteau, Robert Bresson, André Bazin, Maurice Schérer (Éric Rohmer), François Truffaut, Jacques Rivette, Marguerite Duras, and Serge Daney. These are all writers who have engaged with the connection between words and vision, between texts and pictures. The

Diderot text Godard reads is the 1749 "Lettre sur les aveugles" or "Letter on the Blind"; Miéville reads the line from Duras's *Les yeux verts* (which, as I noted in Chapter 1), was a special 1980 issue of the *Cahiers du cinéma* devoted to Duras) where she invokes "Le cinéma différent; l'image écrit; l'autre cinéma" (these are the titles of three separate sections of *Les yeux verts*). These writers are part of what saves cinema from its spiritual death, too. They are Godard and Miéville's ideal companions, figures who share their desire to think through images, to think *via* images. Interpersonal communication in *Deux fois cinquante ans de cinéma français*, whether between Godard and Piccoli or between Piccoli and the young hotel employees, is comically frustrating. Intellectual communication, though, communication that takes place across centuries and through images and ideas, still has some hope. The traces of *Ici et ailleurs* and *Six fois deux: Sur et sous la communication* are clearly visible in *Deux fois cinquante ans de cinéma français*, but Godard and Miéville's voices are mellower now—a bit less urgent but a bit more considered as well. Film culture is dying, yes; but it is the attempt to understand its images (some still, some moving) that will save it from a second, and ultimately more profound kind of death.

Something similar is going on with their 1998 film *The Old Place*, commissioned by New York's Museum of Modern Art (MoMA). Colin MacCabe had a hand in putting this commission together as well, and he writes in *A Portrait of the Artist* of "my two previous experiences of *Soft and Hard* and *2 x 50 ans de cinéma français*. I expected a very rocky ride as we progressed from initial idea to final work of art. I was completely wrong" (313). While MacCabe may be very happy with the way the piece turned out—he also writes in *Portrait* that "[i]t is difficult for me to claim much critical objectivity, but I consider *The Old Place* to be the finest of all the Godard/Miéville essays" (313)—I find this a much more gloomy and ultimately less disciplined, less nuanced work than *Deux fois cinquante ans de cinéma français*. Early in the film, Godard says on the voice-over that "our world has collapsed [around us; *s'est écroulé autour de nous*], and there's not much of it left" (*Four Short Films*, 46/48). He goes on to say that this might not be all bad, that it allows the chance to "*prendre un nouveau départ*" ("make a new start"). But that line hovers over the entire film, which seems preoccupied with collapse, with death, and only superficially engaged with meaning or communication.

One early sequence seems to promise some relief: Godard's voice speaks about landscape over video images of tall green grasslands with little red flowers poking up. But then Godard and Miéville pull the rug out: a little bit of cutting reveals that this scene is actually right next to a noisy freeway. The film is filled with sequences like this, which use images of cinema, painting or sculpture, and the sounds of classical music to suggest the possibility that art can illuminate the world around us, only to pull back in a tone of defeat or vague mockery. Chapter 11, "Les illusions perdues," has Vermeer's *Girl with a Pearl Earring* as part of its montage, but that painting is preceded by a sloweddown shot of the big spaceships from the last scene of *The Empire Strikes Back*. It is difficult to read this invocation of *Empire* as anything other than kitsch, especially given that it is part of a montage of slightly corny paintings of stars and cosmic formations. To say that *Girl with a Pearl Earring* stands out in a jarring way would be an understatement; all it shares with this sciencefiction imagery is its black background, and in terms of aesthetic accomplishment, it could not be more different. The chasm-like difference here makes the sequence feel jokey, absurd, as does Godard and Miéville's voice-over, which has them wondering if a satellite that has been sent to travel beyond the solar system will carry trite, decidedly non-cosmic messages like "don't discriminate against women" or "show a Griffith film at least once a year."

Chapter 12, "Le vieux monde," is harsher still in this strategy. It opens with black-and-white video footage of a horse being shot (it is three shots altogether: a long shot with a brief cutaway to a close-up of the gun being put to the horse's head, and then a return to that long shot as the horse collapses), follows that with two shots of a lovely nineteenth-century painting of two old men holding hands, and then concludes with an excerpt from what looks like a pre-1910 fiction film that depicts a *tableau vivant* of mediaeval torture. Kitsch, then, gives way to dehumanized violence; a slightly sarcastic montage about cinema and painting's ability to capture states both of rapture and naive imagination gives way to a montage that is at first horrifying, then melancholic, then both silly and violent. This all betrays a fairly serious sense of defeat. Art is serving as a mirror of the world in this film, but that world is as often vapid and alienated as it is shimmering or mysterious. Great works of Modernist art abound, but *The Old Place* has a lot of images of death, and distinctly degraded images of death at that. Richard Brody wrote about the film in his 2000 *New Yorker* profile "Exile in Paradise," and while he does not quite offer a judgement, I can hear echoes of my own assessment in his sense that "[i]t is a provocative and disturbing work, and someone who views it in one of MoMA's belowground theatres may be moved to take a long, contemplative detour through the streets and the Park before daring to go up and indulge in the museum's collection" (74).

That said, there are montage sequences here that are genuinely lyrical, as tender as they are complexly evocative. This is certainly true of the sequence in Chapter 13, "Destin des choses," which explores a series of furnishings, presumably part of MoMA's celebrated design collection. Miéville's reads from Paul Valéry's *Mélange* by way of imploring the reader to "[l]ook at the angle, the edge that furniture makes with the windowpane. You have to reclaim it from banality, from the unseen visible. To save it ..." (*Four Short Films*, 31/52). The images constitute just such an attempt; the montage begins with an extreme close-up of a painting of a woman's face, but continues as a series of softly lit and impeccably framed shots of furniture: a head-on lamp shot against a stylized vertical line; a table shot from above, revealing the carpet that it has been placed upon; a chair shot against a brown curtain, both of which take about two-thirds of the frame. As Miéville's voice-over speaks of the need to reconcile these objects "*au moindre paysage sublime*" ("to any sublime landscape"), the montage shifts to the images of verdant fields, snowy lakes, and museum exteriors, before moving back to images of furniture and paintings. This is an evocative, richly visual arrangement across media: design, poetry, painting, music, and of course cinema. It is smooth and tactile, capturing the grain of the wood as well as the paint. Even when the music stops suddenly and we get images of a ceiling light and a tabletop (before moving to the landscape shots), the sensuality, the tactility of these images is inescapable. Really, though, it is sequences like these that make the film overall seem pessimistic and defeated. Beauty exists, and Godard and Miéville are capable of showing it to us. Moreover, they are capable of doing that beautifully, but the beautiful must coexist with some seriously awful objects; life exists only in the shadow of death. I have been offering a close reading of this middle section of *The Old Place* because it illustrates that so clearly. Montages of Valéry and furniture follow montages of horse slaughter and mediaeval torture; Vermeer is made to coexist with *The Empire Strikes Back,* contemplation of the cosmic ends up pro ducing only trite pieties about politics or film culture. Art continues to live, but an understanding of art, a real connection to it, is always being drowned out by the banal. That analysis is not far from the one we find in *Histoire(s) du cinéma*. But it is quite distant from what we find in films like *Deux fois cinquante ans de cinéma français* or *Pour Thomas Wainggai, Indonésie*.

TWO LAST FILMS: *DANS LE NOIR DU TEMPS* AND *LIBERTÉ ET PATRIE*

This sense that art continues to live but its understanding remains elusive is equally far from the analysis of the last two works that Godard and Miéville collaborated on, *Dans le noir du temps* and *Liberté et patrie*. Both pieces are from 2002, and each one shows, in its way, what Godard and Miéville were up to during this last decade of their collaboration. *Dans le noir du temps* is closest of all to *The Old Place* (which it quotes) inasmuch as it uses montage as a way of mourning the possibilities of art, and is finally best understood as an intensely melancholy work. This is not true at all of *Liberté et patrie*, which is a lyrical, essayistic meditation along the lines of *Le rapport Darty*, *Pour Thomas Wainggai, Indonésie*, or *Deux fois cinquante ans de cinéma français*. Because both *Dans le noir du temps* and *Liberté et patrie* came out in the same year, it is difficult to know which is the "last" Godard and Miéville film. Really, though, they are both the last work; together they embody the basic dialectic of this period, the tension between a cinema of interiority and defeat, and one that struggles to engage with the world as they find it.

Dans le noir du temps was one of a two-part anthology film called *Ten Minutes Older* that was divided into two parts: *Ten Minutes Older: The Trumpet* and *Ten Minutes Older: The Cello*. Each film was supposed to use the eponymous instrument as a means to consider the passing of time; for Godard and Miéville, that passing is mostly a matter of a meditation on Godard's own filmmaking. The film is a dense combination of text and music film excerpts, and, like *The Old Place*, a lot of the imagery settles on the degree to which art, and certainly cinema, has been defined by images of violence and suffering. Thus, we begin with a clip from Godard's *La Chinoise* (1967) where a young revolutionary is shot and stumbles around comically, but Godard and Miéville move in fairly short order to degraded video images of extreme violence (followed by a shot of garbage bags being dumped in front of their office in Rolle), and eventually to footage of Allied soldiers carrying the skeletal corpses of concentration camp victims. Even the meditations on Godard's own work are fairly dark: one crucial excerpt is the torture scene from his 1963 film *Le Petit Soldat*. All that said, there are certainly more optimistic elements of the film, both at the level of art and autobiography. The soundtrack is dominated by the Estonian composer Arvo Pärt's 1978 composition *Spiegel im Spiegel* for violin or cello and piano, and it is certainly easy to see the connection between the film's visual minimalism and Pärt's musical minimalism that often is summarized by Pärt's recalling his fondness for gentle tinkling of bells, which is certainly in evidence here.[2] And late in the piece, Godard and Miéville excerpt the sequence from *The Old Place* that features a mechanically dancing screen designed by Swiss artist Jean Tinguely, known worldwide for his whimsically Rube Goldberg-esque contraptions. But the overall argument here is that time has passed, and the world has become more harshly violent, and moments of real communication or connection are more and more rare.

The connection to *The Old Place* seems to me quite clear, and equally so to Richard Brody. He writes that in that earlier film:

> Godard and Miéville use texts and works by artists in order to analyze art visually into two components: a lesson in looking at the world, whether a field of flowers or the way the light hits one's living-room furniture, and

> the documentation of suffering; and their argument is that the two are inseparable. The point was amplified in a second short film by Godard [sic], *Dans le noir du temps* (In the Dark of Time), which was premiered at the Pompidou Center in Paris, together with *The Old Place* (MoMA did not show the film until 2002). (613)

The pairing was a smart one, for, as I wrote about *The Old Place*, *Dans le noir du temps* betrays a fairly serious sense of defeat. It sees art, and indeed Godard's own filmmaking, as a mirror of the world in this film, but it is a world defined mostly by pain and alienation, and only occasionally by shimmering mysteries like a dancing screen. It would be very easy to see this film as a summary of Sonimage's end, as a handmade, autobiographical, home movie-esque montage, but one that is defined not by the possibilities of a truly independent cinema, but by the inability to move beyond mourning the death of its very medium.

Something very different is going on in *Liberté et patrie*. This was another commissioned work, this time made for the 2002 Expo nationale suisse (specifically for the Arteplage mobile du Jura, a floating exhibition site built into an old barge).[3] Its use of montage is similar to what we saw in *Dans le noir du temps*, although its ends are very different. In short, the film is a kind of meditation on the relationship between Switzerland and France, and on the historic and ongoing independence of the Canton de Vaud, *terre natale* for both Godard and Miéville and home of their production company since the late 1970s. They are again using images of Godard's own films, but also the literature of Charles-Ferdinand Ramuz, the landscape of the Jura mountains and Lac Léman, and images of French aggression to present the place as a territory defined by mixture. The elements of this mixture—France, painting, literature, cinema, Swiss regionalism, Romanticism, Modernism—are all part of the place that formed these two, all of it coming together in ways that are difficult to explain clearly but never less than fecund.

The title of the film is taken from Vaud's motto, "*Liberté et patrie*," and Vaud is the only canton in the Swiss confederation to have its motto emblazoned on its cantonal flag (it takes up the upper, solid white half; the lower half is solid green). The canton's relationship with France is a complicated one. As we saw in Chapter 2, from the 1500s until 1798, Vaud was a subject of the canton of Berne rather than a full member of confederation. The territory was reconstituted as the Canton de Léman during the République helvétique, which lasted from 1798 to 1803. This is the period when French forces invaded Switzerland and established a sort of puppet state there, sweeping away the country's federal traditions. Only upon the ouster of French forces and the return to the Confédération suisse did it become the Canton de Vaud. Thus, it is hard to read the film's fourth chapter, titled "Aux armes, citoyens," in any terms other the vertiginously ironic. This is a typically dense montage (which again employs the kind of video mixing so common to these essay films) of the French TGV train (a train that goes between Paris and Lausanne, seat of the Canton de Vaud), Delacroix's painting of Marianne raising the tricolour, the frontispiece of Ramuz's 1915 novel of the Napoleonic wars *La guerre dans le haut-pays*, two clips from Francis Reusser's 1999 film adaptation of the novel that are superimposed on each other. As I mentioned in Chapter 3, Reusser had collaborated with Miéville on the experimental television series *Ecoutez voir* in 1977). We also see details from landscape paintings that suggest Ramuz's novel about a young vaudois artist who returns home after study in Paris, *Aimé Pache, peintre vaudois* (1911). The film's voice-over (which is in the form of a dialogue between a man and a woman who do not sound like Godard or Miéville) remarks that only here did the tyrant of Europe free rather than enslave, and mentions how "it was the French who liberated the country from the Germanics [*les Alamans*]." While, throughout Switzerland, the République helvétique period is generally seen as a kind of national degradation and de facto occupation, in Vaud, the sense of it is more complicated. If you walk down the main street of Rolle, for instance, and you will see a plaque that commemorates Frédéric-César de la Harpe, born in Rolle in 1754 and eventually sympathetic and indeed complicit with French forces, all in the name of securing independence for Vaud from the canton of Berne.

This historical, political, and aesthetic density is what defines the entire film. Throughout, Godard and Miéville are balancing an engaged regionalism that is utterly specific to Switzerland, a genuine affection for France that is more widely accessible, and analogies in cinema and landscape imagery that offer a more general mode of address still. These references unfold as part of a genuine montage, as both the soundtracks and image tracks are almost always densely layered. So, what finally emerges from this montage, and what synthesis is being offered? Godard and Miéville are, in essence, arguing for the need to see the regionally specific together with the genuinely universal. Arguments about vaudois regionalism can only be understood alongside meditations on landscape. These green mountains look even more stunning as a train rockets through their valleys, but we cannot ignore the fact that it is a *French* train. Colour and line dance in these paintings as in these film clips, and it is the voice-over that reminds us that many painters had to leave their homes, that so many films are turning to dust. This is a version of the dialectic that has defined Godard and Miéville's work since the very beginning: regional distinctiveness and political conscience; withdrawal from the metropolis and the search for engagement; the Marian narrative presented in quotidian terms; a long talk on a sofa that is inseparably linked to Broch's obsession with "the realm of beauty at the remote periphery/accessible only to the glance." *Ici et ailleurs*: we could say that their work together was defined by that most Bazinian desire to engage with physical reality but with the romantic desire to connect it to the places we have not seen, to concepts that are beyond our sight. It was defined, we could say, by a belief that art can show us what we cannot possibly imagine and, at the same time, make us understand the feel and the contours of the places that make art fully realized, rich and unique: *Liberté et patrie*.

Chapter 6
CONCLUSION

I began this book by contrasting the fame of its two subjects: Jean-Luc Godard, the hero of the French New Wave, and Anne-Marie Miéville, the interesting but less well-known Swiss filmmaker. What I have tried to do throughout is to show that, together, they have been something else entirely—neither a hugely popular golden child nor a regional curiosity. Together, they have been a pair responsible for the most searching and nuanced negotiations of cinematic form in postwar Europe. Together, they understood the changes that television and video had brought to cinema, the ways in which that transformed medium could refresh ideas both about the local/quotidien and the political/spiritual, and the ways that these sorts of dialectic relationships could, at the same time, forge a new kind of montage and a new kind of realism. And they understood all this in a way they never seemed to in the work they did on their own. There are films that Godard made on his own that move in these directions: *Lettre à Freddy Buache* (1981), *Passion* (1982), *JLG/JLG: Autoportrait de décembre* (1994). That is also true of some films Miéville made on her own: *Papa comme maman* (1977), *Nous sommes tout encore ici* (1997), and *Après la réconciliation* (2000). These, like those Godard films above, are highly sophisticated both at the level of cinematic form and of ideological and philosophical rumination. But the films that they made together, from *Ici et ailleurs* (1974) to *Liberté et patrie* (2002), are quite different. The difference lies not simply in the evidence of collaboration, although that is often integrated into the works themselves. It can be summarized following in three statements: their work together is rooted; their work together is dualistic; and their work together is moderate.

I will explain the last one first, since it seems so counterintuitive. Really, it takes us back to Serge Daney's idea of "Le paradoxe de Godard," which I discussed in Chapter 1. "There is nothing revolutionary about Godard," Daney wrote in that 1987 essay, "rather, he is more interested in radical reformism, because reformism concerns the present" ("Le paradoxe de Godard," 7/"The Godard Paradox," 71). That has been most true when he has worked with

Miéville, a figure whose arrival as a collaborator ended the pseudo-revolutionary silliness of his Dziga Vertov period and its immediate aftermath. That set the tone for a collaboration that both evolved over the course of almost thirty years and retained a core set of formal and philosophical concerns. In terms of both form and ideology, the work that Godard and Miéville have done together never fully departs from conventions of realist representation. At the level of visuals, the work is never fully abstract, and at the level of structure, it never departs from something that is either recognizably narrative or essayistic. This is in vivid contrast to Godard works like *Meetin' WA* (1985) or *King Lear* (1987), both of which are interesting in some ways but neither of which are more than superficially engaged with the generic conventions of documentary or narrative.[1] The opposite is true of a Miéville film such as *Lou n'a pas dit non* (1994), which has very little in the way of formal distinctiveness and often feels like an unintentional spoof of a talky, pretentious art film. When they have worked together, though, they recognized the rules but sought to radically reform them, evincing both impatience with dialogue-heavy illusionist narrative and a desire to enrich and disorient realist form without ever fully displacing it. In this way, they are at the core both Modernists and Bazinians. Colin MacCabe, in his contribution to a recent anthology on Bazin, argues that Modernism is central to his poetics, writing that:

> For Bazin, in all great cinema there is a fundamental "gain" of reality, the ability to allow the spectator to explore reality further. This notion has little to do with empiricism because the reality that the camera grasps is not independent of that camera.... In the sequence of essays that constitute the first volume of *Qu'est-ce que le cinéma?*, Bazin moves between documentary and fiction while trying to elaborate the criteria by which films develop the ontological possibilities of the image ... ("Bazin as Modernist," 70)

That is not a bad way of describing Godard and Miéville's aspirations: to move between documentary and fiction while trying to elaborate the criteria by which films develop the ontological possibilities of the image. That is an intensely Modernist project, both in the way that it tries to move film language forward and in the way that it illustrates Douwe Fokkema and Elrud Ibsch's maxim, which I discussed in Chapter 1, their sense that "the syntactic code of Modernism is no more than a one-sided emphasis on particular syntagmatic options ... *which in general are provided by the linguistic system and only rarely are newly invented*" (34, emphasis mine). The break with the formal (or syntactic) options of narrative or documentary cinema is almost complete in Godard works like *Les enfants jouent à la Russie* (1993) or *Film socialisme* (2010). That is not the case at all with *Ici et ailleurs*, *Sauve qui peut (la vie)*, or *Liberté et patrie*. These signature works of their collaboration move *between* narrative and documentary rather than rejecting them entirely. They are as radical as any figure in European Modernism, and, at the same time, they are also as reformist as any such figure.

This Modernist dialectic between radicalism and reform speaks to a larger dualism in their work together, a dualism that is both informal evidence of their collaboration and further indication of the Modernist quality of the films themselves. Characteristically, it is the American critic Jonathan Rosenbaum who hit this nail right on the head, in his *Chicago Reader* piece on Godard and Miéville's 1985 video *Soft and Hard* (which, I argued in Chapter 4, deserves a central place in any discussion of their work together). Describing Miéville's contribution by way of contrast to work Godard had done on his own, he wrote there that "to my mind she saves both Godard and this video from the unchecked neo-Goethean excesses of self-regard and melancholia that characterise his more recent *JLG by JLG*" ("Godard in the Age of Video," 50). Something very similar is going on in *Ici et ailleurs* (1974), where Miéville is often a skeptical and interrogative presence, and in *Deux fois cinquante ans de cinéma français* (1995), where Godard's performance is quite clearly at odds with the voice of the film overall. He is slightly obnoxious rather than Goetheanly self-regarding or melancholic. Their work together is, in short, a montage—both literally at the level of visuals, and structurally in the way that it is always, inescapably, the product of more than one voice. It is not that I want to simply present Miéville as the sensible woman who saves the tortured art boy Godard from himself (although I think there may be something to that, and Rosenbaum seems to think so as well). Rather, I think it is essential to understand the distinctiveness of their work together as being in no small part a function of its multiplicity. These films, videos, and television programs are not clear pronouncements or smoothly efficient narrations. They are always chunkier than that, always the product of two minds fully, and sometimes painfully encountering one another.

If these films, videos, and television programs are so clearly the product of two voices, then it is no surprise that one element that unifies them is their sense of rootedness, their tendency to incorporate the places where Godard and Miéville are sharing as they work on them. This is true of the material that they made in their 1970s "Communication" period, and it becomes fully realized in an intellectual and aesthetic sense in the period that begins with *Sauve qui peut (la vie)* (1979), the subject of Chapter 4. Richard Brody saw this film as a turning point as well, especially because of the way that it used landscape as a centrally important visual element. While I object to the characteristic effacement of Miéville's role, I find Brody's assessment in his 2000 *New Yorker* profile of Godard to be otherwise invaluable:

> With its first shot, a searching view of wispy clouds and vapour trails in a deep-blue sky, "Every Man for Himself," announces one of the principal motifs of Godard's later films: some of the most sumptuous and awestruck images of nature ever put on film. The presence of nature is simply the presence of Rolle. But the pictorial richness and density can be traced directly to Godard and Miéville's constant video production in the mid-seventies. Now that Godard had his own studio, he was intimate with his tools and was able to exercise a craftsmanlike virtuosity in every aspect of his art. Starting with this film, Godard, like a painter painting the same apples or model or coastline for twenty years, developed most of his full-length projects from increasingly complex elaborations of a small number of obsessive themes, ranging from the grandly philosophical to the painfully intimate. (71)

Throughout this book, I have been trying to connect Godard and Miéville to a project of regionalism, a project that, I argued in the Chapter 1, actually points to the degree to which their work is more Swiss than French. This regionalist sensibility first emerges in the late 1970s, a period where, as Alain Bergala recalled, "Jean-Luc Godard and Anne-Marie Miéville dreamed of being directors-hosts-technicians on a little local television channel" ("Ondes de choc d'un pari lointain,"44; m.t.). But it is this 1980s work where a regionalist sensibility becomes mature, where we can see Godard and Miéville growing fully realized worlds in their Swiss garden, where the technical virtuosity that Brody identifies is coupled with a richly complex set of political, philosophical, and spiritual meditations. This emphasis on the local is characteristic of all of their best work: *Sauve qui peut (la vie)* is very much about what withdrawal to rural Switzerland means for the individual conscience. *Le Livre de Marie* and *Je vous salue, Marie* are both about imagining the Marian narrative as Protestant, and in so doing, imagining "*une Marie vaudoise.*" *Soft and Hard* uses the landscape around Lac Léman to great effect by way of presenting the struggle and the passion of shared creativity. *Liberté et patrie* is as much a meditation on the landscape and history of Vaud as it is about art and longing. In Chapter 1, I mentioned how René Prédal has argued that "[i]n leaving the capital, Godard was giving the tedious notion of regionalisation its real sense" (*Le cinéma français contemporain*, 238; m.t.), and the work that Prédal is pointing to there is basically the projects that Godard was doing with Miéville. Like Prédal, I am aware of how drably folkloristic the notion of "regionalism" has become, and aware of how true this is in France especially. But there are no alpine costumes, bearded yodellers, or dancing maidens in Godard and Miéville's work. If we really want to understand what they have been doing together, it is imperative that we see the *places* where Godard and Miéville have chosen to make films, places with their own distinctive histories and landscapes. The dialectic between place and consciousness, so important to Romanticism (across a number of media), is undeniably present here, and in Chapter 4 especially, I tried to explain the complex connection with Romanticism that Godard and Miéville's work has.

Romanticism is indeed one crucial aesthetic comparison; Modernism is another; Realism is the third. That, finally, is the way that I want to present Godard and Miéville's work: as a uniquely ambitious fusion of these three aesthetics. Their Romanticism is indeed driven by a resistance against the totalizing limitations of the enlightenment legacy in a way that is very close to eighteenth- and nineteenth-century figures like Goethe or Turner, both of whom are obvious influences on the way Godard and Miéville represent interiority and landscape. Their Modernism is defined both by a desire to hang onto the conventions of art and communication and a realization that these conventions are not up to the task of representing their contemporary world. They make feature-narratives the way that James Joyce wrote novels such as *A Portrait of the Artist as a Young Man* or *Ulysses*, and they make essayistic films the way that Hermann Broch wrote novels such as *Der Tod des Vergil* (1945). And their Realism is defined by the philosophically searching and aesthetically open engagement with the world around us that was so eloquently and rigorously laid out by André Bazin in the 1950s. I tried to argue in Chapter 3 that it is the figure of Serge Daney who makes the connection between Bazin's Realism and Modernism via their work (especially *Ici et ailleurs*), and tried to argue in Chapter 4 that a lot of the connection between Straub–Huillet and Godard–Miéville can be explained by the way that both pairs combine elements of Romanticism and Modernism. To explain what Godard and Miéville are doing, then, is to invoke the most significant aesthetic movements in post-enlightenment European history and to invoke the most significant names in European film criticism and filmmaking. Godard and Miéville may be riding two bicycles, but they have, for four decades now, been riding in a single direction, one that takes us through the very heart of European culture and navigates some of the most fundamental problems of cinema itself: thematic, formal, and technical alike. The work that they have done together, like the collaborations of Jean-Marie Straub–Danièle Huillet or Alain Tanner–John Berger, deserves a central place in the history of postwar European filmmaking.

Appendix 1:
CINÉMA PRATIQUE'S INTERVIEW WITH JEAN-LUC GODARD

Phillippe DURAND, "Jean-Luc Godard fait le point," *Cinéma Pratique* (Juin 1973): 156–60. (Translated by Jerry White)

In a way, Jean-Luc Godard needs no introduction. But do we really know him?

This long interview that he granted to *Cinéma Pratique*—of which he is a long-time reader—has the benefit of clarifying his current preoccupations. Other filmmakers will recognize their own concerns at a time when sound-image expression is opening up in new directions.

The misunderstanding of technical problems by people who make films seems to him a simple fact. It is in our columns, more than once, that Jean-Luc Godard has found explanations that nobody, in fifteen years of filmmaking, has been able to give him. Beyond an informational role, the originality of *Cinéma Pratique* for him is in the fact of being the only publication that approaches cinema from a technical standpoint.

"For me, technical matters became important," he says, "once I realized that I did not know anything and the technical level of most technicians is very low. But there is a way of speaking of technical matters: saying that it is only the materialized code of a certain societal desire, inasmuch as to speak of machines helps you understand yourself *as* a machine."

"If the computer so resembles man, this is simply because man is a machine. But we do not easily believe that! We admit that the heart is a pump, the kidneys a filter, but these considerations do not go on to other necessities, those of sexuality, for example, or the desire to be together. For my part, I am more willing to think of this Stellavox [audio equipment] as basically an appendage of myself than the reverse, myself being an appendage of some other central thing. To think of my mouth and my ass as the 'entrance' and 'exit' of a recording machine, or to think of synchronization as a unity obtained by the workings of society, helps me think completely differently. It is in this sense that I find technical matters interesting...."

WHAT IS CINEMA?

GODARD: Contrary to aestheticizing, fantasizing magazines, *Cinéma Pratique*—whose strength is that it speaks seriously about technical problems—seems to me attached to a kind of filmmaking actually practised by a lot of people in France; I want to say that your interests make it clear that the real popular cinema is the "home movie," and that, at the same time, it's something that makes the Kodak corporation happy.

This commerce of images is based on the fundamental need that man has to possess an image of himself—it is no accident that Lumière began by making *Le Déjeuner du Bébé*—an image that is always moving; it is cinema, television, and fixed. This is the source of the eternal appeal of the still photo, which responds to the conservation instinct, the desire to freeze the instant. Moreover, the Polaroid and the tape recorder are born of the desire for this image to be immediate. You must not forget that all progress has been made by amateurs, in the sense that they are responding to popular demands.

DURAND: What is your ideal for a magazine that would take account of this reality that you are evoking?

GODARD: First off, let us say that critics are specialists who are paid to sit in the movie theatre for free; thus, their relationship to the image is the inverse of the audience they are writing for.

Otherwise, their work is that of "academics" without a real connection with what I believe to be the real "commercial" cinema. What would really interest me, more than a study of *Wild Strawberries*, would be an analysis of a film made by X, with an Elmo Super-8 some Sunday in Perpignan, an analysis that would explain how what you want to do has to pass though technological considerations, and how the examination of these considerations gets his intentions across more strongly. More important than just commenting on films that are distributed would be to work on films that are not.

You go on holidays, you take some photos, you organize them, you find some captions. In sum, you offer ideas with the images and sounds, and thus you make cinema. These would not be films to shoot, but films made for the pages of a magazine, and they would be a lot more interesting. I am always excited when someone tells me a story they had witnessed; I can see what they see and what kind of film you could have made of it. Through this lens, you realize that a film magazine could explain all sorts of things, speak about everything. But the existing critical magazines are not interested in this role, which would be too high a price to pay.

DURAND: Would not what you are proposing be an irrevocable break with exploitation cinema?

GODARD: At any given moment, there are people who like to talk about *Battleship Potemkin* or *Last Tango in Paris* and then talk about the photo of their grandmother and find connections there. For me, I notice after fifteen years of cinema that the real "political" film that I would like to make would be a film about myself that I would show to my wife and my daughter so they could see what I am—in other words, a home movie. That is the popular base of cinema....

INDEPENDENCE: HOW?

DURAND: What you seem to want now, doesn't that imply a conversion on your part, since you're a professional filmmaker?

GODARD: Effectively, I have to make a detour; I will not suffer because of it. First off, I have to assure myself of a certain independence. In order to do this, I first have to reposition myself into the era of my tools. So, the technology of my day is no longer the photographic image but the magnetic image, whose evolution I can follow.

I must, at the same time, apprentice myself anew to the technology in order to make a film about my grandmother that would not be the one I would make about Mr. Y from Narbonne, because such a film would not be just a repetition of what I have already done, but something that I determine and over which I have control.

Moreover, I have to avoid being tied down by things. Bertolucci, director of *Last Tango in Paris*, said: "*Marlon Brando, c'est moi*"; so why does not he film himself? Because if he did film himself, he would not get the financing he needs since he is not a star, and, in this specific case, he would not be able to make his film. A moment comes when you have a choice only between a film that costs eight million francs and one that costs 30,000; that is my problem right now.

So, if I imagine being able to film at my house with a few friends, with the hopes of interesting 300 spectators a month who each pay ten francs per seat, that would get me the monthly minimum of 3000 francs that I need to live on. That is how, today, I think of the problem of *my* audience.

DURAND: Are you reaching a resolution?

GODARD: I am not there yet. I will maybe get there if there are other social transformations that allow me to get there. But I think of my audience as being what enables me, or will enable me, to live. It is interesting to pose the problem in this way, to think of the relation between the desire to make films and the necessity to earn a living with them. Of course, if you imagine certain types of films in totally different structures, then you are obliged to see things totally differently, to try to conceive of a different cinema.

At this moment, I am interested in the video recorder because I think that it is the only way to survive. Thanks to this technique, a film like *La Chinoise*, filmed in five weeks with four or five actors in two or three settings, could be made for a budget of 60,000 or 80,000 francs.

THE TECHNICAL RANGE

DURAND: What do you do with the comparatively reduced format of the video recorder?

GODARD: You can project a 16 mm film in every theatre in the world; for a video recorder, it is still difficult. Filming in Super-8 is easier than projecting it; it is not much for a family to own a Super-8 projector, but once you move beyond families, I prefer going back to a video recorder.

For another thing, making an hour-long black-and-white film would be less expensive with a video recorder than in Super-8 ... and, at the same time, the sound problem is solved. On the other hand, as regards closed-circuit television, you have to remember that filming in Super-8 is a lot simpler and less onerous than the same filming with television cameras, and, except for distances, gives you an irreproachable image in the telecine.

I have also become a partisan for fixed projection. I think that today, the technology finally permits us to think about the subject and the writing a bit differently. For example, it would be interesting to make certain films with a video recorder, not only from the financial standpoint, but also for grammatical and aesthetic reasons. For a face to face, for instance (shot with two cameras rather than with the shot/reverse shots—that is to say, question and answer), you have to consider the problem of dialogue, and you realize that you cannot write in the same way any more. By the simple act of questioning yourself, this technology makes the approach more complex, while simultaneously liberating and clarifying.

At the same time, I have the impression that, from now on, you can say: this film can be made with the help of slides and projected that way as well. Others can be shot on video; if you have to show it to everyone, it can be kinescoped, and so on. We are thus starting to control the tool rather than being controlled by it; this is very important.

DURAND: How do you deal with the problem of sound?

GODARD: Sound has always been slave to the image, and our group has inversely tried to conceive of an editing desk that, before being a viewing station, is founded on the synchronization between three tape recorders and unspooling loose tape instead of using perforated tape. Until then, using sound with Super-8 still presented difficulties, and semi-professional tape recorders, despite their high cost, offered sound of only mediocre quality that could be used only as wild sound. The problem is that these tape recorders were designed to record many different things, whereas we need to use them with other kinds of expectations.

The material is always promoted along the lines of what has been successful; if *Gone with the Wind* had been successful for ten years, the camera it was filmed with would have been promoted as "The Camera to film *Gone with the Wind*." For *À bout de souffle*, I needed a portable and silent 35 mm camera in order to do direct sound. It has only come out this year, from Arriflex! I remember that at the time, Beauregard, Coutard, and I offered Eclair 50 million francs to make this kind of equipment, but nothing came of the proposal.

Nevertheless, it must be said that most technical innovations have been pushed along as a result of these kinds of needs. It took Jean Rouch—unconsciously representative of a larger demand—wanting in 1955 to make a certain kind of film in a certain way for the manufacturers to discover a kind of camera that would respond to the desires of the amateur market. It must be said, but you also have to go further, or else you reproduce the eternal system and must resign yourself to it; perpetual and encouraged "reproduction" suffocates the very idea of "production."

SHOW AND PRODUCE

DURAND: How do you imagine the distribution of this different cinema?

GODARD: The man who demonstrates the need to make imagery has an evident desire to show it to the largest audience of all. So, the moment arrives when he might want to pose the question in a better way, in different terms: I have to show this image whatever number of spectators will guarantee me a living. So you no longer say, "I need a real success" but, instead, "How will I be able to live from month to month?" And: "How many people will be willing to pay five francs per month to see an image by me?"

So, you have to really acknowledge that this "home movie"—which really is a popular cinema *par excellence*—never has more than twenty spectators and that, at a certain point, *the contradiction is that these films become interesting enough for the problems of one family to be shown to the family next door.* But given all this, we can begin to think of distribution in an entirely different way....

The problem is thus one of subsistence, which is why I can easily imagine taking a part-time job so that I would not be forced to film or not be able to film when conditions are favourable!

DURAND: What role do you leave for the technical crew?

GODARD: It could be the same, and more numerous, if possible! What will change greatly is the hierarchy in the work. Technicians can sometimes spend hours or days feeling like robots, even at ORTF [Office de Radiodiffusion Télévision Française—French state-owned television]. They take orders, and because they are well paid, they do not think any more about it. But the difference is that here, because it is up to me and to a few other conditions, the technicians could say, at the end of an hour or a day, "I have had enough of just taking orders!" It is in this sense that the use of a video recorder has an extremely interesting social role.

Generally, you have to impose a better distribution of technical, aesthetic, and financial responsibilities in your film crew. I need a sound engineer who tells me: "Your lines are bad," and then takes a moment to try to write a few words. As a result, he discovers himself that it is not easy to put one word after the other, and that once you find the right words, you have to impose that on others. After that, he finds himself quite happy to be paid to record, and he does not complain about not producing!

DURAND: Have you imagined that the means of circulation, such as cassettes or cable TV, would be free or, on the other hand, the reality of monopolies?

GODARD: The two situations could coexist; nothing is so simple. Right now, in the West, we have the example of pornography, which is recorded by the cinema but prohibited on television. On the one hand, capitalism has a pretty loose rein; on the other hand, it imposes archetypes. The result is that it can avoid the posing of certain problems on television at the same time that it allows people to think that a certain kind freedom still exists.

For the past ten years, I have wanted to make a film for the small screen. Every time I talk about that, they tell me: "Go right ahead!" But I want to make a news piece on a soccer match, simply because I like soccer and I have played it. And they think: "Weird. He must be hiding something...." But I am not. It is the only film that they will not ever let me make!

GODARD VS. DRUCKER [Reference to Michel Drucker, ORTF's football commentator]

DURAND: Do you have something against the art of filming soccer, like what they do on ORTF?

GODARD: I am only against people filming soccer who do not love soccer, and thus film it badly and uninterestingly for the viewers. Overall, I reproach them for being parasites: under the pretext of not wanting to violate the sacrosanct 180-degree law, the cameras are placed only on one side of the field. By multiplying the points of view, do you not risk the audience confusing the teams?.... You treat people like they are imbeciles!

What is more, the role of the commentator is really to be a dummy. Try this: tape the sound of a weekly match, change the name of the players, and then use the same soundtrack with the image of the next week's game. I believe that everything will unfold without any surprises. The responsibility of the commentator never changes; he always has the same relationship with whatever he is commenting on because what he is doing does not interest him.

It is the same situation for other sports. We never actually see this famous "human effort" about which we hear so much. What is beautiful in the 5000 metres is the ability to follow it all. Television has the means; it can put little carts in place. But no! The people in ORTF ask no questions. They film whatever, however. You can really see this when, almost by accident, they get a nice shot, and all of the sudden, you understand better, and you get excited!

As for the multiplicity of cameras, why do this? What would be interesting would be to use two cameras together, not to make a choice between a close-up and a group shot, but because you need two cameras together to really understand a character: their masculine and feminine sides, their child and adult sides, their fascist and revolutionary sides, their voice that says yes and that little voice inside them that thinks no. *Yes and no, for me, are two cameras. Two cameras is not "number 1" and "number 2," but something completely different.* And, in that case, I have no use for six cameras or more! But, have you noticed? All the little amateur rules suggest six cameras—which are, because of their price, an impossible luxury. The manufacturers know full well that their customers watch TV: "Make your own little ORTF in your own home!" Just as before, those who make a business out of amateur cinema are implicitly suggesting: "Make your very own little *Gone with the Wind*!"

In response, it seems to me that the only work for me to do is to explain, at every moment and from A to Z, how you make *Gone with the Wind*. But again, critics do not do this work.

THINKING DIFFERENTLY

I want to give another example of things that could be done differently. When I go to the countryside, I read the local newspapers. The only photos inside them are of things like inaugurations, banquets, lawn bowling greens, firemen's balls, and so on—things that completely bore me. On the other hand, if I see the same events on the small screen in my hotel room (where I only see news made in Paris or on the Parisian model), it really interests me! So, you put that stuff in the newspaper, but you should really put something else there.

You reply that that is just one way of using it. In the old days, the slave was just using it. And then, a moment came when someone thought that this was a strange way of using it, one that took a lot of time. That is the way things are; you do not think about it. But what do you think of? For me, ever since I began shooting, I start by asking *"To what end?" and not "What shot?"* [*"En vue de quoi?" et non "Quelle vue?"*] "To what end?" is something else entirely, and, at the end of that day, that is the question that I unthinkingly answer about every moment of my life: when I get up, when I go to work, when I make love ... I always have this question in my mind: "To what end?"

Finally, what is the image? A surface where traces are inscribed. We who must be scholastic [*solentifiques*], we analyze traces. You cannot remain rigid in the face of such a surface. In the theatre, those 500 very particular kinds of telescopes that are the spectators have to work from moment to moment and then react.

You have to talk about all this. There are, at any rate, moments where you come to speak about cinema in a slightly different way and then get the people who are listening to you excited. But this is work that is in no way systematic in that you have to always be finding a way of talking person to person. And sometimes I despair and I think that I am pushing up against inevitably abandoning what we call "the cinema," and I still do not know in what other way I can pursue my aims. And yet, when I talk about this with other people, no matter who, in the street, wherever, I feel sure that there are more and more people like me, or rather that I have become one of these kinds of people!

So, there is, in some way, a common ground that should be a starting a point....

Appendix 2
INTERVIEWS WITH ANNE-MARIE MIÉVILLE

Janine EUVRARD, "Entretien avec Anne-Marie Miéville," *24 Images: La revue québécoise du cinéma* 76 (1995): 12–16. (Translated by Jerry White)

The almost tactile sensual richness of *Lou n'a pas dit non* offers itself to the eye and ear as a rare and moving poetic experience entirely directed at the trembling intimacy of things, held out to life itself. It recalls the experience of being dazzled by the short film *Le livre de Marie* (which preceded Godard's film *Je vous salue, Marie* in theatres). Thus, today, this second feature film by Anne-Marie Miéville, after the superb *Mon cher sujet* (1989), confirms the maturity of this distinctive filmmaker.

EUVRARD: The beginning of *Lou n'a pas dit non* is a bit upsetting. Is it meant as an homage to Rilke, especially to *Die Aufzeichnungen des Malte Laurids Brigge*?

MIÉVILLE: There is a sort of homage to Rilke and to Lou Andreas-Salomé, because the sequence with the little boy and his mother is a dream of Rilke's (published in *Die Aufzeichnungen des Malte Laurids Brigge*) that I wanted to film. There is also the sequence with the little girl and her father that is a memory pulled from a biography of Lou where she recounts a scene between her and her father. Also by way of homage, I find it interesting to try to show— and this is something that I will maybe one day develop into another film—a scene from the childhood of the protagonists of a film that (without wanting to fall into intense psychoanalysis) leads them to see a certain number of elements: a climate in which a child bathes and which would be a preamble to the story.

EUVRARD: Gallotta's ballet—very strong, even obscene at certain moments— comes before another, opposing scene, that of the perfectly pure dance in the apartment. Why this opposition?

MIÉVILLE: When Lou dances alone, it is her body's expression after this night that she has spent with Pierre where there were stormy discussions, very tender scenes and a move toward reconciliation at the end where they both decided to go on a pilgrimage to Rilke's tomb. It is true that her body expression to the little tune by Rossini, when she gestures alone, is a bit florid, like the dance of the Gollotta couple, which is not only a duet but a real coupling scene. If I let the dance go for ten minutes, it was not only to illustrate a moment of getting together. It was really because it is a certain moment where these two dancers become important characters, characters who, for 10 minutes, express a whole palette of situations, emotions, and tensions between men and women, and who do that through choreography, with movements and with gestures.

Each of their movements, often inconsistently, tries to exercise some power over the other. Among men, there is perhaps an involuntary brutality, while among women, there is calculation because she takes back control of things. When I saw the production of *Docteur Labus*, I was very touched by this duo, who I found to be very strong.

EUVRARD: You could say that this ballet was made to order, made for the film.

MIÉVILLE: There are a certain number of elements that come into the construction of a film that I harvested before and that will be present at the film's birth, things like dance, sculpture, Rilke. It is true that this dance is one of the first elements I harvested in preparing the film. I saw *Docteur Labus* in 1989, and I told myself that I had to do something with this. A bit later, I had a commission from the Louvre for something on the statue of Mars and Venus, and this was also an idea of the couple. Bit by bit, the idea of the couple came together, and the dance inserted itself into the film. So, I found it an environment that responded to it and valued it.

EUVRARD: Being sensitive to music, I generally find it very badly treated in cinema. In *Mon cher sujet*, it finds an important place through song. How have you worked with music?

MIÉVILLE: It is true that, generally speaking, music is treated weakly in films. You add it a bit like you add a spice; you ask it to strengthen slightly weak sections of the film, you summon it in a cavalier way. I myself have often tried, even in my short films, to make the music a real character. Music can serve the *mise en scène*, to give birth to a scene or to accompany it.

EUVRARD: The place of Art, with a capital A, is very important in your film. Could you say that art can save the world, can save the cinema?

MIÉVILLE: Save the cinema, the poor thing. I do not know, but I think that art has long helped the world to live, to not give over to its destructive furies. There is a good side of cinema that invites the other arts and lets them enrich it without pretending to speak for them. The arts are invited to share, to reflect, to accompany. That statue of the couple—which is a very old Roman statue—indicates that there is also a time that constitutes this art and that leaves traces that last to today.

EUVRARD: Are you not looking in the other arts for what cinema cannot provide?

MIÉVILLE: Probably. A bit. It is too bad. I do not see very many films. I live in Switzerland, where programming is calamitous; aside from American films, we do not see much. I try to see films in Paris, but now I can say that I do things that make me see things. From time to time, there is a meeting of minds. A Kiarostami ten days ago, a François Girard fifteen days ago, with a remarkable film about Glenn Gould. You say to yourself, like with the film from Girard, that cinema can give back the taste of music. There is everything to gain by seeing what you can do with cinema and what the other arts can bring to it.

EUVRARD: This film on solitude, non-communication, is paradoxically made positive. I often thought of Antonioni's *La Notte* or *L'Avventura* when seeing *Lou n'a pas dit non*.

MIÉVILLE: That is remarkable because tonight (January 10, 1995), I am at the Ursuline Studios where they are showing my film at the *ciné-club*; they asked me to show another film, and I had chosen *L'Avventura*, but because it's a bit long, I chose *La Notte* instead.

EUVRARD: Your viewpoint is not as dark as Antonioni's. Are you more serene?

MIÉVILLE: I think that I am a happy pessimist and that, buried by unhappiness, by miseries, you can find a positive dimension in painful parts of life: grief, for example. Rilke, in one of his elegies, writes as much. What would we know without these problems? There is, in essence, a way of trying to see the bright part of the shadow. We are in the shadows more often, especially Antonioni, maybe because he is a man.

EUVRARD: There are, in fact, four couples in your film: Lou and Pierre, the ballet dancers, Mars and Venus, and Lou and Rilke. Why this choice?

MIÉVILLE: There is Lou and Rilke because, at the time, I was reading a lot of Rilke, as well as the psychoanalytic books of Lou Salomé. The other elements—the ballet, the sculpture—were added a bit at a time. I wanted to deal with the couple, with the moments of coupling, with the difficulties and impossibilities, while still staying on a positive note. In other words, I wanted to deal with our desire for the couple to work, with the ideal image of a functioning couple. It was the idea that you have to try to love in another way, to continue, to develop a relationship.

EUVRARD: I would like to compare *Mon cher sujet* and *Lou n'a pas dit non*. The first one is a vertical film, that is to say, a film about family relations, about generations; it begins with the grandmother and continues until the daughter and her husband are expecting the granddaughter. The second film strikes me as structured more horizontally, because it is a film about a couple, about their relationship. Is this because for you, as a woman who makes films and has a certain feminine specificity, the problem of family relations is resolved and that you now have to move onto something else, to complementarities, for example?

MIÉVILLE: What you say is interesting, and I had not thought of that. It is true that the structure, the configuration of *Mon cher sujet*, on the level of cinematography, was more connected to family relations, which was at the heart of the film's questions. I had a mother, I have a daughter, who in her turn has children. With *Lou n'a pas dit non*, the structure is more free. Meanwhile, there is grief. The preceding generation has disappeared, and you still need to work through this grief along with the sorrow that remains. But, at the same time, there is a certain form of freedom. The character of Lou is a liberated woman.

EUVRARD: She is freer than Pierre.

MIÉVILLE: Yes, that was in the script from the beginning. The woman needed to be a bit older than the young friend, and because of this age, this maturity, she is on a less arduous quest, one made clear by her own reflections.

EUVRARD: This is maybe the first time that we have seen a film where poetry is so important, where it is being honoured. Can the cinema give credibility to poetry?

MIÉVILLE: Does it need that? It is true that people do not read much. I am happy that you have had this feeling about poetry. For some years, I have read Rilke very regularly, and he is, for me, an absolute, monumental poet. I wanted to pay tribute to him. I think that cinema is an art that can put poetry forward.

EUVRARD: Is your dialogue well served by Rilke texts, as Lou Salomé is well served by Rilke?

MIÉVILLE: Not really. From the beginning, there was this desire to pay tribute to Rilke and then forcefully to Lou Salomé.

EUVRARD: Is Pierre the incarnation of Rilke, a reflection of his personality?

MIÉVILLE: There is maybe a bit of that at the beginning, but as I worked on the film's construction, I abandoned the characters; it just did not do to make a modern incarnation of Rilke and Lou.

EUVRARD: The actors are superb. How did you choose them?

MIÉVILLE: I take particular care with the choice of actors, in that I take my time. You have to avoid quick casting, where you content yourself with finding a person who corresponds to the character (to her age, to a certain profile), or who is free during the dates of filming. In all the films I have made, the shorts as well as the features, I have sought a real meeting with an actor who has the age and the capacity to interpret a character—that is to say, who has the capacity as a performer, who has a need to play this character rather than another. When I settle on an actor, when there is this appropriateness, a big part of the work is already done. The spirit of the proceedings is established and the filming goes well. At first, I worked with a young woman who specialized in casting, and I soon met Marie Bunel. I did some video tests, and I immediately felt this finesse, this grace, this emotion, and this equilibrium that she possessed. She really is a great actress, but she had not yet found roles that were up to her powers. For the boy, that was a lot less easy. There was a meeting with Manuel Blanc, but he was not available; he was making a film about Algeria and had shaved his beard. We made the film in two periods: a first one without him and with other guys who could not recognize themselves in this role. The filming was harmonious, and the actors were genuinely agreeable.

EUVRARD: The rhythm of your film gives us the time to see, to feel, to live with things. There is nature, roses—

MIÉVILLE: Those are Rilke's roses. You are speaking of time, and although the film is very short, it is an hour and eighteen minutes. It is in the interior of this relatively short time that you can settle in the interior of these situations. There are quick situations and others that take the time to examine things slowly in real time.

EUVRARD: This is a film that advances in fragments. *Lou n'a pas dit non* is not entirely linear.

MIÉVILLE: In comparison with *Mon cher sujet*, I am much less concerned with linearity, to have a main thread. Very quickly, there is this need to show certain moments of a story that you must not show others.

EUVRARD: For two years, a lot of films by women have been released. They are not just confined to festivals. Is this a battle that women have won, or is it just a flash in the pan?

MIÉVILLE: It is not a flash in the pan, but it is too bad that this access comes at a time when the cinema itself is endangered. It is true that there are a lot of films by women, very different films, like those of Pascale Ferran, or Tonie Marshall, who each have their own style. But I do not think that it is going to get any easier for women. We are all in the same boat. When you want to make a film, you have to find money, and that is very difficult. There is less and less, and breakthroughs are more and more rare. In Switzerland, for example, *Lou n'a pas dit non* had a hard time getting into theatres. Of thirty films in theatres, there were twenty-nine American films, and they were in the multiplexes. We have to look to the small theatres, and there is really nowhere else left. It is unfair. I say that, with a few bucks, you can still manage for a few years, but distribution is becoming extremely difficult. I was just reading a newspaper article about Swiss television's new policy. There were three film nights, and they want to get rid of two. That means that they will also eliminate the production part, the part with which we make our films. And what is more, the films that they do make are broadcast at two in the morning, when everyone is asleep.

Danièle HIBON, *Anne Marie Miéville* (Paris: Éditions Jeu de Paume, 1998). (Translated by Marcy Goldberg)

THE FIRST SHOTS ...

How to enter into the heart of the matter, starting from the first image, the first sound, with only a few clues? With *Mon cher sujet*, for instance, I asked myself: "But how does it begin?" There are all those shots of Agnes walking, that forty-year-old woman, halfway between her mother and her daughter ... who goes on, who has to continue. Then there is her first encounter, during a funeral service—because in *Mon cher sujet* there is death, birth, death, birth. How does the idea emerge, how does the process start? How to cut into the fabric, how to begin? How to present something explicitly but without being heavy-handed, while at the same time quickly establishing the context? That is more or less the idea of the "prologues," in other words, the way in which I put together the opening sequences of my films. In *Lou n'a pas dit non*, those sequences provide clues about the characters of Pierre and Lou, about their personalities—clues that have to do with psychoanalysis.

THE MUSIC ...

In the case of *We're All Still Here*, I handled the question of the music afterwards. But in all my other films, the music came at the same time as the research and the development of the script, and certain sequences were actually born out of a piece of music. In *Le Livre de Marie*, the little girl dances to a movement from a Mahler symphony, and there is also the Chopin concerto that she listens to with her father and which leads to an exchange, to a scene. Similarly, in *Lou n'a pas dit non*, there is Rossini's *Petite Messe solennelle*, which Lou and Pierre listen to after a night of discussion, confrontation, and finally reconciliation, before they leave on their trip to Rilke's tomb. It was the music that made me write those scenes. When I heard that "Little Mass," which is so stirring, I got up from my chair and started to move. The music had brought me the idea for that sequence. It is true that the music has always come of its own accord, or does me the honour of joining me during the planning stages of the work. I have never used music like a spice to be added afterwards, in the sense of, "This is a sad passage, let us use some violin, and that passage is upbeat, so we will add a fanfare." No, the music is always there right at the start and during the development of the project, and at times, it has even given birth to certain sequences.

I have a passionate amateur's knowledge of music and lyrical expression. During my childhood, it was a way of expressing myself. In that petit bourgeois milieu, people did not express themselves, did not really talk to one another. For me, discovering physical self-expression and singing was very important. I did a lot of singing in my childhood and in my youth, and I even made some records, but I never dreamed of being a lyric singer like Angèle. My daughter used to sing as well; in fact, in *Mon cher sujet*, she sings the very beautiful song she wrote herself.

It is true that I am very sensitive to women's voices, even if one cannot forget men's singing, men's voices—I am thinking of Corsican singing, for instance. There are forms of masculine vocal expression that are more poignant, but women's vocal expression has a much greater quantitative presence. Women talk a lot, scream out their pain while giving birth, and their vocal expression generally has a greater presence; men, even if they talk, do not do it the same way, and I myself am more sensitive to women's voices. I hear not only the beauty of their voices, but also something feminine that emanates from them.

THE DIALOGUE ...

In general, it is a rather long and painful process. In constructing a film, you have an idea of what you would like to express using certain movements, certain characters. Then you look for a title and try to develop a structure out of a number of different sequences that begin to come together and form something. I already have a notion of what should be said at those moments, but finding the way to say it, well ... I know that many critics often find my dialogues too literary, too psychological. But since dialogue is a form of writing, I find it physically difficult to write the way people talk in everyday life. Still, what I write is going to be put into the bodies and mouths of the actors; so it should more or less fit. For example, with *Lou n'a pas dit non*, I was criticized because "people do not talk like that in real life." But if it is all about copying what happens in real life, we could just film ourselves at home and watch ourselves on Sunday evenings. In order to develop a thought expressed as dialogue, it is always necessary to use a form that displays a certain respect for language. Our language gets poorer by the day. I feel that I have a task to accomplish, and this seems to me like a good occasion for carrying it out.

A LABORATORY ...

Making a film is like a laboratory for a whole thought process, a place where one can take stock, not only of one's own personal development, but also other people's. It is a very privileged creative space where something can be grasped that might otherwise drift off like smoke and disappear. However, at times, I have dreamed of doing something completely different because filmmaking is the work of sublimation, as they say, and therefore restrictive. Afterwards, there is not necessarily an exchange or a return that could keep things alive. You have to start over and begin creating again immediately. If you stop, things get very quiet.

The cinema is a form of artistic expression that is also an industry. Like a busy beehive, a group of people try to assemble their skills and their efforts, in the course of one day, to bring one shot, or a few shots, into existence. That moment, even when it is plagued by difficulties and pitfalls, is an ideal image of sharing in creating something.

When a film is finished, you continue the process of distribution and presentation. You enter into a system—which, at least for the kind of film I make, is constantly shrinking and will soon cease to exist. It is a circuit of mostly unchanging traditions: you take the train; you go, for instance, to Lyon to present the film; you go to the hotel; you meet five journalists; you are interviewed on the radio; you have dinner with a city dignitary; you are propelled into a theatre in the midst of spectators who have just seen your film and who must ask questions in order to play their role, and you must answer them.

However, real moments of encounter are rare. For me, they occur only with those people who talk about what they felt and who are brave enough to express it in a sentence or two ... I would not be able to travel with a film for a year or more, as other filmmakers do; after a while, I feel that the film now belongs to others, that they can make of it what they will. You have to cut the cord, or you go crazy. It usually happens after a minimum of two years of work—a long time, in other words. What is sometimes painful with the cinema (because it is an expensive form of expression) is not being able to start over again right away. You are a little worn out, and you need to replenish yourself with real life in order to find ideas and build something anew. You are stimulated, you want to begin again right away, and it is impossible: you have to write, produce dossiers and papers.... There are empty moments where I regret that there is not more contact between filmmakers.

NOTES

NOTES TO CHAPTER 1

1 For my discussion in this book, I have had cause to draw on the filmographies in MacCabe's *Portrait of the Artist* (compiled by Sally Shafto), Bellour and Bandy's *Jean-Luc Godard: Son + Image*, Michael Witt's dissertation *On Communication*, Brenez et al.'s *Jean-Luc Godard: Documents*, the second volume of Alain Bergala's *Jean-Luc Godard par Jean-Luc Godard*, and Antoine de Baecque's *Godard: biographie*. The "Communication" chapter of this book is organized around the idea that three features were followed by two television series, and the order of these first works that I give here is basically consistent with all of these filmographies except Shafto's. Shafto specifies that *Numéro deux* was released on September 24, 1975, that *Comment ça va?* was "[p]resented at the Venice Film Festival August, 1976, and released 28 April 1978," and that *Ici et ailleurs* was "released in September 1976" (358–59). *Six fois deux*, she (among others) specifies, was broadcast from July 25 to August 29, 1976. The 1976 Venice Film Festival ran from August 24 to September 7. It is fair to say that for Shafto, *Ici et ailleurs*, *Comment ça va?*, and *Six fois deux* are, for the purposes of release dates, more or less simultaneous. This is at odds with the dates in the filmographies in *Jean-Luc Godard: Son + Image*, *Jean-Luc Godard par Jean-Luc Godard* and *Jean-Luc Godard: Documents* (which all put *Ici et ailleurs* at 1974), as well as those of *Godard: biographie* (which puts it at 1973–76) and *On Communication* (which puts *Ici et ailleurs* at 1974, although specifies that it was "first released in 1976" [331]). The order that I have here is, essentially, going with the majority view on *Ici et ailleurs*' date.

2 Godard's feature film *Je vous salue, Marie* (1985) and Miéville's short film *Le livre de Marie* (1985) were released together, and so while neither one is a collaborative work in the same way that *Soft and Hard* or *Ici et ailleurs* are, they are inseparably linked. I lay out this argument in a more detailed way in Chapter 4.

3 It is, unfortunately, worth noting that the English-language version of *Six fois deux* distributed by Electronic Arts Intermix, in addition to being extremely expensive, is available only as a DVD, whose transfer is so poor as to render the work borderline illegible at the best of times.

4 *Sympathy for the Devil* concluded with the performance of the Rolling Stones's song of that title, the rehearsals for which form a sort of backbone of the film. Godard famously and angrily disowned this version, although he also said in a 1971 interview that "there's not much difference I think, except the ending" (Goodwin et al. 12).

5   Membership of the Groupe Dziga Vertov seems to have been more extensive than just Godard and Gorin. The 1972 interview between Godard, Gorin, and Goodwin et al. has the following exchange: "*How many people are in the Dziga Vertov group?* GORIN: For the moment, two—but we are not even sure" (10). Discussing the breakup of the group, Antoine de Baecque's *Godard: biographie* describes the various post-Groupe careers of Gorin, Armand Marco, Claude Faraldo, and Isabel Pons (517). Sally Shafto's filmography in Colin MacCabe's *Portrait of the Artist* gives extensive credits for all of the films, and some of the names include Claude Nedjar (producer on 1969's *Pravda* and, as I discuss in the next chapter, the producer who brought Godard to Quebec) and May 1968 student leader Daniel Cohn-Bendit (script on 1969's *Vent d'est*); see MacCabe 355–56. Tom Luddy was their "American connection"; he told Brad Stevens that "JLG asked me to coordinate tours—involving himself and Jean-Pierre Gorin—with Dziga Vertov films, which I did—I think twice—as a kind of agent or unofficial US member of the Dziga Vertov Group: Yale, Illinois, Minnesota, Iowa, Berkeley, Ann Arbor—big audiences." See Brad Stevens, "The American Friend: Tom Luddy on Jean-Luc Godard."

6   An excellent English-language introduction to Rouch's work can be found in Joram ten Brink, ed., *Building Bridges: The Cinema of Jean Rouch* (London: Wallflower Press, 2007). Rouch's own writings on cinema and ethnography have been translated and collected as Jean Rouch, *Ciné-Ethnography*, Steven Field ed. and trans. (Minneapolis: University of Minnesota Press, 2003). In French, an excellent introduction can be found in *CinémAction* 17 (1981), a special issue edited by René Prédal called "Jean Rouch, un griot gaulois."

7   Jonathan Rosenbaum has explored these issues in his online article "The Place(s) of Danièle." Detailing the ambiguity around Straub and Huillet's co-authorship, he writes that "Danièle only began to be credited as co-auteur belatedly, after their first few films. But was this because she gradually became more active as a filmmaker or because the two of them began to place a higher value on her participation? Again, I have no idea." Rosenbaum has also pointed out that Godard had "*contribué financement*" to Straub–Huillet's *Chronik der Anna Magdelena Bach*; see his "À propos d'*Inside/Out*," Brenez et al., *Jean Luc Godard: Documents*, 376.

8   Lothringen is the German name for Lorraine. Straub was born in Metz, now part of France and the seat of Lorraine. The Alsace–Lorraine region has switched between German and French control for the last several centuries; bilingualism is very common, and the forms of German native to the area are highly dialectal.

9   La Fémis (Fondation européenne des métiers de l'image et du son) was formerly known as IDHÉC (Institut des hautes études cinématographiques). As Brody writes, Godard was, in 1989, asked by French culture minister Jack Lang "to establish a studio on the school's premises in Paris for the purpose of producing films in which students would participate, including additional chapters of *Histoire(s) du cinéma*" (546). It was Lang who, at this juncture, suggested that they call their production company Peripheria. Aside from that, though, the project did not go well; see Brody's *Everything Is Cinema* 545–48. Godard's 1991 "Rapport d'inactivité," in addition to containing the summary of their "Sonimage practice" that I quote momentarily, is mostly a lament for this project; see *Jean-Luc Godard par Jean-Luc Godard* t.2, 249–51.

10 Upon Brakhage's death in 2003, the *Telluride Times-Journal* produced an unpaginated supplement to their annual special edition for the Telluride Film Festival consisted of excerpts from Brakhage's letters to the Pences (co-founders of the festival), written to them between 1975 and 2001. It was called *Blessings: Letters from Stan Brakhage*.

NOTES TO CHAPTER 2

1. The online journal *Nouvelles vues* has recently (in number 14) reprinted an interview that Godard gave to the Montreal film magazine *Objectif 65* (it is from number 33, August-September 1964). In it, Godard has little to say about Quebec, although the interview's last question concerns his plans to make "*un film sur les mouvements indépendantistes au Canada*." Godard demurs, saying, "Yes, but I have other stuff I have to do. Maybe if it's still like this next year, if the separatists haven't taken power yet.... It's good for us French, to defend the French language through someone else." The interview is available at http://goo.gl/wz5gL. That issue of *Nouvelles vues* also has an essay by Alain Bergala called "Godard/Groulx: quelle partage du cinéma?," about Godard and the Quebec filmmaker Gilles Groulx, specifically on Godard's *Le petit soldat* (1960) and Groulx's *Le chat dans le sac* (1964), the latter a key work of Quebec cinema. That is available at http://goo.gl/jffDZ.
2. The Johnson family produced no fewer than three premiers of Quebec, albeit from three different parties. Daniel Johnson Sr. was premier from 1966 to 1968 for the Union Nationale. His younger son, Pierre-Marc Johnson, was premier for two months in 1985 for the Parti Québécois. His older son, Daniel Johnson Jr., was premier for seven months in 1994, for the Liberals.
3. As I note later on, these lectures were published in 1980 *as Introduction à une veritable histoire du cinéma*. The Montreal publisher caboose is planning to put out an English translation of this book, but it was not yet out as of this writing. The caboose edition is to have an introduction by Godard scholar Michael Witt, and caboose's website includes an unpaginated excerpt from that introduction that is a fabulous source of information about Godard's Concordia project. On May 28, 2013, that could be seen at http://www.caboosebooks.net/node/64.
4. "Shot/reverse shot" is basically the backbone of conventional film editing. Ira Konigsberg's *Complete Film Dictionary* defines it this way: "A technique of cutting developed by the Hollywood studios in which the camera switches between two conversant or intersecting individuals" (321).
5. Godard seems to be confusing the University of California/San Diego (UCSD), a huge public university that is part of the University of California system, with the University of San Diego, which is a small Catholic university. Ira Schneider talks of his appointment and his sharing of an apartment with Gorin in the audio introduction to his short video *A Weekend at the Beach with Jean-Luc Godard* (1979), which is a kind of home movie record of Godard's visit to the beach in Del Mar, California. Tom Luddy, Alice Waters, Gorin, and Wim Wenders all appear in the video. We also get to see Godard in his swim trunks wearing a very silly sun hat. The video is distributed by Electronic Arts Intermix and was included in a compilation of Godard-related films tucked into *The Believer* 61 (2009).

6   I am not really sure what to call this camera. In the version of the "Genèse d'une camera" dialogues published in *Cahiers du cinéma* 348–49 and 350 and reprinted in *Jean-Luc Godard par Jean-Luc Godard t.1*, nomenclature varies. Bergala's introduction speaks of "*la caméra dont Godard a besoin et qu'il a baptisé alors la 8-35*," although when that dialogue was translated by Lynn Kirby for *Camera Obscura*, we read "the camera Godard wanted and which he christened the 35-8" (165). During the dialogue, Beauviala uses the term "35-8" (521 *inter alia*), as does Godard (530 *inter alia*). Brody's biography also uses the term "35-8" (421). A sketch that accompanies the dialogue "Genèse d'une camera" dialogue uses the term "AATON 8/35" (532), and that is the term that Godard's poetic lament for the failure of the camera uses as well (538). The opening titles of *Prénom Carmen* have a credit for "*Caméras: Aaton 35/8 Arriflex*." In the second part of the dialogue, Romain Goupil uses the term "8-35" (546), and section 6 of the "Genèse d'une caméra" dialogue has the title "De « Voyage en Italie » à la 8-35" (553); 8-35 is also the term Antoine de Baecque uses in his *Godard: biographie* (546, 607).

7   Article 70 of the Swiss constitution reads as follows: "*Les langues officielles de la Confédération sont l'allemand, le français et l'italien.*" Article 101, however, reads as follows: "*Les langues* nationales *sont l'allemand, le français, l'italien et le romanche*" (emphasis mine). Romansch, a Romance language close to Italian and spoken by around 35,000 people, mostly in the canton of Graubünden (known in French as Grisons), enjoys considerably less status than the three *official* Swiss languages. It is unusual to encounter an official document in Romansch outside of Graubünden. It remains important as a national symbol, though, as it is spoken nowhere outside of Switzerland, even though few Swiss, as we see in Buache's letter, pay much attention to it. It is in many ways analogous to the place of Irish Gaelic in the Republic of Ireland.

NOTES TO CHAPTER 3

1   This is a pun in French, combining the words for "terrorized" (*terrorisé*) and "theorized" (*théorisé*), which are pronounced nearly identically.
2   Michael Witt's 2001 article "Going Through the Motions" is a meticulous discussion of the series' use of this effect.
3   Sorting out the author's real name is no simple task. Jean-Pierre Bardos' "Postface" to Librairie Belin's 1977 facsimile edition recalls that the book was originally given to Belin by the philosopher Alfred Fouillée, but that "the author was his own wife, Madame Alfred Fouillée, born Augustine Tuillerie, mother by a first marriage to the philosopher Jean-Marc Guyau, himself the author of scholarly books published by the press A. Colin" (313; m.t.).

NOTES TO CHAPTER 4

1   Like *A Weekend at the Beach with Jean-Luc Godard*, this two-part, fifty-minute interview was included in a DVD compilation of Godard-related material tucked into *The Believer* 61 (2009).

2   I feel the same way about *Scénario vidéo Sauve qui peut (la vie)* that Fredric Jameson does about *Scénario du film Passion*; of that film he writes that it "should rather be considered an independent work in its own right, and something of an aesthetically autonomous satellite to *Passion*, rather than some mere accompanying document" (161).

3   What Daney says is "Prosper est un narrateur efficace: pas de graisse, que de nerf et du yop-la-boum." He is alluding here to a Maurice Chevalier song called "Prosper (yop la boum)," a song that was also being used as a jingle in a commercial for gingerbread in the France of the 1980s.

4   This passage is quoted, with this translation, in Laugier 29. It is also cited, in the same words, in Brody's, *Everything Is Cinema*, 460; Brody does not mention Laugier but does give the same date-only citation of *Nouvel observateur* that is found in Laugier's endnotes. Neither one mentions that the article was actually about the release of *Prénom Carmen*. Drillon's piece is also found in *Godard par Godard*, t.1, 582–87.

5   This is repeated, unattributed either to Brody or the interviews in *Studio* and *Télérama* that one finds in Brody's endnotes, in de Baecque's *Godard: biographie*: "les romantiques allemands sont recommandés par Paul Godard, qui fait découvrir à son fils Robert Musil, Hermann Broch, Thomas Mann" (27).

NOTES TO CHAPTER 5

1   There is a version of this dialogue in the book *2x50 ans de cinéma français: phrases (sorties d'un film)*. This reproduces parts of the soundtrack from the film in short lines that make it seem like poetry. This passage appears as "pourquoi / célébrer le cinéma / parce que / il n'est pas assez célèbre" (10). The dialogue in the film has Godard saying, "Pourquoi célébrer le cinéma? Il n'est pas assez célébré déjà?" Thus, the book is not an equivalent of a published screenplay; the lines are not always precisely reproduced, and not everything from the film is found there. P.O.L. has published books like this for *JLG/JLG*, *For Ever Mozart*, *Allemagne neuf zéro*, *Les enfants jouent à la Russie*, *Éloge de l'amour*, and *Film socialisme*.

2   This musical choice was clearly influenced in part by Manfred Eicher, ECM's founder. ECM has a long-standing relationship with Pärt, and Eicher has a long-standing relationship with Godard. Brody writes that during the production of 1990's *Nouvelle vague*, Eicher "sent Godard some CDs of music by Arvo Pärt and David Darling in the hope that he might find it useful for a film." Brody reports that Godard felt very connected to Pärt's music, and goes on to say that "*Nouvelle vague* and almost every film Godard subsequently made features recordings of music produced by Eicher" (528).

3   There is no doubt a story here, although I am not sure this is the place to tell it. Expo 2002 was hosted by four cities: Bienne, Neuchâtel, Yverdon-les-Bains, and Morat. All but Morat are in the Jura mountains, and the "Arteplage mobile du Jura" sailed in three lakes of the region (Bienne, Neuchâtel, and Morat). The "du Jura," however, clearly refers not to the mountain range but to the *canton* of Jura, whose flag flew on the Arteplage mobile. The Francophone-majority République et Canton du Jura was, as I discussed in Chapter 3, created in 1979 as a result of a struggle for independence from the German-speaking-majority canton of Berne that goes back at least to 1815. The name "Jura" still conjures

images of regional insurgency in Switzerland, and Godard and Miéville cannot have been unaware of this, especially given the strong vaudois regionalism of *Liberté et patrie*, which I discuss above.

NOTE TO CHAPTER 6

1. I certainly do not mean to dismiss either film. To my mind, *King Lear* is one of Godard's strangest works, and I mean that in the most positive way. The way that he weaves together elements is unlike anything else in his body of work, even though the slightly mad quality of it all does feel seminally Godardian. The film mixes European high culture (Shakespeare), the avant-garde (Peter Sellars as "William Shakespeare Junior the Fifth" and as a co-writer), American popular and highbrow culture (Norman Mailer as another co-writer, Molly Ringwald as Cordelia, and Woody Allen and Mailer as stars, albeit ones who were barely onscreen at all and who quit the production in frustration, respectively. *Meetin' WA* is a deliciously funny film, a sharp, precise, and utterly unconventional study in the ways that artists genuinely interested in each other's work sometimes cannot quite connect. Tom Luddy told me (in a phone conversation on May 6, 2011) that the idea for *Meetin' WA*, which is made up mostly of an interview between Godard and Allen (translated by an off-screen Annette Insdorf, whose good efforts are often highjacked by Godard), was suggested by him. Allen's just-finished *Hannah and Her Sisters* was about to premier in Cannes (at that time, Allen famously never went to Cannes and thus never gave a Cannes press conference), and Luddy thought that a film like this would be an interesting way of making up for that. To that end, Luddy convinced Cannes's then-director, Gilles Jacob, to put up some of the money for its production.

BIBLIOGRAPHY

Adorno, Theodor. *Moments musicaux. Neu gedruckte Aufsätze 1928–1962.* Frankfurt am Main: Suhrkamp, 1964.

———. *Essays on Music.* Trans. Susan H. Gillespie, ed. Richard Leppert. Berkeley: University of California Press, 2002.

Andrew, Dudley, ed. *Opening Bazin: Postwar Film Theory and Its Afterlife.* Oxford: Oxford University Press, 2011.

Azoury, Phillipe and Olivier Seguret. "Miéville et Godard racontent leur harmonie sur le tournage: 'Jean-Luc a insisté pour jouer'." *Libération,* 27 December 2000. 23.

Barthes, Roland. "La mort de l'auteur." *Roland Barthes: Œuvres complètes,* Vol. 3. Ed. Éric Marty. Paris: Éditions du Seuil, 2002. 40–45.

———. "The Death of the Author." Trans. Steven Heath. *Modern Theory and Criticism.* Ed. David Lodge. London: Longman, 1988. 167–72.

Bazin, André. "On the *politique des auteurs.*" Trans. Peter Graham. *Cahiers du cinéma: The 1950s, Neo-Realism, New Wave.* Ed. Jim Hillier. Cambridge: Harvard University Press, 1985. 248–59.

———. *Qu'est-ce que le cinéma?* Paris: Éditions du Cerf, 2000.

———. "De le politique des auteurs." *La politique des auteurs: les textes.* Ed. Antoine de Baecque. Paris: Cahiers du cinéma, 2001. 99–117.

———. *What Is Cinema?* Trans. Timothy Barnard. Montreal: caboose, 2009.

Beauviala, Jean-Pierre and Jean-Luc Godard. "Genesis of a Camera (First Episode)." Trans. Lynn Kirby. *Camera Obscura* 13–14 (1985). 164–193.

Bellour, Raymond, and Mary Lea Bandy, eds. *Jean-Luc Godard: Son + Image 1974–1991.* New York: Museum of Modern Art, 1992.

Bensimon, Jacques, Christian Rasselet, and Pierre Théberge. "Les cravates rouges. Entretien avec Jean-Luc Godard." *Nouvelles vues* 14 (2013). Available at http://goo.gl/wz5gL.

Bergala, Alain. "Le juste milieu." *Cahiers du cinéma* 307 (1980). 39–42.

———. "La passion du plan selon Godard." *Revue Belge du cinéma* 22–23 (1987). 134–50.

———, ed. *Jean Luc Godard par Jean-Luc Godard.* 2 Vols. Paris: Cahiers du cinéma, 1998.

———. *Nul mieux que Godard*. Paris: Cahiers du cinéma, 1999.
———. "Ondes de choc d'un pari lointain." *Cahiers du cinéma* 583 (2003). 64–66.
———. "Godard / Groulx : quel partage de cinéma? Le Chat dans le sac comme film-charnière." *Nouvelles vues* 14 (2013). Available at http://goo.gl/jffDZ.
Berger, John. *Ways of Seeing*. London: Penguin, 1971.
Bickerton, Emilie. "The Mage of Lake Geneva." *New Left Review* 68 (March / April 2011). 151–58.
Bonitzer, Pascale. "J. M. S. et J. L. G." *Cahiers du cinéma* 264 (February 1976). 5–10.
———. "Peur et commerce." *Cahiers du cinéma* 316 (1980). 5–7.
Bontemps, Jean, Jean-Louis Comolli, Michel Delahaye, and Jean Narboni. "Struggling on Two Fronts." Trans. Diana Mathias. *Cahiers du cinéma: The 1960s, New Wave, New Cinema, Reevaluating Hollywood*. Ed. Jim Hillier. Cambridge: Harvard University Press, 1992. 294–99.
Brakhage, Stan. *Brakhage Scrapbook: Collected Writings, 1964–1980*. Robert Haller, ed. New Paltz: Documentext, 1982.
Braucourt, Guy. "*Ici et ailleurs* et *Six fois deux*." *Écran* 51 (1976). 56–57.
———. "Young and Dynamic." *Jump Cut* 18 (1978). 8.
Brenez, Nicole, et al., eds. *Jean-Luc Godard: Documents*. Paris: Centre Georges Pompidou, 2006.
———. "The Forms of the Question." Ed. Michael Temple, James S. Williams, and Michael Witt. *For Ever Godard*. London: Black Dog Publishers, 2004. 160–77.
Bresson, Robert. *Notes sur le cinématographe*. Paris: Gallimard, 1975.
———. *Notes on Cinematography*. Trans. Jonathan Griffin. New York: Urizen Books, 1977.
Brody, Richard. *Everything Is Cinema: The Working Life of Jean-Luc Godard*. New York: Metropolitan Books, 2008.
———. "Auteur Wars: Godard, Truffaut, and the Birth of the New Wave." *New Yorker*, 7 April 2008. 56–65.
———. "An Exile in Paradise: How Jean-Luc Godard Disappeared from the Headlines and into the Movies." *New Yorker*, 20 November 2000. 62–76.
Broch, Hermann. *The Death of Virgil*. Trans. Jean Starr Untermeyer. New York: Pantheon, 1945.
———. *Der Tod des Vergil*. Frankfurt am Main: Suhrkamp Verlag, 1982.
Bruno, G. *Le tour de la France par deux enfants*. Paris: Librairie Belin, 1977. [1877]
Buache, Freddy. "Un cinéaste vaudois." *L'Avant-scène cinéma* 323–24 (1984). 67–68.
———. *Trente ans de cinéma suisse: 1965–1995*. Paris: Centre Georges Pompidou, 1995.
———. "Préambule." Ed. Brenez et al., eds. *Jean-Luc Godard: Documents*. 343–44.
Büttner, Elisabeth. "In the Image Workshop: Jean-Luc Godard, Anne-Marie Miéville, and the Beginning of Sonimage." James and Florian Zeyfang, eds., 61–92.
Crowley, Patrick and Paul Hegarty, eds. *Formless: Ways In and Out of Form*. Berne: Peter Lang, 2005.

Daney, Serge. "Le Therrorisé (Pedagogie godardienne)." *Cahiers du cinéma* 262 (1976). 32–40.

———. "Le paradoxe de Godard." *Revue Belge du cinéma* 22–23 (1987). 7.

———. *Le Salaire du zappeur*. Paris: P.O.L., 1993.

———. *La rampe: Cahier critique, 1970–1982*. Paris: Petite bibliothèque des Cahiers du cinéma, 1996.

———. "Dialogue entre Jean-Luc Godard et Serge Daney." *Cahiers du cinéma* 513 (1997). 49–55.

———. "Theorize/Terrorize (Godardian Pedagogy)." Trans. Annwyl Williams. *Cahiers du cinéma, Volume 4: 1973–1978: History, Ideology, Cultural Struggle*. Ed. David Wilson. New York and London: Routledge/British Film Institute, 2000. 116–123.

———. *La maison cinéma et le monde 1: Le temps des Cahiers, 1962–1981*. Paris: P.O.L., 2001.

———. *La maison cinéma et le monde 2: Les Années Libé, 1981–1985*. Paris: P.O.L., 2002.

———. "The Godard Paradox." Ed. Michael Temple, James S. Williams, and Michael Witt. *For Ever Godard*. Black Dog Publishers. London: 2004. 68–71.

Daney, Serge et al., eds. *Marguerite Duras: Les yeux verts. Cahiers du cinéma* 312–13 (1980).

de Baecque, Antoine. *Godard: biographie*. Paris: Grasset, 2010.

de Certeau, Michel, Dominique Julia and Jacques Revel. *Une politique de la langue. La Révolution française et les patois: l'enquete de Grégoire*. Paris: Gallimard, 1975.

de Goëje, Frédérique. "Godard prétexte à mes balbutiments." Ed. Jean-Marie Touratier and Daniel Busto. *Jean-Luc Godard: Télévision-Écritures*. Paris: Galilée, 1979. 49–54.

Deleuze, Gilles. "Trois questions sur *Six fois deux*. À propos de *Sur et sous la communication*." *Cahiers du cinéma* 271 (1976). 5–12.

———. *Cinema 2: L'image-temps*. Paris: Éditions de Minuit, 1985.

———. *Cinema 2: The Time-Image*. Trans. Hugh Tomlinson and Robert Galeta. Minneapolis: University of Minnesota Press, 1989.

———. "On 'Sur et sous la communication': Three Questions about 'Six fois deux.'" Bellour and Bandy, eds., 35-41.

Diawara, Manthia. *African Cinema: Politics and Culture*. Bloomington: Indiana University Press, 1992.

———. "Sonimage in Mozambque." James and Zeyfang, eds., 93–124.

Dolto, Françoise. *L'Évangile au risque de la psychanalyse*. Vol. 1. Paris: Éditions du Seuil, 1980.

Dolto, Françoise and Gérard Sévérin. *The Jesus of Psychoanalysis: A Freudian Interpretation of the Gospel*. Trans. Helen R. Lane. New York: Doubleday, 1979.

Drillon, Jacques. "La star, c'est le film: un entretien avec Jean-Luc Godard." *Nouvel Observateur* 999 (30 Décembre 1983). 52–54.

Dubois, Phillipe. Introduction to "*Sauve qui peut (la vie)*: Quelques remarques sur la réalisation et la production du film." *Revue Belge du cinéma* 22–23 (1987). 117.

Dumas, André. "À bout de foi." *Cahiers du cinéma hors-série: spécial Godard : 30 ans depuis* (1991). 88–92.

Durand, Phillipe. "Jean-Luc Godard fait le point." *Cinéma Pratique*, June 1973. 156–60.

Fairfax, Daniel. "Birth (of the Image) of a Nation: Jean-Luc Godard in Mozambique." *Acta Univ Sapientiae, Film and Media Studies* 3 (2010). 55–67.

Fanon, Frantz. *Les damnés de la terre*. Paris: Gallimard, 1991. [1961]

———. *The Wretched of the Earth*. Trans. Constance Farrington. New York: Grove, 1994. [1963]

Fargier, Jean-Paul. "Au delà du principe de P. (*Le camion; Comment ça va, Maman Kusters*)." *Cahiers du cinéma* 279–280 (1977). 31–37.

Faroult, David. "Du *vertovisme* du Groupe Dziga Vertov. À propos d'un manifeste méconnue et d'un film inachevé (*Jusqu'à la victoire*)." Brenez et al., eds., 134–37.

Fokkema, Douwe, and Elrud Ibsch. *Modernist Conjectures: A Mainstream in European Literature 1910–1940*. London: C. Hurst. 1987.

Gianvito, John. "Anne-Marie Miéville." Locke and Warren eds., 125.

"Godard et le groupe Dziga Vertov." *L'Avant-scène cinéma* 171 / 172 (1976). 48–53.

Godard, Jean-Luc. *Introduction à une véritable histoire du cinéma*. Paris: Albatros, 1980.

———. " 'Manifeste', El Fatah, Julliet 1970." Brenez et al., eds., 138–40.

———. "*Moi Je*, projet du film." Brenez et al., eds., 195–243.

———. "Refus du projet pour le 700ᵉ anniversaire de la Confédération helvétique." Nicole Brenez et al., eds., 344–57.

Godard, Jean-Luc, and Anne-Marie Miéville, eds. *Cahiers du cinéma* 300 (1979).

———. "*Soft and Hard*: Soft talk on a hard subject between two friends." *Revue Belge du cinéma* 22–23 (1987). 161–67.

———. *2x50 ans de cinéma français: phrases (sorties d'un film)*. Paris: P.O.L. 1998.

———. *Four Short Films*. Munich: ECM Records, 2006.

Goodwin, Michael, Tom Luddy, and Naomi Wise. "The Dziga Vertov Film Group in America: An Interview with Jean-Luc Godard and Jean-Pierre Gorin." *Take One* 2:10 (1971). 9–27.

Grant, Catherine. "Home Movies: The Curious Cinematic Collaboration of Jean-Luc Godard and Anne-Marie Miéville." Temple, Williams, and Witt, eds., 100–17.

Harcourt, Peter. "Le Nouveau Godard: An Exploration of *Sauve qui peut (la vie)*." *Film Quarterly* 35:2 (1981–82). 17–27.

———. "Metaphysical Cinema: Two Recent Films by Jean-Luc Godard." *CineAction* 11 (1987–88). 2–10.

———. "Analogical Thinking: Organizational Strategies Within the Work of Jean-Luc Godard." *CineAction* 75 (2008). 20–23.

Heidegger, Martin. *Unterwegs zur Sprache*. Tübingen: Verlag Günter Neske Pfullingen, 1959.

———. "Sur le cinéma, le Japon et le Nô." Trans. Patrick Lévy. *Cahiers du cinéma* 186 (1967). 46.

———. *On the Way to Language*. Trans. Peter D. Hertz. New York: Harper and Row, 1971.

Hennebelle, Guy. "Un charabia indigeste." *Écran* 51 (1976). 57.

———. "Incoherent Gibberish." *Jump Cut* 18 (1978). 8–9.

Hoberman, J. "Between Two Worlds." *American Film*, November 1983. 14, 75–79.

———. *Vulgar Modernism: Writings on Movies and Other Media*. Philadelphia: Temple University Press, 1991.

Hughes, Alex, and James S. Williams eds. *Gender and French Cinema*. Oxford: Berg, 2001.

"Introduction." *Camera Obscura* 8–9–10 (Fall 1982). 5.

Ishaghpour, Youssef. *Cinéma contemporain: de ce côté du miroir*. Paris: Éditions de la différence, 1986.

James, Gareth, and Florian Zeyfang, eds. *I Said I Love. That Is the Promise. The TVideo Politics of Jean-Luc Godard*. Berlin: B-Books, 2003.

Jameson, Fredric. *The Geopolitical Aesthetic: Cinema and Space in the World System*. London: British Film Institute, 1995.

Jones, Kent. "A Stranger's Posture: Notes on Bresson's Late Films." Ed. James Quandt. *Robert Bresson*. Toronto: Cinematheque Ontario, 1998. 393–402.

Jousse, Thierry. "*Le Rapport Darty*." *Cahiers du cinéma hors-série: spécial Godard : 30 ans depuis* (1991). 98.

Kolker, Robert Phillip. "Angle and Reality: Godard and Gorin in America." Sterritt, ed., 59–68.

Konigsberg, Ira. *The Complete Film Dictionary*. New York / Scarborough: New American Library, 1987.

Larouche, Michel. "Godard et les Québécois." *CinémAction* 52 (1989). 158–64.

Laugier, Sandra. "The Holy Family." Locke and Warren eds., 27–37.

Le Peron, Serge. "*Numéro deux*: entre le zéro et l'infinie." *Cahiers du cinéma* 262–263 (1976). 11–13.

Levi, Pavle. "The Crevice and the Stitch." *Critical Quarterly* 51:3 (2009). 41–62.

Lévy, Patrick. Introduction to "Martin Heidegger: Sur le cinéma, le Japon et le Nô." *Cahiers du cinéma* 186 (1967). 45–46.

Liogier, Hélène. "1960: vue d'Espagne, la Nouvelle Vague est fasciste ou la Nouvelle Vague selon Jean Parvulesco." *1895* 26 (1998). 127–53.

Locke, Maryel. "A History of the Public Controversy." Locke and Warren, eds., 1–9.

——— and Charles Warren, eds. *Hail Mary: Women and the Sacred in Film*. Carbondale: Southern Illinois University Press, 1990.

Luther, Martin. *Christian Liberty*. Philadelphia: Fortress Press, 1957. [1520]

Lyon, Elizabeth. "La passion, c'est pas ça." *Camera Obscura* 8–9–10 (Fall 1982). 7–10.
Lyotard, Jean-François. *La condition postmoderne*. Paris: Éditions de minuit, 1979.
MacCabe, Colin. *Godard: Images, Sounds, Politics*. London: British Film Institute, 1980.
———. "Betaville." *American Film*, September 1985. 61–63.
———. *Godard: A Portrait of the Artist at Seventy*. London: Faber & Faber, 2005. [2003]
———. "The Commerce of Cinema." Temple, Williams, and Witt, eds., 94–99.
———. "Bazin as Modernist." Ed. Dudley Andrew. *Opening Bazin: Postwar Film Theory and Its Afterlife*. Oxford: Oxford University Press, 2011. 66–76.
Mai en Décembre: Godard en Abitibi. Dir. Julie Perron. Office national du film du Canada, 2000.
Maule, Roseanna. "Introduction: Marguerite Duras, *la grande imagière*." *In the Dark Room: Marguerite Duras and Cinema*. Eds. Roseanna Maule and Julie Beaulieu. Berne: Peter Lang, 2009. 23–63.
Mérimée, Prosper. *Carmen*. Paris: Éditions Garnier Frères, 1960. [1845]
———. *Columba and Carmen*. Trans. Lady Mary Lord. London: William Heinemann, 1923.
Miéville, Anne-Marie. *Après la réconciliation: scénario*. Paris: Cahiers du cinéma, 2000.
Morgan, Daniel. *Late Godard and the Possibilities of Cinema*. Berkeley: University of California Press, 2013.
Morrey, Douglas. "An Embarrassment of Riches: Godard and the Aesthetics of Expenditure in *Le Rapport Darty*." *Formless: Ways In and Out of Form*. Eds. Patrick Crowley and Paul Hegarty. Berne: Peter Lang, 2005. 229–37.
Moullet, Luc. "Jean-Luc Godard." *Cahiers du cinéma* 106 (1960). 25–36.
Mulvey, Laura. *Visual and Other Pleasures*. Bloomington: Indiana University Press, 1989.
———. "Marie/Eve: Continuity and Discontinuity in J-L Godard's Iconography of Women." Locke and Warren, eds., 39–53.
———. "The Hole and the Zero: The Janus Face of the Feminine in Godard." Bellour and Bandy, eds., 75–88.
———. *Fetishism and Curiosity*. London: British Film Institute, 1996.
Narboni, Jean. "Laissez rêver la ligne." *Cahiers du cinéma* 316 (1980). 8–9.
Oudart, Jean-Pierre, and Dominique Terres. "Une expérience de Super 8 au Mozambique." *Cahiers du cinéma* 246 (1979). 54–59.
Peary, Gerald. "In Praise of Jean-Luc Godard." *Boston Phoenix*, 31 October–7 November 2002.
Penley, Constance. "Pornography, Eroticism." *Camera Obscura* 8–9–10 (Fall 1982). 13–20.
———. "Les Enfants de la Patrie." *Camera Obscura* 8–9–10 (Fall 1982). 33–58.
Powrie, Phil. "Godard's *Prénom Carmen* (1984), Masochism, and the Male Gaze." *Forum for Modern Language Studies* 31:1 (1995). 64–73.

Prédal, René. "Les trois âges de Godard." *CinémAction* 52 (1989). 12–18.

———. *Le cinéma français contemporain*. Paris: Éditions du Cerf, 1984.

Quandt, James, ed. *Robert Bresson*. Toronto: Cinematheque Ontario, 1998.

Rafferty, Terrence. "Godard as Oscar Provocateur." *New York Times*, 2 January 2011.

Rodchencko, H.A. "Bluejean-Luc Godard." *Film Comment* 23:6 (1987). 2–3.

Rosenbaum, Jonathan. "Eight Obstacles to the Appreciation of Godard in the United States." Bellour and Bandy, eds., 197–204.

———. "Godard in the Age of Video." *Chicago Reader*, 17 November 1995. 50–51.

———. "International Harvest." *Chicago Reader*, 22 November 1996. 38–39.

———. "The Last Filmmaker: A Local, Interim Report." Ed. James Quandt. *Robert Bresson*. Toronto: Cinematheque Ontario. 17–26.

———. "Daney in English: A Letter to *Trafic*." *Senses of Cinema* 13 (April–May 2001). http://sensesofcinema.com/2001/13/daney/ or http://goo.gl/q0zyZ.

———. "The Place(s) of Danièle." *Undercurrent* 3 (2006). http://www.fipresci.org/undercurrent/issue_0306/huillet_rosenbaum.htm or http://goo.gl/k6bQ1.

Roth, Laurent. "*2x50 ans de cinéma français*." *Cahiers du cinéma* 492 (1995). 84–85.

Roud, Richard. *Straub*. New York: Viking, 1972. [1971]

Rowe, Kathleen K. "Romanticism, Sexuality, and the Canon." *Journal of Film and Video* 42:1 (Spring 1990). 49–65.

Sanbar, Elias. "Vingt et un ans après." *Trafic* 1 (1991). 109–20.

Sarris, Andrew. "Godard and the Revolution." Sterritt, ed., 50–58.

Scemama, Céline. *Histoire(s) du cinéma de Jean-Luc Godard: La force faible d'un art*. Paris: L'Harmattan, 2006.

Schrader, Paul. *Transcendental Style in Film: Ozu, Bresson, Dreyer*. Cambridge: Da Capo, 1972.

Steinebach, Sylvie. "Les signes du mal à vivre." *L'Avant-scène cinéma* 323–324 (1984). 4–11.

Sterritt, David, ed. *Jean-Luc Godard: Interviews*. Jackson: University of Mississippi Press, 1998.

Stevens, Brad. "The American Friend: Tom Luddy on Jean-Luc Godard," *Senses of Cinema* 44 (August 2007). http://sensesofcinema.com/2007/feature-articles/tom-luddy-godard/ or http://goo.gl/Aju8M.

Stoneman, Rod. "*Soft and Hard*: Intimations, Insinuations, Implications." *Film Ireland* 110 (2006). 32–34. [Reprinted in French translation in Brenez et al., eds., 316–318]

Tarantino, Michael. "Alain Tanner: After *Jonah*." *Sight and Sound*, Winter 1978/79. 40–43.

Temple, Michael. "Inventer un film. Présentation de *Moi Je*." Trans. Franck Le Gac. Brenez et al., eds., 189–94.

———, James S. Williams and Michael Witt, eds. *For Ever Godard*. London: Black Dog, 2004.

Thompson, Kristin. *Breaking the Glass Armour: Neoformalist Film Analysis*. Princeton: Princeton University Press, 1988.

Thomsen, Christian Braad. "Filmmaking and History: Jean Pierre Gorin Interviewed." *Jump Cut* 3 (1974). 17–19.

Toubiana, Serge. "Le hasard arbitraire." *Cahiers du cinéma* 262–263 (1976). 15–19.

Touratier, Jean-Marie and Daniel Busto, eds. *Jean-Luc Godard: Télévision/Écritures*. Paris: Galilée, 1979.

Vallières, Pierre. *Nègres blancs d'Amérique: autobiographie précoce d'un "terroriste" québécois*. 1968. Paris: François Maspero, 1969.

———. *White Niggers of America*. Trans. Joan Pinkham. Toronto/Montreal: McClelland and Stewart, 1971.

Virolleaud, Camille. "Camille, vingt-cinq ans après." *Cahiers du cinéma* 583 (2003). 66–67.

Witt, Michael. "*On Communication: The Work of Anne-Marie Miéville and Jean-Luc Godard as 'Sonimage' from 1973 to 1979*." Diss., University of Bath, 1998.

———. "Going Through the Motions: Unconscious Optics and Corporeal Resistance in Miéville and Godard's *France/tour/détour/deux/enfants*." *Gender and French Cinema*. Ed. Alex Hughes and James S. Williams. Oxford: Berg, 2001. 171–94.

———. "Shapeshifter: Godard as Multimedia Installation Artist." *New Left Review* 29 (September/October 2004). 73–90.

Wollen, Peter. *Signs and Meaning in the Cinema*. London: Secker and Warburg, 1972.

———. *Readings and Writings: Semiotic Counter-Strategies*. London: Verso, 1982.

Wood, Robin. "Realism and Revolution." *Film Comment* 13:3 (1977). 17–23.

INDEX

2 ou 3 choses je sais d'elle (1966), 72, 103
24 Images (Quebec film magazine), 13
35-8 (experimental camera), 49, 53–56, 186n6
1968, 4, 9, 10, 11, 32, 38, 39, 41–42, 80–81, 90, 184n5

Aaton, 26, 49, 53–56, 186n6
Abitibi (region of Quebec), 42–43, 52
À bout de souffle (1960), 3, 8, 9, 21, 72, 117, 169
Adorno, Theodor, 111
Akerman, Chantal, 16, 28
Alphaville (1965), 21, 145
amateur film, 30–31, 67, 166–68
An American Family (1971), 89
Antonioni, Michelangelo, 175
Après la réconciliation (2000), 7, 13, 137–39, 145, 159
Arriflex, 55, 169
Aumont, Jacques, 56
authorship, 11–16
Azoury, Phillipe, 13

Bach, Johann Sebastian, 122
Band à part (1964), 21, 117
Bandy, Mary Lee, 147, 183n1
Barthes, Roland, 11, 12, 75
Baye, Nathalie, 49, 99–100, 103–4, 142
Bazin, André, 11–12, 15–16, 19, 21, 24, 32, 39, 64, 71–72, 81, 83, 147, 150–51, 160, 163

Beauviala, Jean-Pierre, 2, 26, 49, 53–56, 186n6
Beckett, Samuel, 103–4
Beethoven, Ludwig van, 109, 111, 112
Bellour, Raymond, 22
Bergala, Alain, 7, 29, 47, 54, 59, 79, 88–89, 90, 108, 120, 162, 183n1, 185n1
Berger, John, 89, 163
Bergman, Ingmar, 34
Berne (Swiss canton), 28, 57, 156, 157
Berne (Swiss city), 28
Berta, Renato, 54
Bertolucci, Bernardo, 167
Bickerton, Emilie, 9
bicycles, 13, 24, 102, 106, 163
Birth of a Nation (1915), 23
Bizet, Georges, 110–11
Bonitzer, Pascal, 24, 104–5
Brakhage, Stan, 30–33, 34, 83, 115, 126, 132, 185n10; *Dog Star Man* (1964), 31
Brecht, Bertold, 43, 74
Brenez, Nicole, 6, 46, 140–41
Bresson, Robert, 124–25
British Film Institute, 147
British Sounds (1969), 10, 20, 87
Broch, Hermann, 132–34, 138, 158, 163
Brody, Richard, 4, 8, 14, 26, 39, 41–42, 43, 49, 52, 54, 55, 63, 69–70, 75, 88, 90, 126, 132, 153, 155–56, 161–62, 183n1, 184n9
Bruno, G., 91–92
Buache, Freddy, 56–58, 118–19
Büttner, Elisabeth, 69

Cahiers du cinéma, 8, 11, 13, 17, 19, 22, 26, 54, 71; Marguerite Duras special issue, 17, 19, 151; Godard and Miéville (eds.) special issue, 50, 51–52
Camera Obscura: A Journal of Feminism and Film Theory, 12, 17, 54, 186n6
Canal+ (French broadcaster), 145
Les Carabiniers (1963), 30
Carrière, Jean-Claude, 7
Catholicism, 91, 117–18
Cavett, Dick, 98
Le changement à plus d'un titre (1982), 7
Channel 4 (UK broadcaster), 129, 135
La Chinoise (1967), 9, 155, 168
Cinéma Pratique (French film magazine), 30, 31, 46, 67, 76, 82–83, 165–72
Ciné-Tracts (1968), 21, 30, 39, 81
Comment ça va (1976), 2, 6, 46, 53, 58, 60, 78–81, 83, 151, 183n1
commercials, 142, 144
communication, 3, 11–12, 37, 38–39, 43, 46–47, 49–50, 59–62, 65, 73, 78, 81–88, 94, 96, 99, 130, 135, 147–50, 152, 155, 163, 175
Concordia University, 43, 45, 185n3
Coppola, Francis Ford, 2, 47–49, 101, 108

Daney, Serge, 2, 17, 19–23, 30, 32, 35, 39–40, 70–71, 73, 104, 109, 113–14, 135, 151, 159, 187n2
Dans le noir du temps (2002), 6, 139, 154–56
Darty (French department store), 6, 140–42
de Baecque, Antoine, 4, 7, 8, 9, 14, 26, 37, 39, 54, 56, 63, 88, 100–101, 140–41, 143, 183n1
de Certeau, Michel, 92
Degas, Edgar, 89
de Gaulle, Charles, 40–41
de Goëje, Frédérique, 87
Deleuze, Gilles, 68, 75, 82–84, 88, 90
Le dernier mot (1988), 7

Détective (1985), 6, 21, 97–98, 114–17, 118, 137
Deux fois cinquante ans de cinéma français (1995), 6, 19, 139, 147–52, 154, 155, 161
Diawara, Manthia, 50–51, 52
Dieckmann, Katherine, 14
Dolto, Françoise, 126–28, 135
Drillon, Jacques, 53–54, 126
Drucker, Michel, 171
Dubois, Phillipe, 108
Dumas, Rev. André, 118, 119–20
Durand, Philippe, 30, 165–72
Duras, Marguerite, 17–19, 151

Ecoutez voir (Swiss television series), 60, 157
Eicher, Manfred, 187n2
El Fatah, 63–64, 68, 70
Éloge de l'amour (2001), 3, 13, 137, 138
The Empire Strikes Back (1980), 153, 154
L'Enfance de l'art (1990), 6, 144–45, 148
Les enfants jouent à la Russie (1993), 161
Euvard, Janine, 13, 173–78
exile, 4, 43–45, 114

Faire la fête (1987), 2, 97–98, 135
Fairfax, Daniel, 52
Fanon, Frantz, 44
Fargier, Jean-Paul, 80
Faroult, David, 63
Film socialism (2010), 7, 13, 138, 161
Flaherty, Robert, 64
Fokkema, Douwe, 33, 160
For Ever Mozart (1996), 137, 138, 145, 148
Foucault, Michel, 11
Frampton, Hollis, 125
France/tour/détour/deux/enfants (1979), 2, 6, 25, 30–31, 60, 75, 83–84, 88–94, 99, 107, 116, 137

Le gai savoir (1968), 10, 21, 30, 40–41, 72, 84–85
gender, 16–19, 72–73, 102–3, 180

Geneva, 118
Gianvito, John, 12
Girard, François, 175
Gorin, Jean-Pierre, 1, 9, 20, 26, 30, 47, 63, 78, 85, 117, 185n5
Goupil, Romain, 7, 54
Grant, Catherine, 1, 5, 12, 13
Grenoble, 2, 4, 26, 28, 31, 52, 53–56, 59, 93
Griffith, D.W., 23, 153
Groulx, Gilles, 185n1
Groupe Dziga Vertov, 1, 9, 20, 21, 32, 41, 63, 67–68, 72, 81, 87, 146, 160, 184n5
Guerra, Ruy, 50

Harcourt, Peter, 34, 100, 114, 122, 139
Heidegger, Martin, 126, 130–32, 132–34, 138
Hélas pour moi (1993), 148
Hennebelle, Guy, 86–87
Hibon, Danièle, 13
Histoire(s) du cinéma (1988–2004), 21, 135, 138, 147–49, 154, 184n9
Hitler, Adolf, 66, 67, 68
Hoberman, J., 31–32, 93
Hopper, Edward, 108
Hornuss, 97
How Can I Love (1983), 2, 61, 96–98, 117
Huillet, Danièle. *See* Straub–Huillet
Huppert, Isabelle, 49, 99–100, 103–4, 142

Ibsch, Elrud, 33, 160
Ici et ailleurs (1974), 2, 6, 20, 33, 46, 49, 58, 59, 60, 63–72, 79, 85, 93–94, 128, 148, 149, 151, 152, 159, 161, 183n1
Intermedio (Barcelona DVD label), 7
Introduction à une véritable histoire du cinéma (1980), 43, 49–50, 185n3
Ishgapour, Youssef, 109, 115, 119

Jameson, Fredric, 33, 34, 187n2
Jawhariyya, Hany, 63
Je vous salue, Marie (1985), 6, 14, 16, 58, 93, 94, 108, 117–28, 149, 162, 173, 183n1

JLG/JLG: autoportrait de décembre (1995), 138, 159, 151
Jones, Kent, 125, 131
Jousse, Thierry, 140, 142
Joyce, James, 33, 77, 149, 163; *Dubliners* (1914), 149; *Finnegans Wake* (1939), 33, 149; *A Portrait of the Artist as a Young Man* (1916), 149, 163; *Ulysses* (1922), 77, 149, 163
Jura (Swiss canton), 27–28, 156, 187n3
Jura (Swiss mountain range), 97
Jusqu'à la victoire (1970), 8, 63, 64, 67–68

Kael, Pauline, 14
Kiarostami, Abbas, 175
King, Allan, 89
King Lear (1987), 115, 160, 188n2
Kirby, Lynn, 186n6
Kolker, Robert Phillip, 67
Kramer, Robert 70, 145; *Milestones* (1975), 70

Lacan, Jacques, 126, 128
Lac Léman, 25, 36, 54, 97, 101–2, 123–24, 132–34, 138, 156, 162
Lake Geneva. *See* Lac Léman
landscape, 25, 32, 33, 94, 96, 106, 123–24, 126, 132–34, 138–39, 154, 156–58, 163
Langlois, Henri, 9, 135
Larouche, Michel, 42
Laugier, Sandra, 126–27
Lausanne, 56–57, 99, 157
Letter to Jane (1972), 10, 72, 85
Lettre à Freddy Buache (1982), 2, 56, 159
Levi, Pavle, 68
Lévy, Patrick, 130–31
Liberté et patrie (2002), 3, 6, 15, 28, 33–34, 56, 58, 139, 154–55, 156–58, 159, 161
Lioger, Hélène, 9
Le livre de Marie (1985), 6, 94, 117–28, 162, 173, 183n1
Locke, Maryel, 117
Loin du Vietnam (1967), 9

Losique, Serge, 45
Lotte in Italia (1970), 10
Lou n'a pas dit non (1994), 13, 160, 173, 175–78, 179, 180
Lubtchansky, William, 54, 88
Luddy, Tom, 48–49, 101, 129, 184n5, 185n5, 188n1
Lumière Brothers, 147, 149, 166
Luther, Martin, 118, 119
Lyon, Elizabeth, 17
Lyotard, Jean-François, 148

MacCabe, Colin, 4, 7, 8, 14, 15, 16, 23, 26, 28–29, 30–31, 34, 41, 47, 59, 88, 127, 129, 135, 140, 147, 149, 152, 160, 183n1
Maddin, Guy, 57
Mahler, Gustav, 123
Man of Aran (1934), 64
Marker, Chris, 9
A Married Couple (1969), 89
Masculin féminin (1966), 8, 9
Maule, Roseanna, 17–18
Meetin' WA (1986), 160, 188n2
Meir, Golda, 65, 66, 67, 68
Le Mépris (1963), 3, 8, 108
Mérimée, Prosper, 110, 112
Modernism, 33–34, 65, 71–72, 73, 76–77, 79, 81, 89, 93, 99–100, 103–4, 125–26, 131–32, 138–39, 146, 153, 160–61
Moi je (aborted project), 2, 37, 46–47
Mon cher sujet (1988), 5, 173, 174, 176, 177, 179, 180
Morgan, Daniel, 119
Morrey, Douglas, 141
Moullet, Luc, 23
Mozambique, 49–53, 80
Mulvey, Laura, 16, 72–73, 78, 97, 114, 125–26
Museum of Modern Art (New York), 16, 139, 147, 152, 156

Nanook of the North (1922), 64
Narboni, Jacques, 40, 100

National Film Board of Canada, 40
Nedjar, Claude, 42, 43, 184n5
New Wave, 1, 2, 4, 8, 9, 10, 17, 29, 41, 115
Notre Musique (2004), 7, 13
Nous sommes tout encore ici (1997), 5, 7, 148, 159
Nouvelle vague. *See* New Wave
Nouvelle vague (1990), 7, 9, 148
Numéro deux (1975), 2, 4, 6, 41, 46, 60, 72–78, 93, 100, 117, 128, 151, 183n1

The Old Place (1998), 6, 21, 139, 147, 152–56
One Plus One (1968), 10, 21
One P.M. (1971), 2, 9, 38–40, 41, 48
Ottinger, Ulrike, 16

Palestinians, 8, 20, 63, 72, 79, 151
Papa comme maman (1977), 60–62, 96, 159
Parisienne People commercial (1992), 6, 7, 142–44
Pärt, Arvo, 155
Parvulseco, Jean, 9
Passion (1982), 7, 16, 33, 49, 54, 93, 101, 108, 110, 159
Peary, Gerald, 3
Pence, Stella, 31, 185n10
Penley, Constance, 91–92, 102
Pennebaker, D.A., 2, 38–39
Peripheria, 29, 34
Perron, Julie, 42–43
Petites notes à propos du film Je vous salue, Marie (1983), 128–29
Le Petit Soldat (1960), 155, 185n1
Piccoli, Michel, 149–51, 152
Pierrot le fou (1965), 8, 30, 116
Portugal, 53, 78–81
Pour Thomas Wainggai, Indonésie (1991), 6, 139, 144, 145–47, 148, 154, 155
Powrie, Phil, 110
Pravda (1969), 10
Prédal, René, 3–4, 162–63, 184n6

Prénom: Carmen (1983), 6, 16, 54, 55, 97, 109–14, 118, 126, 135
Protestantism, 118–21, 162

Quebec, 40–45, 49–50, 51, 63–64, 185n1

Rafferty, Terrence, 3
Ramuz, Charles-Ferdinand, 57–58, 156–57
Le Rapport Darty (1989), 3, 6, 140–42, 143–44, 155
regionalism, 27–28, 34, 92–93, 162–63, 172, 187n3
République helvétique, 156–57
Reusser, Francis, 60, 157
right-wing politics, 8–9
Rilke, Rainer Maria, 173, 174, 176–77, 179
Rodchenko, H.A., 143
Rolle, 12, 13, 20, 28, 31, 49, 52, 60, 93, 129, 134, 155, 157, 162
Romanticism, 119, 132, 157–58, 163
Rosenbaum, Jonathan, 19, 28, 125, 131, 147, 161, 184n7
Roth, Laurent, 151
Rouch, Jean, 23–24, 34, 51, 169, 184n6; *Chronique d'un été* (1960), 23; *Moi, un noir* (1958), 23; *Les maîtres fous* (1955), 23
Roud, Richard, 24, 111
Rowe, Kathleen K., 5, 12, 119, 132

Sanbar, Elias, 64
Sarris, Andrew, 1
Sauve qui peut (la vie) (1980), 2, 3, 4, 6, 15, 16, 18, 25, 27, 28, 33, 49, 53, 58, 59, 74, 78, 88, 89, 93, 94, 96–97, 98–109, 110, 114, 116, 119, 131, 137, 142, 145, 161, 162
Scemama, Céline, 149
Scénario vidéo Sauve qui peut (la vie) (1979), 108–9, 128–29, 187n2
Schick commercial, 142
Schrader, Paul, 124

Seguet, Olivier, 13
Shafto, Sally, 7, 88, 183n1, 184n5
Six fois deux: sur et sous la communication (1976), 2, 4, 6, 15, 43, 58, 60, 66, 81–88, 91, 93, 104, 141, 151, 152, 183n1
slow-motion effects, 88–90, 99, 105–7, 115–16
Snow, Michael, 28, 83, 125
soccer, 170–71
Soft and Hard (1985), 2, 4, 6, 7, 20, 25, 58, 94, 97, 99, 108, 128–35, 137, 138, 139, 147, 148, 149, 162
Sonimage, 4, 5, 12, 26, 28–29, 30, 32, 50, 52, 53, 59, 60, 140, 156
Stellavox, 165
Sterritt, David, 14
Stevens, Brad, 48, 49, 184n5
Stoneman, Rod, 135
The Story (aborted project), 2, 27, 37, 47–49, 101
Straub, Jean-Marie. *See* Straub–Huillet
Straub–Huillet, 1, 13, 16, 22, 23, 24–25, 32, 33, 34, 70, 71, 74, 111, 113, 119–20, 125, 163, 184n7; *Cézanne* (1989), 32; *Chronik der Anna Magdalena Bach* (1968), 24, 25, 74, 111, 113, 114, 184n7; *Einleitung zu Arnold Schönbergs "Begleitmusik zu einer Lichtspielscene"* (1972), 70; *En rachâchant* (1982), 32; *Klassenverhältnisse* (1984), 24, 25, 113, 114; *Lothringen!* (1994), 25; *Moses und Aron* (1973), 24, 25, 113
Super-8 film, 50, 51, 53, 60, 86, 166, 168, 169
Switzerland, 10, 27–28, 56–58, 92–93, 97, 99, 118–20, 156–58, 178, 186n7, 187n3
Syberberg, Hans-Jürgen, 32, 48
Syria, 70, 71

Tanner, Alain, 60, 163
Tarantino, Michael, 60

Tarkovksy, Andrei, 32
television, 4, 22–23, 27, 30–31, 39, 41–43, 49–53, 60, 76, 128, 146, 147, 162, 168, 170–71, 178; *France/tour/détour/deux/enfants* (1979), 88–94; *Six fois deux: sur et sous la communication* (1976), 81–88; *Soft and Hard* (1985), 128–35
Télévision Suisse Romande, 60–61
Temple, Michael, 7, 46
ten Brink, Joram, 184n6
Thompson, Kristin, 101
Tinguely, Jean, 155
Torn, Rip, 39
Le tour de la France par deux enfants (1877), 91–92, 186n3
Tout va bien (1972), 7, 20, 26, 46

Vallières, Pierre, 44–45
Vaud, 3, 8, 20, 28, 56, 57–58, 91, 104, 118–19, 156–58, 162
Vent d'est (1969), 87, 184n5
Vermeer, Johannes, 153, 154
Vertov, Dziga, 70, 71, 87
video, 2, 3, 4, 26, 28–31, 42, 46–47, 48–49, 51–52, 108, 115–16, 128–29, 137, 157, 187n2; effects specific to video, 38, 61, 62, 64, 65–67, 75, 85, 86, 88–90, 93, 104, 106, 141, 149, 168–70
Virolleaud, Camille, 89–91, 106–7
Vivre sa vie (1962), 103
Vladmir et Rosa (1970), 10

Waiting for Godot (1953), 104
Warren, Charles, 117
Waugh, Thomas, 45
Weekend (1967), 3, 9, 72, 117
Wenders, Wim, 108, 185n5
Witt, Michael, 1, 4–5, 11, 12, 13–14, 26, 37, 43, 50, 52, 81–82, 88, 106–7, 183n1, 185n3, 186n2
Wollen, Peter, 14–15, 32, 126
Wood, Robin, 77

Yared, Gabriel, 107
Les yeux verts (special Duras issue of *Cahiers du cinéma*), 17, 19, 151

Zoetrope Studios, 2, 48–49, 101, 129

Books in the Film+Media Studies Series
Published by Wilfrid Laurier University Press

Image and Identity: Reflections on Canadian Film Culture / R. Bruce Elder / 1989; Paper edition 2012 / xviii + 484 pp. / ISBN 978-1-55458-469-7

Image and Territory: Essays on Atom Egoyan / Monique Tschofen and Jennifer Burwell, editors / 2006 / viii + 418 pp / photos / ISBN 978-0-88920-487-4

The Young, the Restless, and the Dead: Interviews with Canadian Filmmakers / George Melnyk, editor / 2008 / xiv + 134 pp. / photos / ISBN 978-1-55458-036-1

Programming Reality: Perspectives on English-Canadian Television / Zoë Druick and Aspa Kotsopoulos, editors / 2008 / x + 344 pp. / photos / ISBN 978-1-55458-010-1

Harmony and Dissent: Film and Avant-garde Art Movements in the Early Twentieth Century / R. Bruce Elder / 2008 / xxxiv + 482 pp. / ISBN 978-1-55458-028-6

He Was Some Kind of a Man: Masculinities in the B Western / Roderick McGillis / 2009 / xii + 210 pp. / photos / ISBN 978-1-55458-059-0

The Radio Eye: Cinema in the North Atlantic, 1958–1988 / Jerry White / 2009 / xvi + 284 pp. / photos / ISBN 978-1-55458-178-8

The Gendered Screen: Canadian Women Filmmakers / Brenda Austin-Smith and George Melnyk, editors / 2010 / x + 272 pp. / ISBN 978-1-55458-179-5

Feeling Canadian: Nationalism, Affect, and Television / Marusya Bociurkiw / 2011 / viii + 184 pp. / ISBN 978-1-55458-268-6

Beyond Bylines: Media Workers and Women's Rights in Canada / Barbara M. Freeman / 2011 / xii + 328 pp. / photos / ISBN 978-1-55458-269-3

Canadian Television: Text and Context / Marian Bredin, Scott Henderson, and Sarah A. Matheson, editors / 2011 / xvi + 238 pp. / ISBN 978-1-55458-361-4

Cinema and Social Change in Germany and Austria / Gabriele Mueller and James M. Skidmore, editors / 2012 / x + 304 pp. / photos / ISBN 978-1-55458-225-9

DADA, Surrealism, and the Cinematic Effect / Bruce Elder / 2013 / viii + 766 pp. / ISBN 978-1-55458-625-7

Two Bicycles: The Work of Jean-Luc Godard and Anne-Marie Miéville / Jerry White / 2013 / x + 204 pp./ ISBN 978-1-55458-935-7

The Legacies of Jean-Luc Godard / Douglas Morrey, Christina Stojanova, and Nicole Côté, editors / forthcoming 2014 / photos / ISBN 978-1-55458-920-3

Detecting Canada: Essays on Canadian Crime Fiction, Film, and Television / Jeannette Sloniowski and Marilyn Rose, editors / forthcoming 2014 / ISBN 978-1-55458-926-5

www.ingramcontent.com/pod-product-compliance
Lightning Source LLC
Chambersburg PA
CBHW052025070526
44584CB00016B/1903